8 March
2022

D0865775

Please return/renew this item by the last
date shown. Books may also be renewed
by phone or internet.

🖥 www.rbwm.gov.uk/home/leisure-and-
culture/libraries

☎ 01628 796969 (library hours)

☎ 0303 123 0035 (24 hours)

University

'A chilling post-mortem of 2020's silent epidemic - fear - and
how it was used by a behavioural science apparat to terrify us
into submission. It's a thorough, fascinating and important book
which I absolutely loved – I couldn't put it down!'

'Laura Dodsworth slices open the culture of fear we have been deliberately manipulated to experience in this pandemic crisis with a journalistic forensic scalpel. The role of behavioural science in instilling fear in the UK population is explored through the lens of those involved in developing policies, 'outlier academics', experts and researchers who have questioned the dominant 'fear-based' policy narrative. Analysis of events and expert testimony is interspersed with heart-breaking vignettes of the real-life experiences of fear that people lived with during the pandemic. The events and experiences of this past year will take considerable time for us to unpack and comprehend, and *A State of Fear* is an excellent early analysis of one of the most concerning elements of government policy in this crisis. I was gripped by it and devoured it in one sitting. There is no doubt that our collective 'cognitive roadmap' in relation to fear and risk perception has been completely obliterated in the past year. Naming and acknowledging what has happened is an important first step to recovery. Books like this will help us get there and heal.'
Professor Ellen Townsend,
Professor of Psychology, University of Nottingham

'Laura Dodsworth has a rare and beautiful talent to observe a situation, process its many layers and present it to the world in exquisite, thought-provoking detail. Without hysteria or anger, she has studied and distilled the forces at work throughout the Covid pandemic so that we may see the world more clearly. This is a vital, eye-opening book which provides balance to an otherwise one-sided story.'
Beverley Turner, writer and broadcaster

'What speaks so powerfully in this work are the voices of those affected by the extraordinary social experiment that lockdown has been. Dodsworth draws out their experiences and puts them centre stage, while taking the reader through the techniques and strategies through which fear was made the most potent weapon in obtaining submission. A stimulating and often disturbing read.'
Francis Hoar, barrister

A
STATE
OF
FEAR

ABOUT THE AUTHOR

Laura Dodsworth is an author, journalist, photographer and filmmaker. Her books *Bare Reality: 100 women, their breasts, their stories*, *Manhood: The Bare Reality* and *Womanhood: The Bare Reality* have attracted worldwide media coverage and excellent reviews. Laura and the creation of *Womanhood* were the subject of a documentary for Channel 4, *100 Vaginas*, which has been broadcast around the world.

HOW THE UK GOVERNMENT WEAPONISED
FEAR DURING THE COVID-19 PANDEMIC

LAURA DODSWORTH

*A State of Fear: How the UK government weaponised
fear during the Covid-19 pandemic*

First published in the UK by Pinter & Martin Ltd 2021
reprinted 2021

ISBN 978-1-78066-720-1

Also available as an ebook and audiobook

British Library Cataloguing-in-Publication Data
A catalogue record for this book is available from the
British Library

Printed in the UK by Martins the Printers Ltd.

This book has been printed on paper that is sourced
and harvested from sustainable forests and is FSC
accredited

Pinter & Martin Ltd
6 Effra Parade
London SW2 1PS

pinterandmartin.com

CONTENTS

INTERVIEWS

Names have been changed to protect anonymity.

'The perceived level of personal threat needs to be increased among those who are complacent, using hard-hitting emotional messaging.'

From *Options for increasing adherence to social distancing measures*, by the Scientific Pandemic Influenza Group on Behaviour (SPI-B), 22 March 2020.

INTRODUCTION

T his is a book about fear. Fear of a virus. Fear of death. Fear of change, fear of the unknown. Fear of ulterior motives, agenda and conspiracy. Fear for the rule of law, democracy, the western liberal way of life. Fear of loss: losing our jobs, our culture, our connections, our health, our minds. It's also about how the government weaponised our fear against us – supposedly in our best interests – until we were one of the most frightened countries in the world.

In one of the most extraordinary documents ever revealed to the British public, the behavioural scientists advising the UK government recommended that we needed to be frightened. The Scientific Pandemic Influenza Group on Behaviour (SPI-B) said in their report *Options for increasing adherence to social distancing measures*,[1] dated 22 March 2020, that 'a substantial number of people still do not feel sufficiently personally threatened; it could be that they are reassured by the low death rate in their demographic group, although levels of concern may be rising'. As a result they recommended that 'the perceived level of personal threat needs to be increased among those who are complacent, using hard-hitting emotional messaging'. In essence, the government was advised to frighten the British public to encourage adherence to the emergency lockdown regulations.

And frighten us they did. This book explores why the government used fear, the specific tactics, the people behind them, and the impacts of fear, including stories from people who were undone by fear during the epidemic. Most of all, this book asks you to think about the ethics of using fear to manage people.

Fear is the most powerful of emotions and, as emotions are stronger than thoughts, fear can overpower the clearest of minds. We shouldn't feel bad about being frightened. From an evolutionary perspective, it is key to our survival: it protects us from danger. And that is precisely what makes fear one of the most powerful tools in behavioural psychology.

This exploration of fear led me to interview people who have been too frightened to leave their homes all year, 'conspiracy theorists', psychologists, some of the behavioural scientists who advised government, scientists, politicians, doctors, pandemic planners and journalists.

By the end of March 2021, Covid had been involved in the deaths of 2.8 million[2] people globally. The disease will continue to kill more, even though hopefully the biggest waves are behind us in the UK. The aim of this book is not to refute that Covid-19 is a serious disease that has killed people, most particularly the elderly and those with certain underlying health conditions, especially dementia, Alzheimer's, obesity, diabetes and hypertensive diseases, among others.[3] The aim of this book is to explore our fear response and whether it was ethical and wise for the government to deliberately frighten the population. Was the government's response proportional? Wouldn't people have cautiously tempered their behaviour during an epidemic in the interests of self-preservation and community spirit? What are the unintended consequences of frightening a population? In the years and inquiries to follow, the management of this epidemic must be forensically and honestly examined. *A State of Fear* asks that we also interrogate the behavioural science approach to managing people's emotions and behaviour.

Covid-19 has become another of the many endemic viruses we have to live with. It was known from the beginning to be a 'very mild illness'[4] for nearly all of us. The UK's Chief Scientific Advisor, Patrick Vallance, stated this publicly on 13 March 2020. Experience has proven that correct; Covid was not lethal or dangerous to the vast majority. Vaccines and treatments were developed at miraculous speed to protect the vulnerable. So what are we still afraid of? The third wave, a fourth wave – a fifth wave? – winter recurrences, mutations, future viruses and the unknown haunt us.

From roadside signs telling us to 'Stay Alert', the incessantly doom-laden media commentary, to masks literally keeping the fear in our face, we've become afraid of each other. Humans are now vectors of transmission, agents of disease. We have become afraid of our own judgement about how to manage the minutiae of our lives, from who to hug to whether to share a serving spoon. Apparently, we even need guidance about whether we can sit next to a friend on a bench. But perhaps we need to be more afraid of how easily manipulated we can be.

Some will believe that leveraging our fear can be justified, if it is in our best interests. If you agree that 'Covid-19 is the biggest threat this country has faced in peacetime history', as the government asserted in its consultation document *Changes to Human Medicine Regulations to support the rollout of Covid-19 vaccines*, you might think it was not only acceptable but desirable to scare the British public into complying with regulations that resulted in the greatest imposition on our liberty in peacetime. If you obtained all your information about the epidemic from Number 10 press briefings that might be your mindset.

Tactics to quell debate and censor dissent mean that information presented in this book may feel new, even challenging. It can be psychologically uncomfortable to encounter contradictory information. We don't like to believe we can be manipulated, let alone that we *have* been manipulated – this book may hurt.

People vastly over-estimated the spread and deadliness of Covid-19. One survey[5] in July 2020 showed that the British public thought 6–7% of the population had died from coronavirus – around 100 times the actual death rate at the time based on official figures. That would have been about 4,500,000 bodies – we'd have noticed, don't you think?

It was reported in January 2021 that the Covid epidemic caused excess deaths (to November) to rise to their highest level in the UK since the Second World War. This was headline news throughout the UK media. However, once the age and size of the population were taken into account, excess deaths were at their worst since just 2008.[6] That is very significant, and showed that just over a decade of public health improvements had been undone, but less hyperbolic than the headlines.

In September 2020, the British people were also more concerned about the spread of the virus than people in Sweden, the US, France, Germany and Japan – 83% of us thought there would be a second wave, while only 21% of us thought the government was well-prepared to deal with it.[7] An international study of public attitudes across Europe, America and Asia found that people in the UK had the highest overall levels of concern about Covid.[8] And yet another study reported that Britons were the least likely to believe that the economy and businesses should open if Covid was not 'fully contained'.[9] We were the most frightened population in the world.

By February 2021 we had one of the most rapid and comprehensive vaccination programmes in the world, yet also the most stringent lockdown in the developed world.[10]

People are notoriously bad at judging risk and numbers, but we substantially over-estimated the dangers. And this wasn't helped by the daily reports from the government and media. We heard about new cases, but never recoveries. Hospital admissions but not discharges were reported. We were given numbers of daily deaths, but largely without the context that about 1,600 people die every day in the UK anyway.

By the end of March 2021, just 689 people under the age of 60 with no co-morbidities had died from Covid in England and Wales according to NHS England.[11] The average age of death with Covid is 82.3 years[12] – one year more than the average life expectancy in Britain. Of course, all the deaths associated with Covid count, but if these facts had been widely reported and people had realised it was a disease which was primarily dangerous to the elderly and otherwise unwell, then 'a substantial number of people' would probably not 'feel sufficiently personally threatened'.

One government report said that lockdown could cause 200,000 people to die as a result of delays in healthcare and economic effects, also equating to one million years of life lost.[13] Another study at Bristol University[14] estimated an average 560,000 lives lost caused by the reduced economic activity during lockdown, due to the well-understood link between wealth and health. Quite simply, people in rich nations live longer.

The government, public health bodies and the media used alarmist language throughout the epidemic. Big numbers, steep red lines on graphs, the use of selective information, careful psychological messaging and emotive advertising created a blitzkrieg of daily fear bombs.

This is a book about fear, not a book about data. Nevertheless, some additional data will be required to help you contextualise the threat of the disease with the policies for managing it, and you will find that in Appendix 1.

A few facts and figures assist with framing the scale and dangers of Covid, and subsequently with assessing whether escalating our fear was appropriate, or not. It is partly an issue of proportion and entirely an issue of ideology. But the numbers risk ignoring the more poignant, human costs of the use of fear. I interviewed people who were driven by fear, anxiety and isolation to develop agoraphobia, obsessive compulsive disorders, panic attacks, started self-harming and even attempted suicide. How do we weigh the potential life saved from Covid-19 with a life deliberately ended by overdose in a hotel room or a jump from a bridge? Can we justify protecting someone from physical sickness, fever and fatigue, if the methods of protection caused someone else to develop a fear of leaving their house, or made them waken sick with dread each day?

Epidemics will come and go. Our basic psychology is here to stay. The pressing issue is whether and how we permit behavioural psychologists, the government and the media to manipulate our psychology.

At times, the experience of the pandemic has felt like a story, or like living in a movie. Not a fun one. While the virus was the plot device in our fantastical reality, the motivating force for many of the characters was fear.

The best macabre fairy tales are also cautionary tales. If you can identify the Big Bad Wolf and understand what he represents and wants, you can find your way through the dark woods and be free. We don't know how this will end. But rather than wait till it's all over to tell the terrible story of when the world stopped and humanity was paralysed with fear, I would like to invite you to decide how the story ends. There is still time for us to craft the happy ending of our choice. Shouldn't we be the authors of our own stories?

As Karl Augustus Menninger said, 'Fears are educated into us, and can, if we wish, be educated out.' We need to inoculate ourselves against fear.

'The coronavirus is the biggest threat this country has faced for decades. All over the world we are seeing the devastating impact of this invisible killer … From this evening I must give the British people a very simple instruction – you must stay at home.'

From Boris Johnson's speech to the nation, 23 March 2020

1. FRIGHT NIGHT

I froze. Appalled by the words. Fight and flight are the better known responses to fear. If you believe you can defeat the source of threat you go into fight mode. If you see the danger as too powerful to overcome, you try to run away: the flight response. If you can't defeat the danger or bolt from it, you freeze. Appropriately, considering my foreseeable future would involve not leaving the house, going out to work, or to see my family, friends or partner, I froze on the sofa.

But as I watched Boris Johnson's speech to the nation, as he told us we 'must' stay at home, I also started observing his body language. Why was he clenching his fists so hard? Why the staccato speech? Something seemed 'off' and that triggered alarm bells. Later on I considered my own response. Until that point I had not been unreasonably frightened of the virus, so why was this speech frightening me now? I was sure that the prime minister's language was intended to alarm me, and that in itself worried me.

I have always tended to freeze when I am frightened. I find it a bit disappointing. It's not a very useful reaction. Of all the fear responses, freeze elicits the most uncomfortable after-effect, as it often accompanies attacks and victims can feel ashamed. But if a threat is bigger than you, and you can't get away from it, freezing and just trying to survive it is your only remaining option. We exhibit all these fear responses at different times because they are successful evolutionary mechanisms; they kept us alive.

Once, my eldest son climbed too far up a tree and fell. I had a bad feeling about that tree. I said he shouldn't climb it, because it had dead branches and, well, because I am a mother. I was maybe 50 yards from the tree when he fell. As he plummeted, I felt every quantum of strength and usefulness drain through my feet into the ground. After the first wave of cold sweat, I wobbled towards the tree, finding my strength and gathering pace as I went, to find him lying unharmed between lethal, spiky branches. My husband had leapt instantaneously into action, galloping towards our son while shouting 'Oi! Oi! Oi!' He had beaten me to it.

Looking back, there are two learnings. First, I freeze. Such a weak-kneed response is not much help (there's the shame) unless I encounter a grizzly bear some day. Second, I also learnt my first fears are worth attending to. I should heed my instinct when it tells me something is amiss. My radar is often good.

Like many others, I had done my best to qualify as an armchair virologist by mid-March 2020, and inhaled articles and YouTube videos about viruses, Wuhan and the *Diamond Princess*. So I understood that while this was a lethal and nasty virus, and much was still unknown, it would inevitably behave as all other respiratory viruses before it. Why would it not?

One reason that Boris Johnson's speech alarmed me was because I was worried that the response was disproportionate. Never before had we quarantined the healthy. We were mimicking totalitarian China's response to the virus. How I had pitied the poor Chinese welded into their homes! My mind fast-forwarded to the worst possible economic and social consequences. Should the precautionary principle in this case mean we should lock down – an un-evidenced method of trying to control a virus – or was it more prudent to follow well-rehearsed pandemic protocols, which had never recommended lockdowns? (At this point you may say, ah, but we had prepared for influenza, not coronavirus! In which case please let me assure you that coronavirus was on the *National Risk Register of Civil Emergencies*.[1])

I have to acknowledge my own fear – I am in no way immune. Indeed, I doubt I would have wanted to write this book had I not felt the prickles of fear myself. From the first night we were told to lock down I realised I was more frightened of authoritarianism than death, and more repulsed by manipulation than illness. Like the rest of the nation I stayed put for three weeks. Then three weeks more. And, well, we're still here one way or another. Then the freeze thawed and I started thinking, and then wobbling, towards the source of my fear. That is also what I do. I may take a little longer to arrive, but I want to look my fears squarely in the eyes once I'm there.

What was it that felt 'off' about Boris Johnson's speech? Reviewing it recently I was struck again by the artifice that triggered my radar on 23 March. Johnson is a performer, but he normally performs the 'likeable buffoon'. You would expect such an important speech to be rehearsed, but it felt too contrived and different to his normal presentation. He was controlled, stern, and at a basic level that was hard to pinpoint, it didn't feel genuine.

I asked two experts to help me decode Johnson's body language and style of speech.

Naomi Murphy is a clinical and forensic psychologist who has spent many years working in high-security prisons, often with people who don't always tell the truth. She echoed my reaction: 'His words and some of his body language convey one message, but you sense another message, and that rings alarm bells. He doesn't seem authentic.' She pointed out that there were times when he was giving a message with his head and hands, bobbing his head forwards and gesticulating, but his body was held back, suggesting that personally he did not believe in the essence of his words.

An appearance of inauthenticity could have been simply down to nerves. It would be natural to feel nervous before such a momentous speech to the nation, and that affects behaviour and body language. As Murphy said, 'you can hear his mouth is dry, which is incredible for someone who is used to the limelight. This is a man who likes being liked, and he might be worried that the public will not like him anymore.'

Neil Shah, founder of the Stress Management Society and International Wellbeing Insights, has delivered leadership training which includes how to read non-verbal communication. We watched the YouTube video of the speech remotely over a video call, so that he could analyse it blow by blow. He told me he would be interpreting a blend of signals because 55% of our communication is through body language,

38% is volume and tone and only 7% is the actual words we use.

'Twenty-six seconds in and you can see the tension in his fingers,' Shah commented. 'He is clenching so hard his knuckles turn white.' He pointed out Johnson was hunched and leaning forwards like he was holding on for dear life. I asked what it means when someone clenches their fists so hard. He told me it can be for emphasis, or as an aggressive gesture, but 'it also looks like a tantrumming toddler. The way he is jabbing his fists at us shows tension.'

Johnson also gives the most awkward and uncomfortable smile when he talks about compliance. Shah added that 'it's almost threatening. We smile when things are funny, but also when we are nervous. When he said that no prime minister wants to do this, a grave look would have suited the moment better than a ghoulish grin.'

Like Murphy, Shah thought the prime minister didn't believe everything he was saying: 'There doesn't seem to be congruence between his words and his body language. It suggests he is not speaking from the heart and doesn't believe what he is saying.'

Both believed his body language was more consistent with his words when he was discussing the impact on the NHS, but was incongruent when he was being more authoritarian in his message. The eyes never lie, so they say, even when the mouth does, and these conversations with Murphy and Shah proved to me that body language doesn't either. The prime minister of the UK would probably have been professionally coached to give the speech of his life, but the body betrays emotion and conflict regardless.

Unprompted, both experts offered astonishing analogies. Murphy likened Johnson's speech to 'a forced hostage speech'. Shah asked if I could see the resemblance to the episode of *Black Mirror* (the British dystopia sci-fi TV series) where the prime minister must be filmed for live TV having sex with a pig. I could see what they both meant.

Hindsight provides another level of analysis. We know the thrust of the message was not true. We did not lock down for three weeks. The reason we locked down was ostensibly to flatten the curve, but the mission creeped and we stayed in lockdown. We also now know that the curve might have flattened anyway, regardless of lockdown, since deaths peaked on 8 April, meaning infections peaked before lockdown.[2] When Johnson told us we would shut down the country for three weeks, the authenticity of his body language shut down too, his language and posture forced and aggressive.

Johnson's words were designed to call fear and death to mind: 'invisible killer', 'lives will be lost', 'funerals', and so on. He told us we were 'enlisted' – very specific wartime language, evoking the Blitz spirit, but also emotionally manipulative. At this point, Shah pointed out that we weren't given a choice, so we were conscripted rather than enlisted. Actually, there was no room for conscientious objectors, so I'd go with press-ganged.

My experts and I found this video difficult to re-watch. With time the performance grates more and the words have acquired a bitter taste. Ultimately, whether you believe Johnson gave the most heartfelt and honest speech of his life, or was coached too hard and over-egged it, or was misleading us, it was a frightening speech. His words set the tone for the three weeks to follow and hovered in the air for many months. As Murphy said to me, 'You can't under-estimate the amount of imprinting this speech would have created.' Johnson released a certain amount of fear that night, like an airborne virus, and you caught it one way or the other. Maybe you believed every word and it was an apocalyptic pandemic that would bring society to its knees. Maybe you were suspicious of the motives behind the inauthenticity, and perhaps there was an agenda that you feared would bring society to its knees. But it was frightening.

We were told we must follow the rules to 'save many thousands of lives'. Threats littered the latter part of Johnson's speech. The police would have powers to enforce the rules; we must follow the rules. The threat of power and penalty is designed to frighten us into compliance. But in a dishonest departure from the rule of law, the 'rules' he was ordering us to obey would not be made law for a further three days.

We didn't know this. The nation took the prime minister seriously from that night. Deadly seriously, just as we were supposed to. Murphy told me she hadn't observed Johnson's body language very closely on the night because she was listening so attentively to what we must do. This is a natural response. He is the elected leader of the country. Authority figures command respect, even in today's jaded world. Psychologically, there is a reason for this.

When we're in panic mode our body directs less blood to our blood-hungry brain and more to our limbs so that we are able to fight or take flight as needed. As a result, when we're threatened the brain needs shortcuts; ways to make decisions quickly. On the most obvious level, we listen to authority figures and leaders, and want to trust them in a time of crisis. We also respond to 'archetypes'. Our elected leader fulfils the archetypal role of 'ruler' and at a time of crisis – the archetypal Jungian motif for this crisis would be 'Apocalypse' – we are even more primed to listen and obey in order to survive.

In fact, the priming had started weeks earlier.

DARREN, 64

I grew up in a deprived area in Liverpool and I was a police officer for 32 years. I've done raids on criminal houses, I've carried firearms, I've gone through front doors at 4am, I've policed riots. I'm not saying I'm a tough nut, but not much throws me.

I f I'm being honest, I was alarmed when the news about Covid exploded. I think everybody wondered what was going to happen. You'd have to be quite thick-skinned or a bit daft not to have been worried, especially when they talked about a quarter of a million people dying.

I am on the clinically vulnerable list, so I got a letter off the government advising me quite strongly to shield. That letter upped the ante straight away. I also had a lot of texts about abiding by restrictions, and it had a subliminal effect on me. I have two of the conditions they were talking about – incurable cancer and a heart problem – so I thought I really, really can't go anywhere near this virus.

My wife decided to shield too, otherwise the advice was we should eat in different rooms and clean the loo in between us using it. You can't live like that in a small house with one kitchen and one bathroom. All these messages make you think that this must be such a bad and such an infectious virus.

There wasn't much to do, so we'd watch TV and we saw programmes about disinfecting your shopping when it arrives, and having a safe zone in the kitchen. The nightly bulletins on the TV about death tolls, the big graphs with huge spikes on them, came at us 'boom, boom, boom!' It was a constant barrage of doom and gloom. My fear of the virus went through the roof.

Back then when I was listening to other people's stories of

the outside world, I remember thinking it sounded mad that McDonald's was closed and there were spots on the ground at Tesco telling you where to stand.

It was like the fear we had in the Cold War, but much worse. That was an abstract concept, we didn't think it would really happen, but Covid was something we were told was actually happening.

I stayed at home for 11 weeks. When I went for my first hospital appointment after seven weeks of shielding, my brain overloaded. I was a wreck that day, petrified of my own shadow. I drove rather than walked, because I didn't think I should breathe in air that other people were breathing out.

When I got out the car I didn't know if I could do this, but I steeled myself and I had my mask and gloves on. My fear got compounded because I was greeted by someone at the hospital entrance who told me I had to take my mask and gloves off because they'd come from outside. That made me think it must be really bad.

There were signs everywhere telling you, 'Don't go past this point. Stand here'. Most of the chairs had been taken out. Nurses were in protective gear. They took my temperature which they wouldn't normally. Everything screamed danger.

I didn't feel wobbles or jellies, but my head was racing, 'I'm going to catch it, I'm going to catch it. If I breathe out of place, if I touch the wrong thing, if someone walks past me, I'm going to catch it.' If someone walked past me I would hold my breath.

Hospital workers walked past me when I was on my way out, and in my head I was thinking 'What are you doing?' When the third one walked past me I swore at him under my breath, the rude four-letter word that begins with 'c'.

When I got home I stripped off in the conservatory because I didn't want to contaminate the house with my clothes. I put my clothes in a plastic bag and I threw my shoes away! I sat in the hottest bath I could, for as long as I could, scrubbing every inch of myself. I looked like a lobster when I got out.

The turning point for me was that the government reopened golf courses. My oncologist said I should get out and that we were going to play a round of golf. It was terrifying at first, but crucially, that got me talking to people and that helped me get over the fear.

For a long time I was frightened of everything: the world, the air, other people, physical objects, anything that could transmit the virus basically. Looking back, I can't believe it was me. I think I became agoraphobic.

I'm awfully angry about the fear now. I feel cheated. Ultimately I am angry at Parliament, not just the government, because there was no real opposition to anything. I'm angry at the media too and feel betrayed, they only publish one side of the argument.

It was despicable that the government tried to frighten us. Any other walk of life, you'd be arrested.

2. FEAR SPREADS IN THE MEDIA LIKE AN AIRBORNE VIRUS

A woman in a face mask stands with her shopping bags next to a subway. Suddenly she falls forward, landing flat on her face. She lies immobile and stiff on the pavement. A concerned shopkeeper runs out to check on her.

A man is out cold in the street, as people in white hazmat suits attend to him. Another man lies face up, body straight, alone in a corridor. Another body, two people attending in hazmat suits. A very wide roadblock is manned by people in white lab coats, masks and high-vis vests. Another man lies on his back in a shop. The area is cordoned off. People in PPE look on.

These worrying scenes all appear in a video[1] which paints an apocalyptic picture of collapsed citizens, medics in hazmat suits, concerned bystanders and a city grinding to a halt. It was our first glimpse of a new, deadly epidemic and our first taste of fear. It appeared in the British press, specifically the *Mail Online*, *Metro Online* and *The Sun* on 24 January 2020. The video was out at the same time that the first few hundred cases and the first handful of deaths were reported in China and shortly before the first case was confirmed in the UK on 31 January.

I remember the video being shared on Twitter and Facebook – I'm not the TikTok or Snapchat generation, but the video also went viral there. Fear is contagious and social media offers the perfect conditions for it to spread. Viruses travel fast by air, but fear travels faster – share, share, share!

One description of the video read 'a particularly dramatic piece of CCTV shows a person wearing a face mask standing on the street, before collapsing to the floor as others rush to help.' Watch the video and decide for yourself whether that is a generous, gullible or collusive review. It's striking how 'set up' and fake the scene is. There's even a visible split second when the falling woman falters. Falling flat on your face takes guts and she does a pretty good job, but it still looks like amateur dramatics. Readers' comments ranged from the credulous 'truly frightening' to the sceptical 'complete set up'.

Maybe the journalists also suspected the video was set up, but the lure of clickbait was too great. Journalists should verify their sources: was this video verified? I contacted the journalists who wrote the articles about the video for the *Mail Online*, *The Sun* and *The Metro* to ask about its provenance, and what they had done to check its authenticity. None of them replied.

Another disturbing video showed people in China being dragged from their homes by officials in hazmat suits. Had they refused to quarantine? Were they knowingly infecting people? The video tells us that the Chinese government had started doing door-to-door temperature checks. Were these people being taken because they had a high temperature? Is the whole thing real or fake? We have no idea, yet the video will have played its part in stimulating fear.

Headlines referred to 'zombies', 'killer bug' and 'apocalypse'. Over and over, these Chinese Covid videos were described as 'disturbing' by newspapers and commentators. Horror film and *End of Days* references seeped through. A *Sun* headline 'Zombieland' travelled with the speed of a virulent sneeze through the copycat global media.

In 2020 we learnt that fear sells better than sex. If it scares, it airs. If it bleeds, it leads. Finally, the obsession with women's physical charms took a backseat, but maybe because it was carjacked by fear porn. I could almost reminisce about the days of quaint media sexism and objectification – oh, if all we had to worry about was a celebrity up-skirt shot, or bare boobs in *The Sun*, rather than daily death tolls!

Some news outlets and commentators wondered if these videos were proof that China was hiding how bad the situation was, rather than exaggerating it. But how plausible were they? The epidemic never transpired to look like this. People haven't suddenly fallen flat on their faces, to be immediately surrounded by hazmat-suited medics anywhere except these videos. They depicted a totally overblown horror-story vision of Covid-19. If the rest of the world had Covid, China appears to have had 'Stunt Covid'.

The videos were shared many millions of times, but it's impossible to quantify now, as in some cases they have been removed, including the probable first sources on Chinese social media sites such as Weibo and TikTok. The videos originated in China: were they a prank or were they a psyop (a covert psychological operation)? The fact-checking website Snopes investigated the source of the videos and couldn't find them before the event they supposedly showed, so they might be from January 2020 and that's all we know.

Whether they were plausible, prank or psyop, the videos planted the seed of an idea that the virus had terrifying consequences. They also – at least inadvertently – 'seeded' the idea of a very strong medical and authoritarian response. There will be more on the importance of 'seeding' in Chapter 7, 'The tools of the trade'. If you don't remember the videos, or didn't watch them, I do urge you to view them to compare this early glimpse of 'Stunt Covid' with what actually transpired.

This book focuses on the UK state, Covid and fear, and this chapter is about the UK's media and social media, but it's relevant to mention another Chinese influence before continuing. While I don't wish to plunge you into the murky waters of anything that could be labelled 'conspiracy theory' so early in our journey into fear, the fact is the Covid stunt videos might suggest an attempt to create fear, and there is yet another reason to suspect deliberate spreading of misinformation.

It is difficult to ascertain the extent of undercover social media propaganda, but a 2017 study *How the Chinese Government Fabricates Social Media Posts for Strategic Distraction, not Engaged Argument*[2] estimated that from 250,000 to two million Chinese people are hired by their government to post approximately 448 million 'fake' social media posts per year. These undercover pro-government commentators set out to be ordinary citizens as they steer conversations in the 'correct direction' for the Chinese Communist Party. They are referred to as the '50c army' as they are reportedly paid 50c per post.

Propublica[3] analysed fake and hijacked Twitter accounts and found more than 10,000 suspected fake Twitter accounts pushing propaganda about Hong Kong. Accounts then switched their focus from Hong Kong to Covid-19. These tweets were not aimed at the Chinese living in China, as Twitter is blocked by the Great Firewall. Some were in Chinese and aimed at ethnic Chinese living overseas, but many of the tweets were in English. They were aimed at us. And they waged an unofficial PR campaign in support of the Chinese government's handling of Covid.

Fake Twitter accounts, including bots, unleashed pro-China propaganda when Italy locked down. Italy was the first European country to sign up to China's Belt and Road Initiative, a global trade, infrastructure and cultural network, generally considered to be a way to extend China's economic and political influence. China's medical aid to Italy was described as a 'Health Silk Road' by President Xi Jinping. Twitter was flooded with #forzaCinaeItalia (Go China, go Italy) and #grazieCina (thank you China). These hashtagged messages of support are thought to be from Chinese social media propagandists, the 50c army, not genuine Italian citizens. Is it a coincidence that Italy was the first country in Europe to lock down? And that this followed Italy and China's trade and development agreement? Did this social media campaign influence the public and the politicians?

Michael P. Senger wrote for *The Tablet*[4] about China's online propaganda campaign. He noticed that these 50c army Twitter users were going a step further, taking 'a darker turn', by criticising US Governors who did not issue statewide lockdowns, deliberately trying to influence US policy.

On 11 March 2020, in an interview with the BBC, David Halpern, head of the UK's Behavioural Insight Team, talked about the plan to 'cocoon' the elderly until herd immunity had been acquired.[5] The concept of herd immunity is well-established in science and had not been considered controversial until that point. Interestingly, by 13 March

Chinese state-affiliated Twitter accounts were criticising the approach:

> 'Sweden will not test people with mild symptoms. UK and Germany tried to build a "herd immunity", which will expose many people to the risk of death. These countries are unwilling to invest more resources in epidemic control. What about human rights? What about humanitarianism?'[6]

This is rich from the country that literally welded people into their homes and instigated a brutal and experimental lockdown. And that's without getting started on wider human rights violations, such as the internment of Uygur people in Xinjiang. As a Chinese satirical song that also did the rounds on social media goes: 'After brainwashing, wash your hands and your face.'

Some things naturally proliferate on social media: they 'go viral'. Fear is one of those things. In 2020 it was given wings. Understanding who helped it fly, how and why should be of immense concern to our government and to all of us.

Other countries mimicked China's lockdown. Confusingly, the World Health Organization didn't recommend lockdowns, yet at the same time lauded China's approach. The West was largely horrified by footage of Wuhan residents trapped in their homes, yet we enacted a similar totalitarian policy. *The Sun* reported that 'devastating footage appears to show coronavirus patients being welded inside their homes and "left to die" as China battles to contain the fatal disease'.[7]

The newspapers which shared Chinese videos without verifying their authenticity lacked journalistic rigour. What followed throughout 2020 and into 2021 was an incessant onslaught of doom-mongering through TVs, newspapers, radio and the internet. In the rest of this chapter I will look at the reasons why the UK media might have reported the epidemic in the way it did.

The constant Covid news and daily death tolls meant they dominated our thoughts. In all likelihood, Covid, death, lockdown and the effects of restrictions have been your brain's main go-tos. The availability heuristic, or availability bias, describes a mental shortcut which means that we recall the most immediate examples of things. When a matter is extremely pressing, it crowds out our ability to think of other things. If Covid deaths are talked about every day then you think about them every day, at the expense of other types of deaths, but also at the expense of much of life. Our cognitive roadmap was redrawn in 2020. You may have been driving, but the government and media had control of your satnav.

The media has a responsibility to inform us, but it also has a responsibility to be balanced. The coverage of daily death tolls, the ghoulish headlines and the scary graphs permeated our brains. Some of the people I have interviewed told me about the considerable effect that the media had on their perception of the world and their subsequent mental wellbeing.

The media should serve the public trust and owes its readers and viewers the best available version of the truth, ascertained by careful questioning. The British public expect the highest standards from the BBC, which is probably why it hurt so much that it spread alarm, exemplified by Sarah's mother (p37). Of all the news providers, it is the BBC we would most expect to take a careful step back from the furore and fear and offer a balanced perspective.

I talked to former BBC journalist Sue Cook. She told me she had been surprised and disappointed by the BBC's one-sided coverage of Covid, and the lack of vigorous questioning. A lifetime listener, she even turned off Radio 4 this year because she couldn't bear to listen to it anymore. For such a BBC stalwart it was a bitter discovery that the BBC's 'standards of truth and impartiality have gone'. She said, 'My fear is that there is now no solid, consistent media outlet you can trust. You have to cast around and find people you can trust. It might be someone on Facebook or YouTube, and it's a jungle out there.'

The BBC has a Charter which promises to 'provide impartial news and information to help people understand and engage with the world around them'. In the BBC's guidelines on the 'Use of Language' there are specific undertakings in times of terror, war and disaster. One promise is that 'care is required in the use of language that carries value judgements'.[8] Some of the BBC's coverage of Covid sits a little uneasily with its Charter, although some welcomed the value judgements. BBC *Newsnight* presenter Emily Maitliss received both praise and criticism from different quarters for her 'editorialising' when she criticised Dominic Cummings on 26 May for 'breaking the rules'. There were 24,000 complaints to the BBC, which agreed she had breached impartiality guidelines.

The BBC appeared to highlight stories which would create fear, focusing on negative outcomes rather than recovery. One headline read 'Luton teen speaks of "really scary" time her dad caught virus'. Another read 'I had my funeral planned in my head'.

'Italian economy takes a body blow' is a subtle example of a BBC headline on 1 March 2020 which was less impartial than we might expect. 'Body blow' is a metaphor that conjures a painful impact on the economy. Rather than leading with a fact about the drop in GDP, or the prediction of recession, this headline is a more colourful, editorialised headline. I asked Cook her opinion: 'The term "body blow" is acceptable if it describes a literal fact, but not to dramatise and exaggerate. That's wrong.' The BBC's coverage was so remarkably fear-mongering during the epidemic that in January 2021 *Telegraph* journalist Allison Pearson labelled the organisation the 'Body Bag Corporation'.[9]

I deliberately chose a subtle illustration here because it's easily forgiven. The issue is it wasn't an isolated example: it was one of hundreds of dramatised headlines about a single virus. They all add up to create a more powerful impression. Among a wealth of other articles about the epidemic in Italy, this headline created a feeling of 'doom-mongering', according to Cook: 'All the examples from Italy dramatise things to sound important and make people sit up and listen. I wonder whether the content is less important than the dramatic impact. Ultimately, it's destructive of trust.' I asked the BBC journalist who wrote the story about this choice of headline and for a wider discussion about the BBC's Covid coverage, but he declined to answer.

Sky News reported on 19 March 2020 that army vehicles were brought in to transport dead bodies in Bergamo. This would make you think that army trucks were needed because there were so many bodies. In fact, according to the Italian Funeral Industry Federation,[10] 70% of undertakers had to stop work to quarantine at the start of the outbreak, so the army was drafted in for a one-off transport of 60 coffins. The startling image of the army transporting the dead was not explained, but it appeared on Sky and other broadcasters and in newspapers here in the UK and around the world, seeding the idea of an almost unmanageable number of corpses.

One reason that the same stories proliferate globally, and that sources are not always thoroughly fact-checked by news outlets, is the reliance on news agencies. There are three main global news agencies: Associated Press, Reuters and Agence-France Presse. Much of the text, images and video you see in broadcast and print has come from those three agencies. This means there is far less diversity in reporting than you might think, especially on foreign news. If one of the big three agencies doesn't report on it, as far as most of the Western media goes, it didn't happen. And agency reporting of geopolitical stories can be subtly deduced from a similarity in tone, as well as the same images and sometimes text.

Journalists are human and subject to the same fears as the rest of us. We are all made of the same psychological stuff. Perhaps their fears clouded their judgement and reporting. They might not have had time, in the teeth of the crisis, to thoroughly investigate every image and video supplied by the picture desk. Yet the result was weeks and months of relentlessly emotional bad news that lacked context and rigour.

How did the relentless fear in the media affect politicians? They also read the news and live with the same cultural wallpaper, so they are not immune to the effects. In an interesting insight, Matt Hancock, the Minister for Health, revealed in an an interview[11] on LBC Radio in 2021 that he had placed large orders for Covid vaccines as a result of watching the fictional film *Contagion*. This seems to have turned out well for our vaccine supplies, but it's a remarkable admission about the influence of a sensationalist Hollywood film (about a fictional virus that kills 30% of people who catch it) on the Health Secretary.

Fear and time are two factors that might explain the fear-mongering, but there are two more. I asked a broadsheet comment writer why newspapers used so many doom-laden headlines. 'Narcissism and greed drive this,' he said. 'Pay rises are linked to the top-performing articles. The journalists who get the highest views for articles and the most subscriptions generated for the paper get the biggest pay rises. You want your stories to get the most views.'

I asked him for an example: 'When SAGE came out with the prediction of half a million deaths, the newspaper instantly published it to get the headline out immediately, rather than interrogate it. Within five minutes it's out there as a headline. Then a few hours later there's a more sceptical article. But the first story has had the impact, not the sceptical one. When Whitty and Vallance predicted 4,000 deaths a day in October we knew straight away that would be the headline. But a good journalist should say, this doesn't pass the sniff test, they should research it and not publish it verbatim. Sure, a couple of days later there's an article dissecting the numbers, but it doesn't get the same take up as the first story.' The article gets the views. The journalist gets the pay rise. We have panic. The damage is done.

Not all journalists fed us a constant diet of fear. Like Sue Cook, I also regretfully switched off Radio 4. I found Talk Radio, which had a broader variety of guests. Talk Radio presenter Dan Wootton's motto in 2020 was, 'No spin, no bias and no hysteria.' I spoke to him about his approach on his radio show and also his column in *The Sun*.

Wootton had Covid at the same time as Boris Johnson, meaning he understood it could be a seriously unpleasant illness, but from the beginning he didn't agree lockdown was the right policy economically, socially or in terms of other health costs. He said he thought that on the day the Office for National Statistics revealed that there had been 26,000 non-Covid excess deaths between March and September in homes,[12] the media would 'get it' and balance the harms and costs of lockdown: 'It was close to the Covid death toll at the time. It got some coverage in the newspapers but I remember the news bulletins didn't do it. The reporting has been focused on Covid deaths and the consequences of lockdown have been ignored.' I asked why he thought that was: 'I think there is a groupthink mentality. If the BBC covers a story then ITV and Channel 4 do it too. A lot of journalists will take the easy option.'

A broadcast journalist who spoke to me off the record said that most people on her editorial team had a different perspective on the epidemic to her. She described herself as 'fighting the good fight in the newsroom' but being outnumbered by her team. Maybe they had consumed the information provided by the government more uncritically than this journalist. It was a crusade for her to push for balance, such as for statistics on recoveries to be given alongside deaths, more detailed breakdowns about ICU occupancy in hospitals and PCR false positives.

The Number 10 press briefings were characterised by bland and unchallenging questions from journalists, such as 'When will the epidemic be over?' A *Press Gazette* reader poll[13] concurred. When it asked 'Do you think journalists have done a good job of holding the Government to account during the daily UK Covid-19 press briefings?' 70% said no.

Weak questions fail to hold politicians to account, fail to uncover essential information which should be in the public domain, fail to provide balance (which would settle minds and emotions) and they also damage journalism itself. Another *Press Gazette* poll[14] showed that public trust in journalists had been eroded. When asked 'Do you think trust in journalism has increased since the Covid-19 epidemic?' 48% said no and 19% said it had remained the same. Only 33% said it had increased. Another survey[15] conducted by Edelman's Trust found that, globally, journalists were the least trusted source for coronavirus updates.

In general, mainstream journalists only discussed the epidemic and the lockdown within the framework set by lockdown – they didn't investigate and interrogate from outside the framework. Where journalists provided challenge, the default position was to perform outrage at every opportunity and to play at unelected opposition, but always in the one direction: demanding the government go further, and lock down sooner and harder. Close businesses? Now schools. Tier Three? Why not Tier Four? Perhaps journalists have come to see themselves more as political activists holding populist Johnson to account, in a simplistic morality play of pandemic deaths versus evil Tory politics.

Of course the political and health journalists employed by newspapers, TV and radio had secure jobs throughout the crisis. If they had suffered financially in the same way as the millions of self-employed, or those in hard-hit sectors such as hospitality and leisure, would they have provided more challenge?

Why else haven't journalists asked more challenging questions? There is a complex relationship between the government, the media and the public. Noam Chomsky explained the 'propaganda model of mass media' in his book, *Manufacturing Consent*. One aspect of this is that the proximity of mass media to political and economic power means that the media propagate the world views of the powerful. One simple way this works is that newspapers and broadcasters have to cater to the financial motivations of their owners and investors. Proprietors have a top-down effect on the preferences and biases of the media. Boris Johnson was a popular leader at the start of the crisis and so newspapers might have been sympathetic. Put simply, if Rupert Murdoch liked Boris Johnson at the beginning of 2020, a News UK media brand would be more likely to write supportive articles.

Piers Morgan offers a marvellous example of someone who was supported by the media. He was a vociferous supporter of lockdown, and critical of people who broke the rules or appeared to minimise the dangers of the epidemic on *Good Morning Britain* and through his Twitter account. On 16 December he urged the government to introduce tougher restrictions for Christmas. Yet he went to the Caribbean island of Antigua for his Christmas break. This didn't break the law, but it did breach guidance, and was contrary to his strong words to the nation and Cabinet ministers. You might call it hypocritical. Guido Fawkes[16] broke the story, which was not picked up by the newspapers. Politicians and celebrities who broke the rules were castigated by the media. Piers Morgan is friends with editors and a powerful figure in the media – did they form a silent circle of protection around him?

I spoke to a seasoned investigative journalist from one of the broadsheets about the challenges in political journalism. There is a symbiotic relationship between government and journalists that can – uncomfortably – provide government with the means to partially set the agenda. Firstly, beyond official press briefings, government press officers and SPADs (special advisors to politicians) give favoured information and informal briefings to political journalists. If the journalist writes things the government doesn't like, the journalist is less likely to be kept in the loop. So to an extent, they are under pressure to write about what they are told, if they want to maintain a preferential relationship. Secondly, if information is fed to the journalist late in the day, there isn't always time to thoroughly investigate before it runs. If it's a cracking story, it may be published quite uncritically in order to get the scoop.

The investigative journalist acknowledged that fear is a good story; it's easy for the media to go full throttle into scare mode. Fear engages the reader. That has a short-term positive benefit for the news outlet, but ultimately it disrupts the delicate balance between public, government and media. The longer lockdowns and restrictions go on, the more advertising and sales revenues suffer. Are we now at the stage where that will, finally, drive a change in tone in the media?

There were certainly times when the relationship between the government and the media looked very cosy. The media enthusiastically covered stories which supported the government position, but ignored stories which might harm it.

For example, two studies were released in a short space of time about the immune response to Covid, one negative about long-term immunity and one positive. Guess which one received the most coverage? The BBC reported on the 'negative' study, which showed antibodies fall after a Covid infection, on 27 October 2020,[17] and said 'immunity appears to be fading and there is a risk of catching the virus multiple times'. However, in November it did not report on a study[18] showing that a quarter of us might have T-cell immunity to Covid, which is long-lasting.

Low-quality evidence in favour of masks was all over the media, but the one decent randomised controlled trial (RCT) into mask-wearing was barely reported. It found a statistically insignificant difference in infection between mask-wearers and non-mask wearers.[19] I interviewed one of the study's authors for Chapter 13, 'The climate of fear'. Hospital admissions made headlines, but not discharges. Deaths were reported with grim daily dedication, but not recoveries. Is it any wonder that the UK was one of the most frightened countries in the world?[20] Professor Sir David Spiegelhalter, the head of the University of Cambridge's Winton Centre for Risk and Evidence Communication, which carried out a study into British attitudes, said he was concerned that the UK had become 'overanxious'.

Most news outlets rely on advertising revenue for income, which means there is a degree of unspoken catering to the preferences of the advertiser. There was a 48% decline in traditional advertising spend in the UK in the lockdown period 23 March to 30 June. Public Health England became the UK's largest advertiser, and the government the sixth biggest advertiser, during this time. The chancellor, Rishi Sunak, announced in April 2020 that the UK would spend £35 million on the 'All in, All together' advertising campaign in national and regional newspapers. Did that set the tone for editorial coverage at the outset of the epidemic? Campaign reported that Cabinet Office figures reveal that the government invested in excess of £184m on communications relating to Covid-19 in 2020.[21] What will the final bill be? And do the newspapers dare to bite the hand that feeds them?

As well as editor and proprietor bias, the influence of advertising revenue, the lure of the clickbait headline and the journalist's own tendency to feel the fear and allow that to influence reporting, another worrying factor affected media coverage of the epidemic. On 23 April 2020, Ofcom, the UK's communication regulator, issued strict guidance about Covid coverage. It asked broadcasters to be alert to 'health claims related to the virus which may be harmful; medical advice which may be harmful; accuracy or material misleadingness in programmes in relation to the virus or public policy regarding it'. [22]

That guidance could be interpreted as not permitting anyone to challenge the government's public health policy. Scientific advice evolves, so does government advice, and inhibiting broadcasters from these discussions is dangerous.

Free speech is not just for the good times, it's for epidemics too. In fact, it is in times of crisis that we need to hold these values even closer. As the Free Speech Union pointed out, broadcasters should be able to air different views without Ofcom making value judgements: 'The approach adopted by Ofcom in these cases is deeply concerning. It is true, as Ofcom notes, that this is a time of significantly heightened public sensitivity. It is also a time of substantially increased state powers and restrictions on long-established liberties. However, no such restrictions have been placed by the Government on the right to free speech. In fact, it is vital that this right should be upheld so that the Government's decision to impose wide-ranging restrictions can be challenged by broadcasters and others. This means that any regulator charged with upholding freedom of expression – as is the case with Ofcom – should proceed to restrict that freedom only on a closely-reasoned basis. That is something Ofcom has manifestly failed to do.'[23]

Ofcom's decision may have chilled the inclination of the media to explore theories which were counter to government advice. The state broadcaster, the BBC, refused to challenge state orthodoxy, which is the sort of thing we criticise other countries for. Open debate should have been allowed, in sensible and contextual ways, to inform the public, stimulate scientific debate and acknowledge that consensus moves. There is a word for only sharing information which is biased and is used to promote a political cause: propaganda.

3. FRIGHTFUL HEADLINES

GLOBAL GLOOM

Coronavirus leaves Wuhan a 'zombieland' with people
collapsing in streets and medics patrolling in hazmat suits
The Sun, **24 January 2020**

> Killer Bug Chaos: Man arrested after filming covert
> video showing true scale of body bags piling up at
> Wuhan hospital *The Sun*, **2 February 2020**

Iran's coronavirus mass graves so big they can be seen from
SPACE as 429 die from disease *The Sun*, **13 March 2020**

> Elderly 'dead and abandoned' in Spanish care homes
> *BBC*, **24 March 2020**

Thousands more people may have died in Wuhan than
authorities are saying *Metro*, **30 March 2020**

> US passes 10m Covid cases as virus rages across
> nation *The Guardian*, **10 November 2020**

Swedish surge in Covid cases dashes immunity hopes
The Guardian, **12 November 2020**

> Brutal Covid second wave exposes Italy's shortage of
> intensive care staff *The Guardian*, **18 November 2020**

THE UK'S FRIGHTFUL HEADLINES

UK on 'war footing' as elderly face isolation *BBC*, **15 March 2020**

Three numbers that tell a terrifying story *BBC*, **23 March 2020**

Coronavirus horror: London mortuaries expand to prepare for massive surge in deaths *Daily Express*, **18 March 2020**

End of freedom *The Daily Telegraph*, **24 March 2020**

Heartbreak as healthy 21-year-old dies from coronavirus – 'It's not just a virus' *Daily Express*, **25 March 2020**

NHS Hero's Death on the front line *Daily Mirror*, **30 March 2020**

Don't go out and enjoy the sunshine *The Daily Telegraph*, **4 April 2020**

Boris Johnson fights 'truly frightening' virus as Michael Gove tells of Cabinet shock at PM's condition *Evening Standard*, **7 April 2020**

Intensive care nurse 'going through hell' battling coronavirus begs Britons to stay home *Daily Express*, **11 April 2020**

UK could be 'worst affected' country in Europe *BBC*, **12 April 2020**

Coronavirus: UK must prepare for 'volatile and agitated society' after lockdown lifted, senior police officer warns *The Independent*, **19 April 2020**

Bombshell virus blow to economy with calls for path out of lockdown as output fall 'worse than 2008 crash' *Evening Standard*, **23 April 2020**

Post-Covid UK 'will face twenty years of pain' – The UK's recovery from coronavirus is likely to be slower and shallower than first hoped and Britons will be paying for action to save the economy for the next two decades, a former Bank of England rate-setter has warned *The Scotsman*, **27 April 2020**

UK becomes first country in Europe to pass 30,000 deaths *BBC*, **6 May 2020**

World baffled at how UK got coronavirus so wrong as global headlines blast Government's 'biggest failure in generation' *The Sun*, **7 May 2020**

UK working mothers are 'sacrificial lambs' in coronavirus childcare crisis *The Guardian*, **24 July 2020**

Grim milestone as virus cases top 25m globally *BBC*, **30 August 2020**

NHS has worst week 'in living memory' as doctor warns situation could deteriorate *The Irish News*, **27 October 2020**

Matt Hancock warns that whole population is at risk of 'long Covid' *Daily Mail*, **17 November 2020**

Grim and distressing milestone as Covid deaths in the country pass 5,000 *The Scotsman*, **18 November 2020**

WHO fear Europe will be hit by a THIRD wave of coronavirus early next year due to 'incomplete' response to the pandemic *Mail Online*, **23 November 2020**

Mutant Covid *Metro*, **14 December 2020**

London faces Christmas lockdown TODAY as new super-infectious Covid mutant spreads *Daily Express*, **19 December 2020**

HEALTH SCARE HEADLINES

Britain's youngest coronavirus death: Boy, 13, 'with no underlying conditions' dies alone in isolation in London hospital after testing positive, leaving his family 'beyond devastated' – after UK death toll rises record 381 to 1,789
Daily Mail, **1 April 2020**

> My lungs felt like they were filling with quicksand then all five of my family were struck with Covid-19 hell *The Sun*, **2 April 2020**

Covid-19 found in semen of infected men, say Chinese doctors – Authors claim study based on small number of patients opens up chance of sexual transmission
The Guardian, **7 May 2020**

> 'I've been through 15 weeks of hell': 'Long-haul' Covid-19 sufferers tell of 'debilitating' after-effects *Yorkshire Evening Post*, **6 July 2020**

At least TWO British children have died from mysterious Kawasaki-like disease linked to Covid-19, study reveals
Daily Mail, **10 July 2020**

> People over 6ft have double the risk of coronavirus, study suggests *The Daily Telegraph*, **28 July 2020**

Third of newborns with Covid infected before or during birth
The Guardian, **15 October 2020**

> Celtic star Bitton reveals he couldn't even STAND as he opens up on Covid-19 hell that left him fearing for his health *The Scottish Sun*, **21 October 2020**

People who contract COVID may develop red and swollen toes which turn purple *Sky News*, **29 October 2020**

Coronavirus - every symptom you need to be aware of including 'Covid toes' and hiccups *Daily Mirror*, **30 October 2020**

My Covid hell – student, 20, left in brutal pain from Covid-19 *Leicester Mercury*, **5 November 2020**

Covid 'could damage fertility of up to 20% of male survivors' *Metro*, **12 November 2020**

Baby left with lifelong condition after developing rare syndrome linked to coronavirus *Wales Online*, **15 November 2020**

Damage to multiple organs recorded in 'long Covid' cases *The Guardian*, **15 November 2020**

Is testicle pain potentially a sign of Covid? 49-year-old Turkish man who had no other symptoms is diagnosed with the virus *Mail Online*, **18 November 2020**

A British father is suffering from blindness and paralysis in a hospital in India after being bitten by a snake while battling coronavirus, his family have said *Sky News*, **20 November 2020**

COVID-19 could cause erectile dysfunction in patients who have recovered from the virus, doctor warns *Daily Mail*, **6 December 2020**

THE WEIRD AND THE WAFER-THIN

Bad news for baldies as new US study finds they're 40% more at risk of coronavirus *Daily Star*, **23 July 2020**

Health officials recommend 'glory holes' for safe sex during the pandemic *Metro*, **23 July 2020**

Why your PETS should be socially distancing: Experts warn dogs should be kept two metres away from other canines and cats kept indoors to protect owners *Daily Mail*, **11 November 2020**

Covid survivors could have potentially life-threatening allergic reaction to hair dye *Daily Mirror*, **12 November 2020**

Masturbate during coronavirus lockdown to 'boost your immune system and fight off infection', docs say *The Sun*, **13 November 2020**

Dog-owners face 78% higher risk of catching Covid-19 – and home grocery deliveries DOUBLE the risk, study finds *Daily Mail*, **16 November 2020**

Ice cream tests positive for coronavirus in China *Sky News*, **16 January 2021**

SARAH, 85, BY HER DAUGHTER

My mum is 85 and she has said she doesn't want any treatment if she gets it. She will let nature take its course.

She doesn't have any health issues, there's no reason to be hidden away. She was very active for someone her age and used to be involved in the University of the Third Age and go to a horticultural club, but everything that makes her life worthwhile and gives her forward motion is completely gone.

At the beginning, the ramping up of fear got to her. She began to believe it was inevitable that she would die of Covid. It was foremost in her mind.

We had to tell her to turn the BBC off. I honestly think that because the BBC is so respected and looked to as the voice of calm and reason, it has completely let down its licence payers because it kept up a constant narrative of fear. It has ceased to do its job in giving balance and it didn't question the government fiercely. If you just watched or listened to the BBC every day, what hope have you had?

Then she came back to herself. She was brought up in the war, her family were bombed out and so she understands risk and mortality. She got to the point where she wanted the choice to exercise her discretion. She didn't agree that her choices should be taken away from her.

Sadly I think she has gone downhill – not because of the fear she felt, but because she hasn't had enough to fill her days. The rug has been pulled away from her.

We would break the rules and visit her in the garden with a cup of tea. It was very important for all of us that we keep seeing each other. When I hear about people who let one of their family die alone in a care home, I am amazed that they put away the very essence of being human. How could they have been so compliant?

You have to work out the risks you want to take. We shouldn't let fear manipulate us out of proper reasoning. I think people should be encouraged to be stoic and strong and we've had the exact opposite.

When we are navigating life, fear is not the right compass.

4. FEAR IS A PAGE OF THE GOVERNMENT PLAYBOOK

'Fear is the foundation of most governments.'

John Adams, Founding Father and second President of the United States

Once upon a time, the fear of nuclear war travelled on the wind from a snowy, far-away country, where an abstract red button might be pushed. The Cold War marks a starting point – out of a number you could pick – in the trajectory of the threats we have faced in modern times and the fears they inspired. In this trajectory, the weapons we fear have become smaller and the enemies closer to home.

Covid did not travel on the wind of a weapon of mass destruction: we were told it is a stowaway on human breath. The threat is from the intimate whisper of your lover, pleasantries exchanged with a shop assistant, the convivial conversation of friends in a pub, a hug from your grandchild or silent travellers on public transport. The danger is not an enemy on the other side of the world, but every single person you come into contact with. And that means you are their enemy too.

The 'war on terror' bridged an arc of exploitable fears between the Cold War and Covid. Terrorists could inflict destruction anywhere, at any time. They might be from faraway lands, but they could also be among us in a world of leaky borders, immigration and air travel. Suspicion could be directed at anyone who leaves a bag on the train station platform, or who looks like a 'certain type'. Terrorism is smaller in scale than nuclear war – it destroys a building, or a bus, not a continent or a country – yet it is unnervingly random.

But an infectious virus makes terrorists of us all. Anyone on the train station platform or next to you in the pub could present a danger, not just a 'certain type'. The weapon we find ourselves at war with has reduced in size from nuclear bomb behemoth, to weapons concealed on the body, to the body itself. The enemy shifted from a foreign government, to foreign terrorists, to every single one of us.

Geopolitical borders are now not just between countries but between our own bodies. We must stay apart, observe distances of two metres, wear masks, not shake hands or hug. All for our own safety.

In 2020, *we* became the enemy.

Once lockdown was announced, passersby on pavements danced a nervous minuet, keeping a formal distance from each other, skirting the edges of pathways, or huffing and puffing with ostentatious righteousness into the road. The anxiety was palpable in public in the spring of 2020. Many proclaimed on social media how angry they were when people broke the rules and breached their two-metre perimeter. People were scared, skittish, and defended their new borders from intruders.

Can we be at war with a virus? Politicians and journalists think so. The language is martial: it's the 'greatest threat in peacetime'; we are 'at war' with a virus; we will 'defeat' it; NHS workers are on the 'front line'.

The report *Behavioural Government*,[1] produced for the government in 2018, observed the importance of 'framing' policies and the language used into 'a coherent and comprehensible pattern… by providing a powerful governing image or metaphor.' The report gives the examples of describing crime as a beast, or as a virus infecting the city. Of course, language used by ministers is – at least sometimes – considered very carefully.

Donald Trump kept calling Covid the 'Chinese virus', a foreign threat equivalent to a hostile nation. Angela Merkel said Covid was the greatest threat Germany had faced since 1945. Boris Johnson did his best to channel Churchill. In a speech[2] in the summer of 2020 he compared Gavi (The Global Alliance for Vaccines and Immunisations) to NATO, revealing a seismic paradigm shift in how we perceive our 'enemies'. *The Metro*'s front-cover headline was 'Careless talk costs lives' on 12 January 2021, evoking the Second World War.

Truthfully, no government can believe that the virus can be defeated like an enemy nation; it's a very different proposition. So what do governments hope to achieve with this fighting talk? War appeals to the ego, to the need to exert control. To offer hope of winning when we feel out of control. It's easier to cast a virus in the role of opponent. But viruses are endemic, they are part of our history, our present and our future. In fact, they are part of us. Our DNA actually contains about 100,000 pieces of viral DNA, 8% of the human genome.

Governments may feel obliged to do whatever it takes to steer us through a crisis, and that means we have to swallow it like bitter medicine, even if we don't like it. War requires populations to be resilient, make sacrifices and obey their leaders, like soldiers obeying the chain of military command. Martial language reminds us of this.

This epidemic's course has been measured in deaths and cases. Wars are normally counted in victories, not fallen and wounded soldiers – those counts are saved till the end, but we were the fallen. Daily body counts reminded us of the sacrifice, kept the fear alive, and primed us for compliance. Fear works best in wartime.

History shows us that governments have long used fear to control populations, from the ancient Egyptians to the vast campaigns of terror committed by totalitarian governments in China, Russia and Germany in the 20th century. The 'Reign of Terror' during the French Revolution, and the term 'project fear' used to describe the referenda for Scottish independence and the UK's membership of the EU, did what they said on the tin.

British propaganda was accelerated during the First World War through the War Propaganda Bureau, using films, the press and advertisements. You might be familiar with the graphical depictions of the evil 'German Hun' during the First World War, and with the mobilisation of the UK state apparatus to encourage its people to fight. Since then we have honed our skills. The weapons are sharper.

Following the bloodshed of that period, the pioneering psychoanalyst Sigmund Freud wrote much about human nature; that there was a 'pleasure principle', in which we are driven to pursue gratification, and a 'reality principle', in which society must restrict and control the instinctual desires in all people, to a socially productive end. His nephew, Edward Bernays, who was living in America, took many of these ideas on board and pioneered the 'Public Relations' industry, named as such because he understood the negative connotations with the existing term 'propaganda'. In his book *Propaganda*, published in 1928, Bernays wrote: 'The conscious and intelligent manipulation of the organised habits and opinions of the masses is an important element in democratic society. Those who manipulate this unseen mechanism of society constitute an invisible government which is the true ruling power of our country.'

Just how far do governments go? Edward Bernays offers a perfect example of how it's done and it's worth meandering at this point, away from Covid, to illustrate how a government will leverage fear and propaganda. Bernays argued in the US in the 1950s that instead of reducing people's fear of communism and nuclear war it should be exaggerated, but in such a way that it became a weapon in the Cold War. Essentially, he wanted to weaponise the US population's fear.

In his series *Century of the Self*, Adam Curtis illustrated how Bernays helped to eject the popularly elected Guatemalan leader, Juan Jacobo Árbenz Guzmán, and restore the malleable 'Banana Republic dictators' controlled by the US's United Fruit Company. And he did it in a way that made it look like a victory for American democracy.

He organised a trip to Guatemala for journalists and arranged for them to meet selected politicians who told them that Árbenz was a communist in league with Moscow. During the trip there was a violent anti-American riot, which some believed Bernays arranged. He set up a news agency called the Middle America News Bureau and pushed out news stories saying that Guatemala was going to be used as a beach head for a communist invasion of the US. The *New York Herald Tribune*, *Time*, *Newsweek*, and *Atlantic Monthly* all described the threat and called for US government action. At the same time the United Fruit Company sent favourable articles and reports to Congress members and journalists.

Bernays was also part of a secret CIA plot to remove Árbenz and re-install a puppet dictator. Howard Hunt, CIA officer, confessed that they organised a 'terror campaign'. The CIA ran a psyop to present military defeat as a foregone conclusion in Guatemala, and military support was provided to the new dictator of choice.

Bernays created the conditions in the public and the press to reshape political reality through this cleverly crafted campaign using universities, lawyers, the media, business and government. The reason it all worked? He exploited fear and manipulated people. He believed in democracy, he just thought people were too stupid to be trusted with it and that rational argument was fruitless. He called his process the 'engineering of consent'.

Propaganda, as a heavy blunt instrument, had been used for centuries, but Bernays set out a clear scientific framework for how to engineer the consent of the public, even warning that these tools could just as easily be employed by demagogues. The key point is that Bernays saw himself as a true and liberal patriot, helping benevolent governments and organisations to overcome the irrational drives in their people to reach an altruistic goal. Modern politicians and behavioural scientists might agree with his ambition.

At around the same time, in 1957, William Sargent explained in his book, *Battle for the Mind*, how politicians and religious leaders use 'brainwashing' techniques, specifically highlighting the importance of fear in causing alteration in brain function to increase suggestibility. He gave China's Cultural Revolution as a specific example:

'Fear of continued civil war, or foreign intervention, or both, convinced the Chinese Communist leaders they they must use shock tactics to convert the masses. A more intellectual approach might have resulted in a more stable type of conversion, but it would have taken dangerously long, and been consummated only with the gradual dying off of those brought up in the old ways of thought, and the growing up of the children in the new. To make a new China overnight, emotional disruption was essential; and so effective were the methods used, that thousands killed themselves in despair… leaving the more resilient millions to dance, dance, dance for joy at their liberation from millenniary bondage – until they learned to tremble at the periodic visits of the Household Police who now keep a dossier on the history and activities of every household.'

Between all these examples and the present day, has anything fundamental about humanity changed? That doesn't seem likely. No doubt governments and psychologist advisors are as tempted, and populations are as pliable.

An alarmed populace will desire to be led to safety by its government. The more severe the emergency, the more a population will appreciate strong government. In the US, they call it 'rallying around the flag'. In *Hidden Persuaders* by Vance Packard, which explored the use of depth psychology and subliminal research in post-war United States consumerism, the 'perfect president' is described as a 'father image'. In an obvious and visceral attempt to convey a strong paternal leadership, Boris Johnson said the government would put its 'arms around every single worker' during the epidemic. Some might welcome the embrace of the state, while others feel it as a stranglehold.

People willingly sacrifice liberty for security during a crisis. This is not a simple exchange though. What does security mean? And is liberty returned when the crisis has passed? After a crisis some governments may wish to lengthen the state of fear, or exaggerate it, to keep the population obedient.

Early in 2020, the people of the world realised en masse they would die. Of course, they were always going to die. But they believed they could die then, or soon, as a result of the epidemic. Mortality felt real. It could be that a modern-day death phobia, or at least our disconnect from death, has primed us for an over-reaction. If you haven't accepted you will die one day, you are a sitting duck for policies which claim to be for your safety. There is mixed evidence about the efficacy of lockdowns. We do know that they have cost lives. (For a fuller explanation, see Appendix 2.) Yet people traded their liberty in the hope that the government knew best.

Robert Higgs, the American economic historian, said, 'The masses can be turned around on a dime on the basis of a crisis, even a bogus crisis. The politicians will quickly come running round to exploit on a crisis.' He has good form for predicting the effects of crisis on government. In his book *Crisis and Leviathan* he postulated that the First World War, Great Depression, Second World War, Johnson–Nixon years, 9/11 and the Great Recession that started in 2008 all caused the US government to expand, in a pattern he calls the 'ratchet effect'. Effectively, nothing is so permanent as a temporary government measure.

'A crisis,' Higgs observed,[3] 'alters the fundamental conditions of political life. Like a river suddenly swollen by the collapse of an upstream dam, the ideological current becomes bloated by the public's fear and apprehension of impending dangers and its heightened uncertainty about future developments.' Bewildered people turn to the government to resolve the situation, demanding that government officials 'do something' to repair the damage already done and prevent further harm.

In an interview for *Reason* magazine on 20 September 2001 – nine days after 9/11 – Higgs was asked about the future of the US and its government, based on his studies of crises in the past. He accurately predicted more surveillance, the military increasingly being used for domestic duties, the enlargement of the 'Big Brother' state and that terrorism would not be wiped out.

So, what does Higgs predict will happen as a result of the Covid crisis? In short, associated government measures will leave an abundance of legacies for the worse so far as people's freedom is concerned.[4]

There were significant changes in the UK following acts of terror too. The Prevent policy is one of the most significant of recent years. In 2015 it became a legal duty for public sector institutions to effectively engage in surveillance of the population for signs of extremism and radicalisation. We should remember that extremism and radicalisation are not illegal, and who gets to define them anyway? Let's not forget that the Suffragettes were considered extremists in their time.

The Investigatory Powers Act 2016 followed the controversy over bulk data collection by authorities which had been revealed in the famous Snowden leaks, and aimed to create a firmer legal footing for bulk collection and interception of communications, including your internet browsing histories. It allowed police and other governmental organisations to access information. Effectively it legalised the mass surveillance that Snowden had revealed.

The Terrorism Act 2000 enabled arrest without charge beyond 24 hours and stop and search without suspicion. This basically allows people to be held for considerable periods of time without charge and for that to be extended, whereas normally the police can only hold you for 24 hours without charge. Chillingly, the UK might also have been caught up in torture since 9/11.[5]

What was the risk to the UK population which justified these far-reaching policies of mass surveillance, stop and search and detention? Acts of terror create a whiplash of shock and fear, but in fact from 1975–2018 the risk of dying in a terrorist attack in the UK was one in 11.4 million per year.[6] The risk of being injured was one in 496,464. It's imperative we understand how much fear clouds our perception of risk.

I interviewed Silkie Carlo, the director of Big Brother Watch, about the parallels between the changes to UK law and society after 9/11 and what we are experiencing since Covid. She didn't hold back: 'Covid has given the world an electric shock. It's a time when measures can be introduced and there is little bandwidth for people to oppose. The extent of the changes this year is going to affect everything about being human. The point about liberties is when you restrict them you don't just restrict the legal aspect of liberty, you restrict life itself. The reason we are in the situation we are in now is because of the precedents that were set after 9/11.'

While we talked I felt a recognition in my gut of my own fears this year. She told me that after the war on terror 'we were left with a raft of counter-terror legislation which had implications beyond counter-terror. It justified the global mass surveillance architecture that we passively live under now.' As I had envisaged an arc of fear from the Cold War to the present day, Carlo noted how the state had exploited that fear: 'There were warnings from congressmen during the Cold War when fear was whipped up about 'reds under the bed' that we could take surveillance so far that it would prohibit the possibility for resistance to form. The big change we were left with was the massive internalisation of fear and suspicion. There is a hyper focus on security. It's moved our dial on the preservation of democracy. Fear justifies actions which are purely performative. Someone seizes your tweezers at the airport for safety. And you tolerate it. That is the end of rationality.'

Tony Blair used the threat of terrorism to give him a new moral authority. Fear of the enemy is how politicians maintain power and advance agendas. The Labour government's military intervention in Iraq is believed to have motivated and strengthened terrorist groups and led to terrorist actions in the UK, from the 7/7 London bombings in 2005 to the London Bridge attack in 2017. Those acts of terrorism were in turn used to justify restrictions on liberty.

In *The Power of Nightmares*, Adam Curtis says that politicians will eventually have to concede that some threats are exaggerated and others have no foundation in reality, that 'in an age when all the grand ideas have lost credibility, fear of a phantom enemy is all the politicians have left to maintain their power.' Are viruses and variants to be the phantom enemy?

At the outset of the epidemic, politicians, journalists and even scientists may have over-estimated its deadliness. This is due to lack of knowledge (common early on in an epidemic), caution and even fear. But as the year wore on, it became clear that Covid was less lethal than feared. Globally, the average Infection Fatality Rate (IFR) is 0.15%[7] and the median IFR for under 70 year olds is 0.05%.[8] Yet the UK government pursued lockdowns and strategies which created other impacts on mortality from other causes, cancelled GP appointments, led to businesses closing and jobs lost, children missing school, local elections cancelled, and many basic liberties curtailed.

The focus switched from deaths, to 'R' (the reproduction number), to cases, to hospitalisations, to vaccine rollout. The goalposts also moved: flatten the curve was followed by slowing the spread, then we dabbled with suppression, the notion of zero Covid was floated, there were fears about a second wave, then we were in it (or at least a bad winter surge), then waiting for a vaccine, the vaccine arrived, then we were told that wouldn't mean restrictions could be lifted, the inevitable third wave was mentioned, and fears raised about a new transmissible variant – Covid-21 next perhaps? – then there are variants or 'scariants' as they were termed by cynics. We seemed to be caught in an endless bait and switch.

The virus narrative makes us enemies of each other, which is used to justify impositions on our freedoms and the manipulation of our fears. History shows that people in wars, or considered dangerous, have been imprisoned, put in concentration camps, tortured and suffered the loss of human rights. War and terror justify a security state. The virus justifies a biosecurity state. Is the average person to consider themselves lethally infectious, unless proven otherwise using an enabling test?[9] Are we bio-terrorists? On 26 March 2021, Dr Sarah Jarvis said 'Breathing is an offensive weapon if you are infected with Covid' on Channel 5's *Jeremy Vine on 5* show. Even allowing for a bit of dramatic licence on telly, it is impossible to imagine someone saying that pre-Covid.

On 18 August 2020, Matt Hancock, the Secretary of State for Health and Social Care, announced that the new National Institute for Health Protection's 'single and relentless mission' would be 'protecting people from external threats to this country's health.' And what are these threats? Apparently they are 'biological weapons, pandemics, and of course infectious diseases of all kinds.' Is it the state's role to protect us from infectious diseases of all kinds?

Notice how many governments and organisations,

including the UK government, started referring to the 'new normal' in the spring of 2020. Lockdown legally started on 26 March 2020, and as early as 26 April Dominic Raab, the Foreign Secretary, said that Britain would be moving to a 'new normal'. That term framed our expectations for the future, because it implied that 'normal', our old normal, real normal, was gone and to be replaced by something new. It signalled a move from one type of society to another.

A comparison with the Nazis might invite frustration in the sceptical reader, but consider the name 'Das Dritte Reich'. The Third Reich, was a clever title, because it planted the idea in the minds of the German people that Hitler's style of government wasn't for a term, it wasn't a fad, it was their present and their future.

How did we move so fast from an emergency situation to a term which seeds the idea the future will be forever different? We were supposed to lock down for three weeks to flatten the curve – why would that necessitate a 'new normal'? A three-week intervention and a 'new normal' cannot logically coexist. What made governments think that Covid-19 would be different from every infectious respiratory disease the world has ever known? Respiratory diseases follow a bell curve: they come and then they go. Why would normal have to be permanently altered for this respiratory disease, and why would that be proclaimed so early?

A biosecurity state, where we are advised to follow directives to wash hands, socially distance and remember 'hands, face, space' is one thing. A legally directed biosecurity state which mandates staying at home is another. We have never before quarantined the healthy and impeded so many human rights in one fell swoop. Our rights to liberty, protest, worship, education and maintaining relationships were all impacted. And these are not trifling privileges, but basic liberties: our human rights as established in law.

I experienced the curtailment of the right to protest personally, and I realised that the attitude towards protest in the UK this year has been indicative of a government that wanted to control more than infection.

'Go home now or you'll be arrested!' an aggressive policeman shouted in my face. He barked orders and questions at me. I had attended an anti-lockdown protest in London on 28 November in my capacity as a journalist and press photographer, and witnessed the police using excessive force. I had just been photographing an arrest on a fairly empty stretch of pavement on Oxford Street, a long way behind the protest which had moved on. I showed the police officer my press pass. He wasn't satisfied and demanded my 'password' to check it was real. His intimidating manner flummoxed me and instead of asking what I had done which was unlawful (nothing), I set about retrieving my personal password to my press association. If he didn't believe me he should have just called the number on the back of the press card; it was unorthodox and inappropriate to ask for my personal password. I can't believe I even started looking, but fear clouds your judgement.

After a couple of minutes with the 'bad cop' a relatively 'good cop' took over and was satisfied by my press pass. I had not done anything unlawful after all. After being subjected to several rounds of Kafka-esque questioning, the four police officers who had surrounded me moved on.

Shockingly, another press photographer I spoke to was shoved twice by the police. One time, his camera was grabbed by a police officer who pushed it in his face to move him on.

Allowing press photographers and journalists to do their work is essential to a free press and democracy. The attitude towards us was obstructive and intimidating. Unfortunately, what we experienced was typical of the force and intimidation which was turned on the protestors that day.

There seemed to be a deliberate strategy of making lots of arrests in order to create a politicised media story. Hundreds of police officers picked off protestors from the edges and back of the protest, like sharks feeding off a shoal of fish, and put them in vans which were lining the streets. The peaceful protest saw violence later in the day, which I'd suggest was at least partially caused by the brute and excessive policing.

On the same day there were crowds of people at Borough Market and Chelsea Farmers' Market, to give just two London examples. Two weeks later there were crowds of people on Oxford Street Christmas shopping. Why are some crowds tolerated, but peaceful political marches and protests clamped down on hard? Does the virus behave differently in different types of crowds? Of course not. We have to conclude that the government and the Met Police seemed to be more concerned about political contagion than viral contagion.

Georgio Agamben, the Italian philosopher, has written about the reduction of life to biopolitics. To simply reduce the theory, he says that the man who is 'accursed' can be set apart from normal society, and must live a 'bare life' – life reduced to the barest form.

In the worst examples, the 'accursed' are put in concentration camps, where a state of exception becomes the rule, and normal laws and morals are forgotten. Guantanamo is a modern example. The 'bare life' of the prisoners was such that the only protest left to them, hunger strike, was also dominated by the brutal policy of the wardens, and they were force fed and anally rehydrated as a form of torture. The prisoner's geopolitical border of the body was destroyed by the captor. This is a disturbing example of a government taking away rights and creating fear.

The UK government has said many times that healthy people can still be infectious, therefore we can all be the 'accursed' to a degree. (This is despite numerous studies showing that asymptomatic transmission is not a serious risk,[10] and Dr Fauci proclaiming in 2020 on US television that 'an epidemic is not driven by asymptomatic carriers'.) Has much of the world been turned, without our understanding or noticing, into a 'state of exception'? The camp can also be metaphorical. We don't need to be relocated, we can be locked down at home too. Home is clearly not a concentration camp, there are no barbed wires or machine-gun towers, and I do not want to stretch this metaphor into melodrama, but nonetheless it is a confinement. For those in cramped and inadequate homes, the confinement is more serious. We were presumed infectious rather than healthy, our geopolitical borders were determined to be unreliable, thus our normal rights were restricted, and for some self-isolation felt like a form of torture.

Beyond the metaphorical, China forced 800,000 people into quarantine, and its use of stadiums as mass isolation areas was chillingly reminiscent of concentration camps. In Israel, the publication *Haaretz* described ultra-Orthodox Jews who do not follow the state's rules as 'Covid insurgents' and 'terrorists'[11] in starkly obvious biopolitical language. In a particularly hyperbolic description, 'maskless individuals' are accused of setting off 'epidemiological time bombs'.

We should be alert to similar, albeit less extreme, moves in Europe. *The Times* headline 'Hunt for mystery person who tested positive for Brazilian Covid-19 variant then vanished'[12] evoked a slightly aggressive image of a hunt for a person carrying a new Covid variant, as though a bio-terrorist was dangerously on the loose with a weapon. Four states in Germany announced plans to create detention centres for those who violate lockdown measures, using specially built facilities, a refugee camp and a juvenile detention centre guarded by police. Public health mutated into crime and punishment, all made possible by emergency laws. Some people will believe that if you break the rules you should accept the consequences, tough. But we must remember that these rule-breakers were healthy, not necessarily infectious, people.

The PCR test used to determine 'infectiousness' is not actually a good indication of infectiousness, believe it or not. The management of the epidemic rested strongly on the use of the PCR test. As the Public Heath England document *Understanding cycle threshold (Ct) in SARS-CoV-2 RT-PCR: a guide for health protection teams* says, 'A single Ct value in the absence of clinical context cannot be relied upon for decision making about a person's infectivity.'[13] And as the Centre for Evidence-Based Medicine at Oxford University said, 'PCR detection of viruses is helpful so long as its accuracy can be understood: it offers the capacity to detect RNA in minute quantities, but whether that RNA represents infectious virus may not be clear.'[14]

In guidelines for NHS staff,[15] the government wrote that

staff who had already had Covid should be exempted from mass screening tests because 'fragments of inactive virus can be persistently detected by PCR in respiratory tract samples following infection – long after a person has completed their isolation period and is no longer infectious.' Think of all the people who tested positive and did self-isolate when they may no longer have been infectious. Of those, how many broke self-isolation and were punished? In November 2020, the Portuguese High Court ruled that PCR test results alone could not be used to enforce self-isolation; they must be accompanied by clinical diagnosis.[16]

The legal detention of healthy people is permitted by emergency laws but enabled by a narrative of dehumanisation. People who break the rules are 'dangerous' (they might be infectious), 'stupid', and 'socially irresponsible'.

People have been instructed not to work, have relationships or touch other people. These are rules which would have sounded outlandish, cruel and impossible not long ago. The number of people attending funerals was restricted, the elderly were left unvisited in care homes, and women birthed without their partners, to give just a few examples of exceptions to the normal moral and human rights which were impeded or suspended.

Lockdown itself is prison terminology. Only wrongdoers are locked down. At least in law you are innocent until proven guilty. In our biosecurity state we are assumed infectious until proven healthy.

How do you leave the camp, the world of confinement, social distancing rules and restrictions? In time, when the government determines the epidemic has run its course? Or perhaps the answer lies in a vaccine, to be delivered en masse in 2021? The choice to take a vaccine is a marvellous modern medical blessing, as long as resuming sovereignty of your life does not mean forgoing sovereignty of your body. Beyond choice, we should be vigilant about the danger of mandation and the more subtle, but no less powerful, threat of coercion, for example by offering a return to normal civic and social life with a 'vaccine passport' or 'Covid status certificate', or double-speak 'freedom app'.

The worst threat, mandation, would signal loss of bodily sovereignty, in the same way as a prisoner in Guantanamo Bay tube-fed against his will. Coercion is more nuanced, but over time would it create a two-tier society of vaccinated 'safe' people and unvaccinated 'unsafe' people? Would the unvaccinated be considered reckless, socially irresponsible or stupid? These are values which push them further into a 'less than' status. Note that Matt Hancock linked 'personal responsibility'[17] with the 2021 vaccine rollout, the implication being that the choice not to vaccinate is irresponsible.

Nick Cohen wrote in *The Guardian*: 'it is only a matter of time before we turn on the unvaccinated'.[18] A German doctor[19] called for people who refuse the vaccination to be refused hospital treatment if they become sick with Covid. This is not how national healthcare has been provided in Germany or the UK. It is available to all. Obesity is one of the key indicators of ICU treatment and death from Covid. It would be equally monstrous to propose that the overweight may not be treated in ICU, because they did not show 'personal responsibility' for their health.

The 'accursed' are less than their fellow humans. This is why it is important to always be aware of language and policy which 'others' and dehumanises. The media and social media have reverberated with language like 'covidiots', 'selfish morons' and 'granny killers'. I can personally attest that peaceful protestors were wrongly characterised as 'violent anti-lockdowners'. A study[20] claimed that non-mask wearers were more likely to be psychopaths. History reverberates with examples of deliberate attempts to dehumanise and divide people and it has never ended well.

So, why do governments use fear? Simply, it encourages compliance. A meta-analysis has found that messages with fear are nearly twice as effective as messages without fear.[21] At a time when there is political disengagement, fear cuts through. How do you get your population to take heed? Scare them. Fear suppresses rational thinking and they are more likely to do what they are told.

I spoke to political scientist, Piers Robinson, about fear. He was the chair in Politics, Society and Political Journalism at Sheffield University, leaving in 2019 to focus on his work as co-director at the Organisation for Propaganda Studies. Piers has been 'smeared' for disputing the use of chemical weapons in Syria. So he has studied propaganda and also – depending on your viewpoint – been at the other end of it.

I asked if he thought governments were leveraging fear as a form of social control. He said: 'If something very big is going on in the world, you should always ask if it can be exploited for reasons that are entirely separate from what the primary concerns appear to be. Covid is an event of such scale that there is the potential for actors to exploit it for various agendas. Never let a good crisis go to waste, and so on. You can be open-minded about both the severity of the disease and the potential for exploitation. 9/11 is an example. That event led to 20 years of warfare which wasn't about fighting terrorism but was enabled by the 'war on terror' narrative. When the Chilcot report published communications between Tony Blair and George Bush and they were talking about 9/11 and attacking various countries, it was obvious that the war on terror was to be used as propaganda to fight different wars for other reasons.'

I put it to him that our anxieties have developed in a trajectory from Cold War, to the war on terror to a 'war on viruses'. He agreed, but shot back, 'We destroyed other countries in the war on terror. This time we're destroying our own.'

I asked Robinson how and why a government would destroy its own country. He was keen to clarify he didn't mean 'a caricature of conspiracy theory' but rather 'vested interests and agendas which coalesce. No social scientist would dispute we live in a world where there exist powerful actors with agendas. One of the ways through which agendas are pushed is propaganda. I would call this a major propaganda opportunity.'

Propaganda is Robinson's speciality so I asked how he observed it at play. He was cautious, explaining that this was such a large event it would take months to research fully, but that censorship had raised a red flag: 'Very early on it was clear that eminent scientists were questioning the approach. It's likely the threat was being overplayed because some dissenting and credible scientists were being censored. The utility of lockdown, for example, has been extremely difficult to debate in public. Bad decision-making and groupthink could also be behind this, but there is manipulation of the narrative through propaganda going on as well.'

Censorship is one of the tools of propaganda. Others are false flags – the use of covert operations that appear to be carried out by other states – repetition, manipulation of the facts (lying), and the manipulation of emotions, notably fear.

'People have been gripped by fear in an obsessive way, and to a degree far worse than occurred with fear of terrorism,' said Robinson. 'Propaganda is all about behavioural psychology, manipulation essentially, getting people to do what they wouldn't otherwise do, through coercion, or incentive or deception. Not all persuasion is propaganda, but propaganda is manipulation and it is not democratic. The way some behavioural scientists have acted during the Covid-19 response runs the risk of unethical conduct. I think we should investigate and hold to account the professionals complicit in this. We in academia need to think about the ethics of this more. When I research and write I do not try and manipulate people, I am trying to get to the truth and inform people.'

When will political scientists and historians have a clear perspective on the motives and tactics used in the government's Covid policies, if it took 20 years to understand the war on terror? 'In the fullness of time it will become clearer,' Robinson said, 'as long we don't lose democracy, because it's not inconceivable that we are walking into an absolute nightmare in which freedom of speech and debate become significantly curtailed.'

SUSAN, 15, BY HER GRANDMOTHER

Our granddaughter, Susan, lives with us. We are her guardians. When she realised her mum wouldn't be able to visit her, she got very upset about it. She started harming herself. She would get a sharp object and puts scores on her arms and legs.

I t was very difficult to get her out of her bedroom in lockdown, even into the garden. She became like a hermit. I think she was probably depressed. It was very difficult. She's doing GCSEs and it affected her school work too. She was upset about not seeing her mum and friends and she didn't do any work.

Her and her brother facetimed their mum, but it was really hard. Once we could be in a bubble with her mum it got better. She's also much happier now she is back at school. She has been having counselling at school.

Being inside all the time and self-harming… What were we doing? Looking back, were the rules necessary? I feel really sad and angry. Maybe at the beginning it made sense, but the longer it went on, no.

Susan's mum will stay with us at Christmas, whatever the rules are, to make sure she doesn't self-harm. I think her mum should be able to come over whenever. These days I say 'Sod the rules.'

5. THE BUSINESS OF FEAR AND THE UNELECTED PSYCHOCRATS

'If we understand the mechanisms and motives of the group mind, it is now possible to control and regiment the masses according to our will without their knowing it. In almost every act of our daily lives, whether in the sphere of politics or business, in our social conduct or our ethical thinking, we are dominated by the relatively small number of persons who understand the mental processes and social patterns of the masses. It is they who pull the wires which control the public mind.'

From *Propaganda* by Edward Bernays

Nudge theory is the concept in behavioural science which uses insights about our behaviour to 'nudge' our decision-making. Nudges are not mandates: they are subtle suggestions, and they happen without you even being aware.

We don't always make decisions rationally; we simply don't have time to evaluate each decision we make carefully. If you understand the psychological drivers beneath the surface thinking, you can positively influence people's decisions and behaviour.

The person who coined the term 'nudge', Cass Sunstein, said, 'By knowing how people think, we can make it easier for them to choose what is best for them, their families and society.' Isn't it great that there are people who know what is best for you? And who can change your thinking and behaviour without you even being aware of it? Rest assured, there are many behavioural scientists and their advocates embedded and advising within the UK government, nudging you towards what is best for you.

Britain is one of the pioneers in nudge theory. The Behavioural Insights Team (BIT), unofficially known as 'the Nudge Unit' was set up in 2010 under David Cameron's government. Britain is so good at behavioural insights that we export it all over the world. The Nudge Unit is now a profit-making 'social purpose limited company' with offices in London, Manchester, Paris, New York, Singapore, Sydney, Wellington and Toronto. It has run more than 750 projects and in 2019 alone worked in 31 countries. It has conducted over 1,000 workshops for governments around the world, training 20,000 civil servants in behavioural insights.

Essentially, Britain is teaching governments around the world how to follow its model of nudging citizens into doing what is 'best' for them. Nudge has become a big business and it's still growing. In the autumn of 2020, I noticed 10 new behavioural science roles advertised in the NHS and Public Health England.

I wanted to interview the founder of the Nudge Unit, David Halpern. I sent an email via the Behavioural Insights Team website to explain I wanted to discuss the use of fear to influence behaviour and encourage compliance during the Covid epidemic. Richard O'Brien, the Head of Communications, replied to me to emphasise that the unit is 'operationally and legally separate' from the government, but he said he was a great admirer of my work and would like to build a connection with me. We spoke on the phone and he told me that discussing the use of behavioural science and the use of fear during the epidemic was not 'something David or BIT could comment on'.

I was disappointed by the lack of engagement and transparency. If not the behavioural scientists at the Nudge Unit, then who would comment on the government's use of behavioural science? It was all a bit cloak and dagger. There was also something irregular about our exchange. Richard suggested I might be able to work with BIT on a creative project to showcase their work. I asked him to tell me more and send me a brief so we could talk further, but stressed that it must be kept separate from the questions I wanted to ask him at that point. However, after a dazzle of compliments (he was 'impressed', 'flattered' and an 'admirer') there were no further details and no brief to pitch for. More to the point, I never got that interview.

Could the offer of work, and therefore a fee, have been a ploy to distract me? Had the project materialised, and if I agreed to undertake it, it could have compromised an interview. He must have known that. I wondered though if I had become too cynical? Was I peering so far up the magician's cloak sleeve that I couldn't enjoy the magic held in front of me? I checked in with a couple of trusted contacts to ask their opinion.

I described the exchange to Gary Sidley, a retired consultant clinical psychologist. He chuckled drily, and said, 'It sounds like a way of neutralising you. A classic tactic is to neutralise an opponent by being seen to collaborate.' I also spoke to an anonymous scientific advisor deeply embedded in Whitehall. They told me that flattery is a very common tactic used by the government when people ask difficult questions. This echoed my suspicious gut feeling.

Even without talking to the nudgers, we know a lot about what they do and how they work. A 2018 document, *Improving people's health: Applying behavioural and social sciences to improve population health and wellbeing in England*[1] has the laudable aims of addressing 'the problems currently impacting on population health, such as smoking, poor diet and physical inactivity'. The Department of Health and Social Care (DHSC) launched DHSC Collaborate in 2018 to deploy behavioural science to these ends. The document gives case studies like reducing tobacco use and smoking-related diseases.

It's hard to argue with the value of some of these campaigns, although it has caused political controversy for years. Back in 2015, Claire Fox, Director of the Institute of Ideas, which campaigns for free speech and debate, said: 'Nudge theory is about denying certain choices or making other choices harder. It is used to avoid having arguments and instead to manipulate people without them realising. It is a real assault on people's capacity to make up their own minds. It treats us like mice in a laboratory. If people don't do something, it's not because they are incapable of doing it. It's because they have chosen not to.'[2]

A key difference is that until 2020, the health conditions that the NHS and Public Health England have wanted to target have been well understood, whereas a novel virus is less well understood. The result is that the use of behavioural psychology to encourage compliance during the Covid epidemic could have been heavy-handed if the dangers of the virus were over-estimated, and if its transmission was not fully understood. Also, creating fear and appealing to fear is far more serious than other uses of behavioural psychology. Perhaps because the DHSC's goals in 2018 seemed noble and sensible, and the methods seemed harmless, this blueprint didn't contain any discussion of the ethics of using tools which affect us subconsciously.

In 2010, the authors of *MINDSPACE: Influencing behaviour through public policy*[3] at the Institute of Government, a think tank, included a whole chapter on the 'legitimacy of government involvement in behaviour change' because they know it is 'controversial'. Although they say that 'public acceptability' should not be the determining condition for going forward with behaviour change, they acknowledge that the use of behavioural science 'has implications for consent and freedom of choice' and offers people 'little opportunity to opt out'.

As such, the report conceded that 'policy-makers wishing to use these tools… need the approval of the public to do so.' Yet to date, the public has not been consulted nor formally given approval. A review[4] of Halpern's book, *Inside the Nudge Unit*, postulated that nudge implies a 'sanguine acceptance of a technique of government that has manipulation and even deception as a prominent feature'. Making no bones about it, nudge is clever people in government making sure the not-so-clever people do what they want.

A 2010 House of Lords Science and Technology Select Committee report, *Behaviour Change*,[5] also brought up issues of 'ethical acceptability', concluding that the proportionality of the intervention, intrusiveness, restriction of freedom and transparency were the key considerations. In all the exercises of pandemic preparedness in the past, why wasn't the ethical use of behavioural psychology considered and the public consulted?

Paternalistic policies are presented as being in our best interests. Behavioural economics assumes that we are not rational, that we know this, and we welcome the release from anxiety and guilt. According to the select committee report, when the government guides our decisions for us it 'acts as surrogate willpower and locks our biscuit tins'. Locking up biscuit tins is bossy and patronising. Rationally I know I 'shouldn't' eat too many biscuits – or whatever public health issue you would like to insert into that metaphor – but it is my choice. And I would argue that people should be given factual information to guide choices rather than being manipulated at a subconscious level into making choices the government thinks are best for us. But locking us up is a serious measure with vast repercussions. The behavioural science framework for making the population comply with being locked down involved powerful techniques which deserve public consultation. That the consultation hasn't happened so far is concerning, but now, more than ever, the use of propaganda and nudge needs to be brought into the public forum for debate.

Gary Sidley was one of the few psychologists I noticed airing concerns about the ethics of behavioural science during the Covid epidemic. He was keen to stress that 'covert strategies are interesting and they have a role. For instance, if you can try and minimise the likelihood of vandalism, that seems like it would be a legitimate use.' His concern was that there has been no public consultation about the acceptability of the tools, and they were too contentious for such a major public health policy: 'Using fear, public pressure and scapegoating are probably tools that would be rejected by the British public if we had a vote.'

He told me that none of us are immune to the bombardment of fear. He worried about the continued use of these tactics for his children and grandchildren. I asked where he thought it would take us and he said: 'I don't want to think about that really. It's not a good place. There is something distinctive about using fear to get people to conform which is so distasteful and ethically unacceptable. Fear impacts on every aspect of our being.'

Not all this fear came from the Behavioural Insights Team; there are other actors. As the Nudge Unit wouldn't speak to me I can't pretend I know its role in detail, but I assume it was a key contributor, given it is central to UK government, and that David Halpern is part of SPI-B, the Scientific Pandemic Influenza Group on Behaviour which reports into SAGE, the Scientific Advisory Group for Emergencies. Controlling information, countering disinformation, using behavioural psychology and leveraging fear can be wrought by different parts of the government machinery: the Cabinet Office, the Rapid Response Unit, the Counter Disinformation Cell, GCHQ, the Home Office's Research, Information and Communications Unit (RICU), Prevent and the 77th Brigade, which is part of the army. (An explanation of the units is below.)

I spoke to an independent scientific advisor, deeply embedded at Whitehall, who needs to remain anonymous. I interviewed them about pandemic planning and death registrations (for Chapter 11, 'Counting the dead') but was struck by their anger about the government's use of behavioural psychology. Indeed, it's one of the reasons they wanted to help me with my research. They told me that they are 'stunned by the weaponisation of behavioural psychology over the last five years' and that 'psychology and behavioural science are feted above everything else. The psychologists didn't seem to notice when it stopped being altruistic and became manipulative. They have too much power and it intoxicates them.'

The advisor told me that in their experience, the application of behavioural science in disaster planning used to be more about predicting how people would behave and what they would need, but became more about 'how to make people do what we want'. Essentially, it became about manipulation, 'spin' and 'disaster management for the social media age'.

Off the record we talked about the use of propaganda, not just creating fear, but also shaping positive responses after disasters, and steering 'radicals' in different directions. Government units are created entirely for these purposes and their methods are opaque. 'I never used to be cynical,' my anonymous source told me, 'you couldn't find a more positive person. Now if I see a cute seven-year-old in the news, I wonder which government department is behind it.'

In the advisor's opinion, 'Everything about the government messaging this year has been designed to keep the fear going. The story about a Kawasaki-like disease in children, for example.' Funnily enough, I had noticed the story about a potential link between Kawasaki disease in children, which broke on the BBC[6] the same day as a story about Ofsted saying children should return to school.[7] At the time, incidences of Kawasaki disease were lower than normal for that time of year,[8] probably because children were at home and not catching as many viruses. That context was not part of the dramatic articles about Kawasaki, which lit up social media with alarm. I mused it was odd that two such conflicting stories were in the news on the same day, although of course the news fell in a fast flurry around us all year. But could this push–pull be designed to create confusion? Or were the media and their sources struggling to keep up with confusing and conflicting stories? My source said stories are leaked to the media to help push certain narratives forward.

Another example of that was an article in *The Independent* which ran in February 2021 with the headline 'Hospitals prepare for increase in children suffering rare disease triggered by Covid'.[9] This came out just when the clamour for schools to open was increasing. Honestly, it was a bit of a non-story. Even the sub-heading explained 'Covid-19 triggers inflammatory response in very small minority of children, most of whom will not be seriously affected.' In fact, at this time, more young people were being admitted to hospital with mental health problems than all medical conditions, let alone Covid.[10]

The anonymous scientific advisor said that there had been conversations about the use of fear. It was felt that the fear of death could be leveraged to make people follow the rules. While this source was party to confidential conversations, the idea that the government should weaponise our fear is fact: we know that the idea was officially put forward and minuted as part of the SPI-B recommendations.

Similar tactics were employed in other countries. In Canada, the *Toronto Star*[11] reported that Ottawa's behavioural science 'nudge unit' was mostly operating 'under the radar' producing campaigns to gain compliance with public health measures, helping politicians with their speeches and collecting data. The article accurately observed that a 'massive social-science experiment that has taken place over the planet' had 'given government important clues on how to modify citizens' behaviour for other big global issues – such as climate change, for instance'.

Jacinda Ardern made an embarrassing slip of the tongue when she referred to 'a two-week period of sustained propaganda' that New Zealanders who completed the government's Managed Isolation were subjected to. Devastating truth, or inconsequential misuse of the word? As *Stuff* observed, 'under this slip of the usually very polished tongue is a truth: the Ardern Government has, in fact, been delivering a masterclass in propaganda since Covid began. It has presented the plan that it formulated as the only feasible option, set up rules and language to prosecute that agenda and rhetorically crushed all opposition.'[12]

Gript[13] reported that leaked documents showed that the Irish 'Zero Covid' advocacy group ISAG (Independent Scientific Advocacy Group) was instructed to 'look for ways to increase insecurity, anxiety, and uncertainty', and to 'go after people and not institutions' because 'people hurt faster than institutions'. ISAG members, many of whom are regular guests in Irish media, were told that they could count on 'imagination' to 'dream up' many more consequences' as 'the threat is usually more terrifying than the thing itself.' Although ISAG is made up of independent scientists and doesn't represent a government, these leaks reveal the tactics resorted to by the same type of academics who do populate government advisory panels.

The country with the most striking story was Germany. Leaked documents from the Ministry of the Interior showed that scientists were hired to produce a worst-case scenario in order to justify restrictions on society. *Welt am Sonntag*[14] broke the story of how leading scientists from various research institutes and universities collaborated with management at the ministry to create a computational model to 'get ahead of the situation mentally and in terms of planning', which was to help plan further 'measures of a preventive and repressive nature'. The State Secretary, Markus Kerber, drew a dystopian picture: it was about 'maintaining internal security and the stability of public order in Germany'. Kerber wrote 'without bureaucracy, maximum courage' in his emails. For 'without bureaucracy' you could substitute 'without honesty' or 'without scientific rigour'.

The scenario paper itself was more damning than the UK's SPI-B paper, which was comparably freer of the dirty details. It said that to create the desired 'shock effect', the specific effects of an infection on human society must be made clear. Here are two of its astonishing suggestions:

'Many seriously ill are taken to hospital by their relatives, but turned away, and die in agony at home gasping for breath. Choking or not getting enough air is a primal fear for everyone. The same applies to the situation in which there is nothing you can do to help loved ones who are in mortal danger. The images from Italy are disturbing.'

'"Children are unlikely to suffer from the epidemic": Wrong. Children are easily infected, even with exit restrictions, e.g. from the neighbours' children. When they infect their parents and one of them dies in agony at home and they feel they are to blame for forgetting to wash their hands after playing, for example, it is the most terrible thing a child will ever experience.'

The German government, and the scientists it employed, collaborated to bring images of people choking to death at home, and to inflict fear and guilt on children, in order to make the population follow rules for an epidemic which had been deliberately exaggerated. This makes the concluding lines of the report even more unpalatable:

'Only with social cohesion and a mutual distance from one another can this crisis not only be overcome with little damage, but also be future-oriented for a new relationship between society and the state.'

Would German citizens happily consent to such a 'future-oriented' relationship of manipulation and fear? Would the British public if the same type of leaks came to light? Science was politicised rather than independent, and the German government was most certainly not 'following' the science but rather dictating it. Might a similar scenario have happened in the UK?

In researching this book I found a number of people who were keen to talk to me because they were deeply concerned about government policy, but they had their own fears we had to work around: fear of losing their job or contract if they appeared critical of the government, or fear of being seen to be contrarian or an outlier and therefore being judged. Fear influences us in many ways and we are motivated psychologically by the need for social conformity. While it's not as satisfying to quote anonymous sources, this is how it has to be, and they are our flies on the wall in the corridors of power.

A friend offered to connect me with a government official, someone who is in and out of Number 10; someone who was sick of what they saw every day at work. Like the scientific advisor I spoke to, this government official told me exasperatedly that they were 'at the end of [their] tether' over the 'indefensible' policies enacted this year.

Also like the scientific advisor, this government source was cynical about the motivations behind the policies: 'The government wasn't worried about the virus, they were worried about the way the virus might ruin their PR credibility over the NHS. It all stems from the election campaign they ran on saving it. We had to make sure the NHS runs really well. Two months into government and this issue comes along which could fuck up the NHS. Lee Caine and Dominic Cummings had put it at the centre of the campaign and they couldn't lose support and let that fail.'

Aside from Boris Johnson's treatment in hospital, it's easy to see why the government was so enthusiastic about the weekly 'Clap for Carers'. Tribalism is an inherent part of human history. Football fans chant and sing, and sometimes they even pray for their team to win. (Is God really supposed to pick a side?) Building tribalism builds cohesion and conformity. People are more emotional and less rational when they are tribal. The weekly pot-banging was a tribal show of solidarity, venerating the NHS and its workers, who were central to the government's election campaign, but there was also a Stalinist rhythm to it, which some felt but were nervous to confess to.[15]

The fears about the NHS might help explain the change of direction from the early plans to create 'herd immunity' and 'cocooning' the vulnerable to a full lockdown. But were ministers not frightened about the impact of the virus as well? In the main, my source said, 'there was a fear of losing voter support,' but, yes, 'the health department was the most worried. Hancock is quite paranoid and a total "wet". He's a real panicker. He's the kid in the playground who wouldn't want to get hurt. And he's in charge of the response.'

Over time, they said, the fear spread from the health department to the other departments, and they all fell under the spell of the SAGE scientists foretelling doom: 'They've drunk the scientists' kool aid. They're scared. The government don't have a malicious agenda, they just don't know what they are doing. They don't have a plan. The ministers in the cabinet think the vaccine is the best way to end it.'

The 10pm curfew for pubs was hugely controversial and it turned out was not evidenced. So why implement it? Transmission is not particularly driven by hospitality.[16] My source said that the 10pm curfew decision was made even though 'they knew they had no evidence. It was just considered a political win against the scientists, because the scientists

wanted a full lockdown and the curfew was a compromise.'
I wonder what publicans will make of this compromise. The
SAGE scientists' spell might be breaking.

Just as some of the sources in this book decided they
must remain anonymous for the safety of their careers, it
is inevitable that politicians keep an anxious eye on their
prospects. They are not anonymous. Every decision, every
mistake will be examined under the media's unforgiving
magnifying glass and the inevitable future inquiry. The source
who spends so much time at Number 10 tells me that our
ministers fear 'they'll get hauled through the press for their
own mistakes and that's worse for them than ruining people's
businesses. They are scared of their own inquiry. And MPs
don't vote against the government's lockdowns and tiers
because they are worried about not being promoted.' There is
a lot of very human, very fallible fear behind the government's
decision to frighten us.

I spoke to MP Steve Baker in the summer of 2020. He
also told me that the scientists had too much influence over
the Cabinet Office, describing ministers as being 'under a
spell like King Theoden under the influence of Wormtongue'
in *The Lord of the Rings*. Baker may be a polarising figure,
thanks to his well-documented support of a hard Brexit, but
the issues around science, health, and behavioural psychology
should transcend politics. The fact is that the response to
Covid became hyper-partisan, as I discuss in Chapter 13, 'The
climate of fear', and few politicians were expressing concerns
about lockdown and the behavioural science aspects as early
as Baker.

Baker told me that he considered lockdown was a
'justifiable incursion' on the liberties of the British people,
in the context of a disease with significant consequences. In
effect, the restrictions were justified at the beginning of the
epidemic. How we were incited to follow the regulations was a
different matter. When I asked him what he thought of the use
of fear to encourage compliance with the rules he replied that,
'in a free society we ought not treat people as if they are things
to be managed. We ought not to use behavioural psychology to

lead people in this manner. What's happening now is consistent with dystopian novels. If it is true that the state took the decision to terrify the public to get compliance with rules, that raises extremely serious questions about the type of society we want to become.'

He has concerns about where we are heading: 'Throughout all of this, what we had to do was be proportionate. It's very difficult for me to say what should have happened, I wasn't in the room and able to ask questions of officials. I'm clear that ministers should have had greater respect for civil liberty, the economy and other health concerns. I now think we're into disproportionate territory. If we're being really honest, do I fear that government policy today is playing into the roots of totalitarianism? Yes, of course it is. I went almost as far as saying that when I made a speech. Is this a totalitarian government? No. Do they believe they are liberals? Yes. And the pursuit of safety is our greatest danger at the moment.'

The pursuit of safety is our biggest danger, driven by fears and exaggerated fears.

The use of unelected advisory groups in 2020 is a technocratic style of government, a command-and-control model of public decision-making that is reliant on scientific expertise rather than political debate. Added to that, there has been limited transparency about the scientific advisors, the modelling they use, and the data ingests. Before key votes on emergency legislation, MPs were not given the data they asked for. For example, 70 conservative MPs asked for a full cost-benefit analysis before a parliamentary vote on a strict three-tiered system to follow lockdown,[17] and when a flimsy analysis followed it contained very little in the way of quantifiable costs and benefits.[18]

Within this technocratic style of government, we are subjects of a 'psychocracy', where the policy-making is dictated by psychological expertise. This is even more top-down and opaque, because redefining our behaviour by using stealthy psychology techniques means we aren't always aware, let alone able to comment on, consent to or participate in policy-making. One of the aims of this book is to alert you to the tools and influence of the psychocrats.

We did not elect the psychocrats that operate and advise within the heart of government. We do not even know how each governmental unit leans on behavioural science, but there are behavioural insights teams in at least 10 government departments.[19]

Crises 'justify' political institutions and governmental units and the accretion of power above democratic oversight. All of these units operate in ways which are not transparent to the population, nor even to MPs. You will find little information about them. I approached the Cabinet Office to discuss the Rapid Response Unit and the 77th Brigade several times and never received a response. I asked MPs for introductions or insights and they were unable or unwilling to help. So, aside from the Nudge Unit, here is a brief overview of the departments that form the shadowy 'Business of Fear'.

RICU

The Home Office's Research, Information and Communications Unit is a strategic communications unit within the Office for Security and Counter Terrorism in the Home Office. It works across a range of public security issues, including counter-terrorism and serious and organised crime.

One paper seen by *The Guardian* set out RICU's ambition to use 'strategic communications aims to effect behavioural and attitudinal change'. The unit apparently attempts to covertly engineer the thoughts of people by using chosen 'grassroots organisations and NGOs, providing financial and technical support from the government for the production of their multimedia campaigns which purport to be 'grassroots'.[20] I interviewed someone who worked for an agency employed by RICU for Chapter 8, 'Controlled spontaneity and propaganda', and gained some fascinating insights.

THE RAPID RESPONSE UNIT

Based in Number 10 and the Cabinet Office, this unit was especially created to drive rapid response on social media to help support the 'reclaiming of a fact-based public debate'.[21]

Its role during the Covid epidemic has included: 'direct rebuttal on social media, working with platforms to remove harmful content and ensuring public health campaigns are promoted through reliable sources'. It claims to be dealing with up to 70 incidents a week.

COUNTER DISINFORMATION CELL

The cell falls under the Department for Digital, Culture, Media and Sport.[22] It brings together experts from various government departments and engages with social media platforms and with disinformation specialists from civil society and academia. Along with the Rapid Response Unit it tackles 'fake news'. (Their work seems to overlap for some reason.)

We have little understanding about what the Counter Disinformation Cell and Rapid Response Unit actually do, but they seem to be working behind closed doors to control and censor otherwise lawful things people say online, despite the UK's extensive laws about free speech and censorship. Obvious examples are the removal from YouTube of videos by doctors and scientists which supposedly contravene WHO official guidance. As Silkie Carlo of Big Brother Watch said to me, 'I have to pinch myself sometimes that doctors have been removed from YouTube for talking about their medical experience of treating patients.' Not only does this not allow people to think for themselves, but the WHO itself has changed its thinking a few times during the epidemic – not unusual as scientists learn about a new disease. A banned video which contravenes today's guidance might be compliant next week when scientific consensus changes.

GCHQ

Government Communications Headquarters is an intelligence, cyber and security agency. During the epidemic it has been engaged in a 'cyberwar on anti-vaccine propaganda'. This work is supposed to be directed at foreign actors not UK citizens online. *The Times* reported on a 'Whitehall source who emphasised that GCHQ was able to gain permission to tackle disinformation that originated only from state adversaries. It is not legally permitted to disrupt online content written by ordinary citizens. "You wouldn't get authorisation to go after cranks. People have a right to say batshit stuff online," the source said.'[23]

THE 77TH BRIGADE

The 77th Brigade is an army unit which combines former media operations and psychological operations, specialising in 'non-lethal' forms of psychological warfare. It works with social media companies to counter disinformation. Would you believe that Twitter's Head of Editorial in Europe, the Middle East, and Africa also served as a part-time officer for the 77th Brigade and the Ministry of Defence would not reveal his current rank when asked by *Middle East Eye*?[24] MP Tobias Ellwood is a reservist lieutenant colonel in the 77th Brigade.

Many people believe the 77th is giving direct rebuttals to UK citizens who speak out against lockdown on social media. If you search for the hashtag #77th on Twitter you will find scathing comments from people who believe they have identified the 77th at work. My question for the 77th Brigade was, would it attack British citizens online while reinforcing the government message? The old saying goes, 'Sticks and stones may break my bones but names will never hurt me', yet 'pile-ons' can feel like ferocious verbal and psychological attacks, which lead to anxiety, withdrawal from social media and even threaten job security. Are the military harassing British citizens?

I called the 77th Brigade and spoke to Major Bruce Weston who handles media enquiries. He was very friendly and very slick and, unsurprisingly, wouldn't directly answer my questions. I referenced the many negative comments about the 77th on Twitter and he did acknowledge that 'what you will get from Twitter is the perception that the 77th is people sat behind computers dealing with cyber'.

He did tell me that the 77th 'have provided a small team from the information and outreach unit, and are supporting the Rapid Response Unit'. I asked how exactly and he retorted that I would 'have to ask the Cabinet Office'. But do their policies permit direct engagements with British citizens to attack their views on social media, I wondered? 'We are part of the 6th Division of the army,' he said, 'and we are bound by policies and frameworks that all parts of the army will work within.' I approached the Cabinet Office as he suggested and got precisely nowhere.

Humans are naturally excellent at some forms of identification. We recognise sex, for instance. Obviously that's handy from an evolutionary perspective. We also recognise inauthenticity in language and communication. A sad fact of social media is that it is now littered with accounts that appear to be 'bots' or deceptive accounts of some kind. Bots are automated accounts, running on code, and can be bought in bulk for covert use. Subtle linguistic clues can give them away. Deceptive accounts, troll accounts (like the Chinese '50c army') are more intensive and expensive to operate as they are run by humans. Their giveaways are 'eggs' and handles with weird names composed of numbers (as with bots), also accounts who engage with others but people don't initiate communication with them, and timelines which are 'one note'. Are some of these run by the 77th? We have no idea.

SAGE AND SPI-B

SAGE is the team of advisers that coordinates scientific advice given to the Cabinet Office decision-makers who attend COBRA (Cabinet Office Briefing Rooms) meetings. (Don't those acronyms sound impressive? I think we are meant to deduce that SAGE members are wise and COBRA can strike like a snake.) The government will ask questions of SAGE which then coordinates the advice and answers from across multi-disciplinary experts drawn from academia, government and industry.

The SAGE team is the spearhead of three sub-teams working together: New and Emerging Respiratory Virus Threats Advisory Group (NERVTAG); Scientific Pandemic Influenza Group on Modelling (SPI-M), Scientific Pandemic Influenza Group on Behaviours (SPI-B).

SPI-B is the team of behavioural scientists and

academic specialists in health psychology, social psychology, anthropology and history, which provides 'behavioural science advice aimed at anticipating and helping people adhere to interventions that are recommended by medical or epidemiological experts'.[25]

SPI-B is not tasked with assessing which interventions are effective or analysing the data ingests, but purely with advice to encourage people to adhere to the law and guidance.

To start with, the membership of SAGE was secret, purportedly due to national security. It's worth noting that there have been many criticisms of the make-up of both SAGE and SPI-B. Remarkably, SAGE does not include disaster recovery specialists, and there is a lack of expertise on risk management and the psychology of risk.

Did the government hide behind the phrase 'following the science'? Did they hide behind the unelected psychocrats?

JANE, 68

I've had anxiety before, but nothing like this. I would try and talk myself down, but a deep part of my brain was telling me I was in terrible danger. It has felt like a bad dream.

T he first couple of days of lockdown I was very nervy and scared, I had a cloak of anxiety over my shoulders. To start with I thought it would be six weeks of lockdown, we were in it together and we'd be alright. I think a lot of us felt the same. It's how it was told to us.

I'd put the news on as soon as I got up in the morning. I don't know if the media peddle the bad news because they think it attracts us, but I watched every day hoping for good news, something that would make me feel a little less bleak. It never came. I don't put the news on in the morning any more.

Every single feed said we were going to die. *Sky News* was the worst. There were so many gruesome headlines that came at you thick and fast. There were Ferguson's predictions that 500,000 would die. Graphs have completely lost their meaning. I watched every Downing Street briefing. There was one press briefing when they talked about a vaccine, and the one about dexamethasone. They were the only two things that I can remember. All the dreadful ones have just merged.

I can't understand why no one talks about how many people have recovered? People would have loved headlines about recovery.

A tipping point for me was Boris Johnson's first unlocking speech. I thought, 'Jesus, he doesn't know what's going to happen.' After that, I could feel my mood going down.

One morning I woke up with my whole body in a state of

shock. I was trembling from head to foot and I had a shushing noise in my ears. My whole body felt in a state of agitation. I was dizzy when I got up, I nearly fainted. My pulse was regularly over 100 and my blood pressure was high. I thought I must have Parkinson's or MS or something, but it was anxiety. It's hard to believe anxiety made me feel so terrible.

For weeks, I was like this every morning. Most symptoms would begin to resolve by the evening and I'd hope I would be OK the next day, but the following morning there they all were again. I would stay in bed or on the sofa all day.

I grew up in the Cold War. We had ads on TV showing houses being blown away. But it wasn't as constant as Covid, we weren't talking about it all the time. Now we have adverts about the virus and the news in your face every hour, every day.

I don't know if I will listen to the government again if there is another epidemic. We don't have the types of statesman that we had in the past. I don't have confidence in our government's strategy and intentions.

There has never been a medical end to a pandemic. The only illness we have ever eradicated is smallpox. We haven't got rid of bubonic plague or Spanish flu. Societies end pandemics, not science. I think we are in Covid phobia phase and next we'll go into Covid fatigue phase and then it will end because people will want to go to the shops or whatever and we'll get our herd immunity anyway.

The whole of society is riven with fear. We've all become each other's enemy. For the first time, everyone has become a threat to everyone else. Will we look back and say it was collective hysteria? There was a dancing plague in the 1500s. I think we are passing hysteria between us more effectively than a virus.

I feel depressed about the winter ahead. It feels incredibly bleak.

6. THE SPI-B ADVISORS

'The way we have used fear is dystopian.'
SPI-B advisor

The idea of going back to so-called-normal is a major area of consideration. There's a climate crisis coming and that's going to have to be dealt with. The way we have gone about adapting to the virus has been quite beneficial in terms of working patterns and reducing carbon – all the things we are going to have to go through to adjust to the new future. As the New Zealand prime minister put it, we need to "build back better". There are challenging times ahead of us for the next 20 or 30 years, God help us. The most major crisis of humanity is starting. I see the weather patterns changing around me. I believe in climate change. It's already getting bad. These will have major impacts on the nature of the world around us.'

'The new future'? My blood chilled. I'd asked Clifford Stott if SPI-B had been tasked with thinking about how to bring the population out of lockdown, climb down from fear and back towards a normal society.

Clifford Stott is a Professor of Social Psychology and an expert in collective violence and riots, policing issues and management of crowds. He is one of the four members of SPI-B who agreed to speak with me. Another nominated her colleague who produces work which is fed into SPI-B. A SAGE advisor also agreed to be interviewed and, as before, the anonymous scientist who advises at Whitehall had plenty to say.

I hadn't imagined that a SPI-B advisor would mentally segue from Covid to climate change when asked how to end lockdown. I silently wondered if he envisaged future lockdowns to reduce CO_2 emissions. Boris Johnson made some drastic environment promises during the epidemic, pledging to 'build back better', including commitments to wind power and switching to electric vehicles.[1] And this is where we tap into my fears.

If you ultimately concede that lockdown is a useful tool, you must concede that the tool may be used again. The government, wielding the tool, develops muscle memory. So do we. Covid-19 is not the last novel virus. It's not the last crisis. Would you accept another lockdown for a future epidemic? Could we do another lockdown without laying waste to our economy and society? Would you go along with another lockdown for a run on the banks, an act of terror, or a food shortage? How about regular lockdowns to reduce CO_2 emissions? How about every winter to reduce deaths from flu? Would our fear be deliberately elevated again to make us comply? Welcome to my raw nerve, strummed by Stott's answer.

If you think this is an exaggeration, Speaker Lindsay Hoyle demonstrated an appetite for a 'lockdown' or restrictions of some sort, for the environment. At the G7 Speakers' Meeting in September he said, 'If one lesson from the pandemic is that taking serious action in a timely manner is key – then shouldn't this also be true in terms of climate change? With Covid, what surprised many of us in the UK was how engaged most of the population became once the seriousness of the situation was made clear. People were prepared to accept limitations on personal choice and lifestyle – for the good of their own family and friends. No one could ever imagine that we would be wearing masks so readily and that we would all be so compliant. Perhaps we ought not to underestimate the ability of people and communities to work together for the common good, if there is united and clear leadership.' They never imagined we would be so 'compliant'.

It's widely accepted that the government uses polling company YouGov to 'test the waters' before announcing new policies. In mid-January 2021, YouGov started probing how lockdowns might have affected public concern for the environment. The survey tested agreement with attitudes such as 'The short-term positive impact Coronavirus has had on wildlife and ecosystems has encouraged me to make better environmental and sustainable decisions' and the importance of reducing your carbon footprint since the beginning of the Covid pandemic.

To understand how our fear had been leveraged against us in the UK, I needed to get to know the people who suggested frightening us. I approached most of the advisors on SPI-B for an interview. Nearly all of them ignored me or turned me down. They probably fielded many media requests alongside their advisory work and regular jobs, but it wasn't necessarily wise to nail my lockdown sceptical colours to the mast in a series of articles and tweets in 2020 before writing this documentary book – my contributors might have thought me biased because I clearly wasn't a lockdown supporter. The fact is, we are all biased: it is unavoidable. The point is to be clear about it to yourself and in your work, as far as you are able. Fortunately, previous work must have spoken of my genuine willingness to embrace a story and all its nuance, because several agreed, during this very busy time, to speak with me.

I asked all my interviewees if they had been commissioned to think about helping people manage their fear and the ending of lockdown. A SPI-B paper put forward the idea of elevating fear, so I assumed that they would have considered the exit plan. Fear impacts us mentally and physically and it would then impede the reopening of society – surely that would make an exit plan essential? They all seemed surprised to be asked. The idea was obviously not on the table yet. Perhaps they had been too busy fighting one fire at a time. Stott said to me that he couldn't speculate because he was 'far too busy in the here and now'. That is understandable. But if this was an experiment in a lab, researchers wanting to scare you would need a plan for how to manage your emotions afterwards. At the end of the experiment, they would probably show you a happy film and give you a slice of chocolate cake, at the very least. You would not leave the lab scared and unhappy. The psychologists running the experiment would have been through a very rigorous ethics process. We would have signed consent forms to agree to be frightened. I know I didn't sign a consent form. It would seem that this live experiment has no ethics committee and no exit plan. (Actually, I doubt it would get past the ethics committee.)

Stott was careful to point out that his answers were personal reflections, but that's partly why I was worried. I had a breakthrough – it seems very obvious in retrospect – when I realised this group of experts were bringing their own personalities, biases and beliefs to the table. In effect, they were fully-fleshed out humans, not faceless experts. In the early days of the epidemic, SAGE and SPI-B members were anonymous. The summaries of meetings were published, but they were fairly 'clean'; you don't know who said what, how easily they reached consensus or when they disagreed. You'll never know which informal conversations 'outside the room' gave the biggest policy decisions dynamite.

Because of that infamous SPI-B document, some people have assumed that SPI-B advisors are powerful, caricature villains. They are well-thought of in their fields, and highly qualified. The power is harder to ascertain, because their role is to provide answers and proposals in response to COBRA and SAGE requests. In the papers, you can sometimes discern the political persuasions and biases of the SPI-B team. For instance, right-wing libertarians would be unlikely to reach towards 'collectivism' as often as SPI-B does. The papers read like proposals from mainly left-wing academics. In the questions behind the papers you can read the political intent of the policymakers. In the obvious example of *Options for increasing adherence to social distancing measures*, SPI-B has been asked how to make people adhere to the rules. One answer is obviously to legislate. The advisors are telling the politicians what they want to know, as well as giving behavioural insight about how to achieve that. It would be remarkable indeed if the advisors went in a completely different direction. It is well known in advisory circles that scientific advice is inherently political. Where the SPI-B advisors have sometimes wielded an additional and weighty power is speaking to the press and from their own social media pulpits.

A very consistent source of discontent among the SPI-B team is that the government often ignores their advice, which means that they aren't quite as powerful as people on the outside might think. As Stott said to me, 'It's self-evident that government policy is at odds with the advice they are given.'

It was apparent to me from the SPI-B documents that one of the government's biggest fears was social unrest, even riots, and Stott would have the experience to anticipate and advise. 'One of the first concerns was that there could be protests or riots in response to lockdown,' he said. 'The idea in February of ending football matches, shutting pubs, making people not go to work for months on end, closing schools seemed unprecedented. Unthinkable. Our advice revolved around inequality and not doing things to amplify perceptions of illegitimacy. Within all of this the people who suffer the most are the poor and where they suffer harm as a result of control measures, the potential for police to exacerbate social conflict would be quite profound.'

There have been protests, but not the dreaded riots. I commented to Stott that there was a strange pivot in the country's attitude to protest in the summer. One day, the general attitude was that we needed to protect the elderly and vulnerable by staying inside, 'old lives matter', and the next, people were protesting 'Black Lives Matter', and the world took to the streets. Stott retorted it was simply about 'priorities' but he obviously disapproved of inhibiting the right to protest: 'The right to assemble is a basic human right. It's protected under the European Convention of Human Rights. Any government that takes the right away is taking massive steps in what we think of as democracy.'

He was excoriating on the emergency legislation to prohibit protest and the fines for organising and attending. 'It's a very pernicious piece of legislation,' he told me, 'and it has massive and negative implications for the reach of government.' He was also disapproving of the large fines for breaking self-isolation. A common theme from the SPI-B advisors was that encouragement is more effective than punishment.

The conversation took a frosty turn when I asked him about the effect of groupthink within SPI-B. This is a phenomenon where the natural desire for harmony within a group means that people will set aside their personal beliefs and adopt (at least outwardly) the beliefs of the group. The SPI-B papers only reflect consensus and I wondered if they always achieved that in their meetings. He threw me when he said, 'Groupthink is a completely flawed concept, developed around the inherent pathology of the group that undermines rationality and critical thinking. That is not what is going on. Groups don't have a tendency towards conformity, and I can absolutely guarantee you that groupthink is a myth.' I told him I'd look this up.

Indeed, I checked with a couple of psychologists who were surprised at the idea that groupthink had been so confidently 'debunked'. Naomi Murphy, clinical and forensic psychologist, told me that within the NHS, teams try and guard against groupthink as they are aware of the dangers. She made an additional interesting point that video calls will be affecting group dynamics in ways we can't fully understand yet. These behavioural insight 'war room' meetings are not happening in a room, they are happening in disparate studies and sitting rooms around the country – how does that affect communication and consensus?

The National Association of Scholars (NAS) in the US published a report in 2018 entitled *The Irreproducibility Crisis of Modern Science*.[2] Sadly, I don't think the UK government, civil service or the advising scientists appear to have read it. The NAS and the report's authors are concerned with the use and abuse of statistics, irreproducibility of results and political groupthink in science, saying that the intersection between these issues is very much what is 'wrong with modern science'. They summarise that 'an entire academic discipline can succumb to groupthink, and create a professional consensus with a strong tendency to reinforce itself, reject results that question its foundations, and dismiss dissenters as troublemakers and cranks' and that this 'particularly affects those fields with obvious policy implications, such as social psychology and climate science.' The problem is, the scientists in the midst of this don't see it.

My video call with Stott ended swiftly after my next question, which was about the use of fear. I asked him what he thought of the ethics of fear being used to influence people. He said: 'At the time it was about what might be necessary going into lockdown. We'd have been asked to consider what level of behavioural changes might be needed.' I tried again, specifically querying the trade off in making people more frightened if it is 'for the greater good'. He responded that it was 'a reflection on people who might not think Covid will affect them.' Again I probed, pointing out that statistically most people won't be much affected, that Covid will not be serious or lethal for the majority – therefore is it acceptable on that basis to make people think they are more at risk than they are? He said, 'There you go then,' and our video call dropped from frosty to arctic and we wound up.

SPI-B's remit does not involve questioning the data, the government-provided 'facts' that they work with, and Stott didn't like my train of questioning. If your SPI-B advisor, or civil service behavioural psychologist thinks the country is facing the apocalypse to end all apocalypses (and presumably they were told to treat the Imperial College London modelling as de facto) then they might think the ends utterly justify the means. Although you would hope they would still be constrained by the ethics of their professional bodies and training.

Robert Dingwall, a Professor of Sociology who sits on various government advisory panels, was far more open on the subject of fear. In his view, fear 'passed its sell-by date by the end of April', although he took a nuanced view that 'fear might have been an appropriate tool at the beginning when we thought the virus might be an existential threat.'

His concern was that since then, there had not been a wider debate about alternative strategies and that 'the narrow base of advice given to the government was following a very narrow sub-set of science'. A struggle is happening within government between those who think the policies are disproportionate and the medics who have 'colonised the expert panels'. While I have postulated in this book that aspects of our government resemble a technocracy, or a 'psychocracy', Dingwall worries that the upper echelons of government and advisors are leaning towards 'iatrocracy', a system whereby the doctors and scientists are in charge.

It is understandable for doctors and scientists to be dedicated to the pursuit of health, but Dingwall sees the problem as 'a lack of challenge and diversity'. Ultimately he believes we 'need to learn to live with Covid. We have never thought it necessary to inflict social distancing and mask-wearing for influenza even though that can carry off 50,000 people in a bad year. We live with the threat of infectious disease at a minor level every day.'

The anonymous scientific advisor deeply embedded in Whitehall I interviewed in Chapter 5, 'The business of fear and the unelected psychocrats', believes the 'narrow base of advice' Dingwall talked about has been deliberately cultivated for years: 'There used to be rebels, and that was good, because you can learn from the rebels. Labour liked the rebels. During the coalition under Cameron, rebels became a little less popular. Then they disappeared.' They think the teams of experts have been recruited for their unified approaches and in order to align with political intent. Once the panel is assembled, they 'are given the injects as facts'. In the first instance in this epidemic it was that '500,000 would die' and it was not their job to consider whether the facts were correct or not. Quite simply, questions are not welcomed. 'You aren't allowed to fight the information,' they said.

The anonymous scientist characterised a homogeneity of thinking and groupthink among the SPI-B team: 'SPI-B interpret dissent as bad. Rosa Parkes didn't get off the bus. SPI-B would not have liked Rosa. The behavioural psychologists are arrogant and they have no rebellion in them.'

I certainly got a sense from all my interviewees (admittedly this is only through several conversations with several advisors) of common themes and a consistency in approach among SPI-B. They liked terms like 'co-creation', 'co-design', 'co-production', 'collectivism', 'in it together' and 'solidarity' – words which are strewn throughout the SPI-B documents on the government website. Depending on your ideological perspective, these might be seen as admirable qualities, but I can see how they could accompany a dislike for 'dissent'. They must also have in common a belief in the appropriateness of a behavioural science approach to an epidemic, or they wouldn't be on the team. And I detected politicisation in their approaches and advice, which is arguably inevitable, but could be skewing their advice disadvantageously.

My chat with Dr Daisy Fancourt was very pleasant. I think she would have been OK with Rosa Parkes. She is an Associate Professor in Behavioural Science and Health at UCL and runs The Covid Social Study, a longitudinal social and psychological study into the impact of the epidemic and lockdowns. She feeds research into the advising panels including SPI-B. She was recommended to me by Susan Michie, Professor of Health Psychology & Director of the Centre for Behaviour Change at UCL. Michie didn't have time for an interview, which is not surprising as she sits on SAGE, SPI-B and 'Independent SAGE'.

Fancourt told me that one of the strengths early on in the pandemic was that we were 'all in this together'. She believed that had encouraged compliance and social cohesion. My impression from some of the interviewees was that they liked collectivism for itself, but also because it breeds adherence to the rules.

I asked her about the use of fear as a tactic to encourage adherence. 'One of the things that was effective was increasing the idea that you shouldn't pass it to others,' she said, 'as people are concerned about spreading the virus to neighbours and families. Some of the less effective policies are on the threat to yourself. Appeals to collective conscience are more effective.' That made sense, but then she uncritically mentioned one of my personal bête noires, 'don't kill granny', which was 'good for compliance'. For one thing, some young people will have lost grandparents during the epidemic, making this quite an insensitive catchphrase. Back in March 2020, Neil Ferguson said that two-thirds of the people who would go on to die from Covid might die anyway during the year because 'these are people at the end of their lives or have underlying conditions'.[3] Given that, should children and young people be burdened with this level of responsibility in order to encourage compliance?

Fancourt told me about the 'huge role' of psychology and behavioural science as the epidemic continues. She thinks they can be used to heal trauma and grief, ease mental health problems, treat frontline healthcare workers experiencing trauma and heal the divisions sown by the epidemic. In her opinion, behavioural science would be needed to 'encourage people to use vaccines. We won't get out of this unless people have vaccines.'

She expanded: 'Most people are worried that because the vaccines have been developed quickly, safety stages have been missed out, and they have not. We need to make sure the information about vaccines comes from different sources, it mustn't look like it's propaganda. It needs to come from faith leaders, influencers, local leaders. "Anti-vaxxers" aren't bad people they just have concerns that need addressing. We need to make people want to have the vaccine, not feel like they must have it.' Wouldn't simply seeing the full data from trials and post-launch convince people? Wouldn't longer-term safety data be part of that, because despite Fancourt's assurances that safety stages have not been missed out, people will be aware that medium and longer-term side-effects won't have emerged? And was she basically saying that propaganda is acceptable as long as it doesn't look like it's propaganda?

On 22 October 2020 SPI-B published a paper entitled *Role of Community Champions networks to increase engagement in context of COVID-19: evidence and best practice*,[4] which is ostensibly about 'Test and Trace' but puts forward the general idea that 'community champions are volunteers who, with training and support, help improve the health and wellbeing of their families, communities or workplaces.' While the document pushes the idea of 'co-creation' often mentioned by the SPI-B advisors, it's about how to use champions to influence, rather than genuinely 'co-create'. The question came from government, the strategy comes from SPI-B, and the next step is lining up the champions, who presumably will tailor the messaging, but not the objectives. The term 'community champions' also has a slight ring of the block policing that has been, and still is, widely used in Communist regimes, where individuals are asked to report anti-social behaviour and promote pro-social acts by their neighbours.

Two of the SPI-B advisors who agreed to talk to me were adamant they could only be fully honest if they were anonymous, to protect their reputations and future careers. I'm going to call them SPI One and SPI Two. (I know, this is not ideal.)

SPI One is high up in their professional body and, as such, I was very keen to talk to them. Like Fancourt, they also brought up the vaccine, telling me, 'Without a vaccine, psychology is your main weapon. You have to restrict ways in which people mix and the virus can spread. Psychology has had a really good epidemic actually.'

I asked them which psychologists had particularly stood out. They mentioned Susan Michie, who had been unable to speak with me, and told me that she is 'particularly fantastic on the messaging'. This brought me on to the intersection of scientific advice and politics. Michie is a member of the Communist Party of Britain,[5] which wants a 'revolutionary transformation of society' to end capitalism and create a socialist state of Britain. I had been surprised that a Communist Party member was advising the government through two important advisory panels. Might such revolutionary views influence her advice? She praised China's response on Twitter on 14 March: 'China has a socialist, collective system (whatever criticisms people may have) not an individualistic, consumer-oriented, profit-driven society badly damaged by 20 years of failed neoliberal economic policies. #LearnLessons'

I'm not sure the people who were welded into their apartments in China would agree with this rose-tinted view of collectivism, or the Uygurs, or those who are blacklisted ('once discredited, everywhere restricted') using China's government surveillance social credit system.

'It's interesting how people's personal politics sit with this,' said SPI One. 'Susan Michie, who I think's been outstanding, is a member of the Communist Party, yes. I'm not sure how helpful her criticisms of the government are. The attack on neo-liberalism and the whole culture of individuality is rooted in the collective, the 'we', group identity – this is powerful psychology at the moment. In general, the pandemic hasn't exactly always brought the best out in people and the science/politics interface is both very interesting and problematic.' I asked if personal politics interfere with the quality of advice. SPI One turned it round, saying that they believed the more right-wing and populist governments had not managed the epidemic as well.

As *The Irreproducibility Crisis of Modern Science* notes, 'Some of the groupthink afflicting scientific research is political. Numerous studies have shown that the majority of academics are liberals and progressives, with relatively few moderates and scarcely any conservatives among their ranks'. Politicised groupthink can bias scientific and social-scientific research in any field that acquires a political coloration.

SPI One warned me that 'people use the pandemic to grab power and drive through things that wouldn't happen otherwise.' They were concerned about some of the policies the government were enacting, possibly using Covid as a proxy: 'We have to be very careful about the authoritarianism that is creeping in.'

They told me that there was a more pressing problem with science and politics. The advice might depend on who pays the advisors. (Frankly, I was surprised there was not more of a clamour to understand the financial interests and funding behind the various advisors to government during the epidemic.) More interestingly, they observed that 'psychologists tend to be more on the neurotic end of the spectrum. I personally have been taking Covid very seriously. I go in shops, but I don't go in cafes. There is a madness in psychology at the moment. Suddenly every psychologist and undergraduate in the country is at looking this. And that is partly an anxiety management thing.' Perhaps the strategy to frighten the country was ignited in the crucible of the psychologists' own anxieties.

I asked my standard question: had it been ethical to frighten people 'for the greater good'? 'You need to frighten people,' they affirmed, 'there is something frightening about pandemics. The number of deaths in Italy meant it was responsible for the public to be informed about how dangerous it was, for their own safety. Young people, particularly people under 55, seem to be quite safe. How do you alert people to the fact there is a serious life-threatening illness they can get without putting the fear of God into them? We live with the knowledge we are going to die but we don't normally think the person we are going to shake hands with could kill us.'

This seemed at the heart of the issue ethically – is it acceptable to implement a campaign of fear when the threat does not apply equally to everyone? One SPI-B paper spelled out clearly that 'the messaging should be transparent about uncertainty where present, in order to earn trust,'[6] but this had not been reflected in ministers' speeches, or in scientific briefings, or in advertising. As an example, one government advertisement, targeted at the young, showed teenage lads sitting in a park, with the message, 'Don't meet up with mates. Hanging out in parks could kill.' Providing tabulations of relative risk in advertisements wouldn't work, obviously, but does over-stating risk to people who are clearly not in the risk category engender trust? It doesn't take long for young people to suss out they aren't at risk, so what was to be gained long term by pretending they were? The government tried to democratise the risk of Covid, when in fact it was highly patterned and age-stratified. I thought of how Jane (p76) said she wouldn't trust the government again if there was another epidemic. She was just one example of how simple messaging – which may have the best intentions – can backfire if not honest.

I mentioned Jane to SPI One and said she suffered panic attacks every morning for weeks, and scoured the news for stories of hope. Had SPI-B ever been commissioned to give people hope? Apparently not.

Another call for transparency came from SPI-B member Gavin Morgan, an educational psychologist. With his educational focus, he worried about the impact of school closures on children's mental health and learning, especially 'the more needy kids' with mental health issues and behavioural problems. He said that the longer lockdown went on, 'the more kids will be affected. The more broken pieces there will be to pick up.'

He did a lot of work with SPI-B to get schools in a position where they could reopen in the summer, but he found the willingness was not there. The government had created so much fear that there was 'a lot of misplaced concern' from parents and teachers about the risk level. In his view, 'This stems from the government's concern that people wouldn't follow lockdown rules. They went overboard with the scary message to get compliance. They were pushing at an open door, because there was already fear. Effectively, locking down schools was easy and unlocking was very difficult because of fear. The government's campaign was too effective.'

I asked if a more honest and transparent communication of risk might not have reduced the difficulties with schools. He agreed, and used the term 'co-creation' again. In his opinion, the Department for Education, teachers and parents should have jointly developed plans, which would have led to more honesty, a better understanding of risk, and ultimately they would all have been invested in the plans and 'owned the solution'.

His great success with schools was preventing the use of masks in schools, at least initially. He was adamant that teachers and pupils should not wear masks in classrooms, telling me, 'younger kids' speech and communication needs are predicted on being able to see an adult's mouth when they are talking. We take in so much when we interact with people: the non-verbal, eyes and mouth. It's massive if you take away half of people's faces. There isn't any empirical evidence because this is all new, but we can relay theories about human development. Young people and children could be hugely affected. Masks dehumanise people.'

Given that he thought masks dehumanise people, and that the evidence that they help prevent transmission is weak, I wondered how the SPI-B advisors felt about them? I was not surprised that he told me that the group was split. As he said, 'they are not a panacea and the evidence is not clear cut'. But he told me that some of the group like masks because they convey a message of 'solidarity'. In other words, there is a behavioural science 'reason' for wearing masks, to increase a sense of collectivism. This is a feeling favoured by the psychologists that is entirely unrelated to the scientific evidence regarding transmission. Essentially, they want us to feel like we are 'in it together'.

During the course of writing this book I spoke to Morgan a few times. I liked him. He was open, where others were sometimes guarded, and he enjoyed the process of our 'interviews' because they encouraged him to look at different perspectives. When I spoke to him again in early 2021 I got the impression his involvement had been dialled down a little.

The government gave very strong guidance that secondary school pupils should wear masks in classrooms when schools reopened on 8 March 2021. I asked him what was behind this new policy. 'It's gone quiet. We've gone from regular meetings to just being commissioned for different projects,' he said. 'There was no consultation about face masks in schools.' I asked him why. 'I don't know. I have raised the questions a few times with other SPI-B members and with people who also sit on SAGE. We don't know why we weren't consulted.'

It seemed strange that the government had a willing educational psychologist ready and waiting to provide pro bono advice, and not to take advantage. I asked if he thought he wasn't being consulted because he gave the 'wrong sort' of advice. He paused and then offered a diplomatic answer: 'It's becoming more streamlined which is sensible.' Right, but he'd fought hard to prevent masks being used in classrooms before – were they weeding out the wild cards? 'Maybe,' he agreed.

I wondered what he thought of this U-turn on masks in

classrooms. He reiterated the same kind of points he'd made before, perhaps expressed even more strongly. He pointed out that, 'masks aren't even questioned any more, it's like a seatbelt in a car.' What the public would tolerate, accept, and even wanted, had shifted.

At this stage, an unevaluated mass-testing programme had also started in secondary schools, with pupils taking three tests to return to school, and thereafter two per week. I asked him what he thought about the impact of this. 'It's one more thing that schools are being asked to do,' he told me. 'Fair play to teachers, they are doing it, but they do roll over without any challenge. It assuages the government; they are trying to keep parents on board and reassure people it is safe to go back to school.' But what about the pupils? How did he think this might make them feel? 'Anything invasive like that feels like a threat. We don't send children to school to be prodded. And for what end really? I don't know if mass testing will do any good.'

Morgan was the only SPI-B advisor I spoke to who emphasised that we should have been thinking about the finish line from the beginning: 'There was a lot of positive goodwill about wanting to lock down and we rushed into it. I cautioned that we would need an exit plan.'

I asked if they were thinking yet about the exit plan? He said no. Depressingly, he commented that, 'We've seen how much people are willing to give up their freedom since March.'

I asked him how we would alleviate fear and get back to normal. I had the feeling that he agreed with me that we should try and get back to normal, in contrast to Clifford Stott. He hoped that a vaccine and 'track and trace' would help, but ultimately the greatest aid to encouraging compliance and reducing fear would be 'open, honest and truthful' government. He didn't seem at all convinced we'd get that.

We talked about the fear that enabled this trading of freedom for a sense of security. Morgan admitted to me, like SPI One had, that he had feared catching Covid at the beginning. People seem to enjoy being scared – at times – and I mused that perhaps the response to Covid had revealed a craving for existential crisis that had not been met since the

Second World War. Was there a deeper psychological need being expressed through this fear? He responded that 'people like being scared. Think about rollercoasters and horror films. They are enjoyable because we know they are safe but provide a vicarious sensation of fear. We don't have to go out hunting any more, we're not scared of being attacked anymore.' So perhaps the muscles of our evolutionary fears needed flexing...

By the autumn Morgan's fears had evolved and he worried that 'important aspects of human society are being taken away. If this goes on much longer we will lose our culture. If that's taken away, then what are we? My fears have changed over six months.'

SPI Two is the other member of SPI-B who could only speak to me honestly if I agreed to conceal their identity. They had grave concerns about the use of fear: 'In March, the government was very worried about compliance and they thought people wouldn't want to be locked down. There were discussions about fear being needed to encourage compliance and decisions were made about how to ramp up the fear. The way we have used fear is dystopian. We have a totalitarian government in respect to propaganda. But all governments engage with propaganda. The use of fear has definitely been ethically questionable. It's been like a weird experiment. Ultimately, it backfired because people became too scared.'

We talked about propaganda during the Covid epidemic, which SPI Two felt had reached 'sinister' levels, and they shared their suspicions with me about 'Clap for Carers'. 'I never joined in with Clap for Carers. I was relieved when it was over. I would say it was "created", invented, I don't think it was grassroots,' they confided. 'We never discussed it in SPI-B, it wasn't our policy or recommendation, I just think someone, somewhere dreamt it up. It was ready to go. Something about it struck me as artificial. I bristled at the rainbows in people's windows. It felt more like a clap for Boris rather than a clap for the NHS. I think the government used it as a shield.'

I felt goosebumps. I had interviewed the 'founder' of Clap for Carers, Annemarie Plas, for an article I wanted to write, and had felt a strange hunch. Instead of pitching the story and portrait to a magazine as planned, I had felt stuck, unable to confirm my inklings one way or the other, so I'd just dropped it. SPI Two's conjecture echoed my hunch, and it was not the first time someone close to government had shared suspicions that Clap for Carers was not the grassroots sensation it seemed.

It might be that Clap for Carers was invented by one of the covert propaganda units in the government. Or maybe it really did originate with Plas (she seemed genuine, I do believe her on this) but was turbo-charged to become a visible nationwide campaign with government help. It injected the early days of the lockdown with a feeling of hope and humanity. It encouraged the collectivism so beloved of the behavioural scientists. But something felt off, 'artificial', as SPI Two said. The government has form for manipulating emotion this way, which I explore in Chapter 7, 'The tools of the trade' and Chapter 8, 'Controlled spontaneity and propaganda'.

We concluded our thought-provoking conversation. SPI Two told me they felt we had lost the balance between protecting people from a virus and protecting what makes us human. Again, this resonated deeply with my fears for the future when we first locked down. I asked how this could have happened. After a pause, SPI Two confessed: 'I don't want to contemplate it. We've allowed ourselves to be governed in this way.' I pressed on – didn't they want to know? They were part of the propaganda engine, so didn't they want to know where we were being driven and why? 'It's in the name of the unit I am in – it's behaviour. You could call psychology 'mind control'. That's what we do,' they said. 'Clearly we try and go about it in a positive way, but it has been used nefariously in the past. Psychology has been used for wicked ends. I don't want to get too into this because it's dystopian and it's what wakes me up at 3am.'

AUSTIN, 75

I am 75, overweight, diabetic and my kidneys don't work properly. That's four strikes against me. My wife has asthma. I am the primary carer for my 98-year-old mother who lives with us and she is housebound. She doesn't have any underlying health conditions other than she will be 99 in December. We have to keep anointing her skin or it would get dry and cracked.

I would not find it easy to live with myself if she caught coronavirus. She'll die at some point in the next two weeks to 10 years, but I don't want to be the agent of that.

Between my wife and myself we do everything for her. I do all the cooking. We don't have any carers going into the house because we don't want to import anything. She can go to the loo on her own but she is almost double incontinent.

Our washing machine has broken down. I don't want a new one delivered because that would mean a person coming into the house and a washing machine coming in which might have coronavirus on its shiny surfaces. We've been hand washing for longer than I would like. I have become very good at wringing out towels and sheets in the garden.

It's getting a bit more oppressive now we're seven months in, but I can continue living the lifestyle that I have set up for myself almost indefinitely. We get food delivered, we get stuff in the post, I read a lot, I can do the gardening and put the bins out.

What is hard for me is not seeing people and getting out, not having hugs. I have had lots of Zooms. My daughter and one of my sons come by every now and then and wave outside the living room window. It's better than nothing, but it's hard.

I feel a slump a couple of days a week, but then it gets better again. We have foxes in our garden and it's glorious to watch them. Little things like that are moments of joy and keep you going.

I haven't had fear and angst, but I do have high levels of concern. My fears centre around the incompetence of our government and the disinformation. They claim to be led by science, but their lack of strategy has made me concerned. I am fed up with lies and misinformation. The writing was on the wall when Cummings was not in trouble for travelling up north. I cannot believe that this government are as incompetent as they appear. I have to believe that the misinformation is deliberate. It doesn't make sense otherwise.

7. THE TOOLS OF THE TRADE

'I'm stunned by the weaponisation of
behavioural psychology over the last five years.'
Anonymous scientific advisor deeply embedded in Whitehall

C ovid-19 is not the first time the UK government has
frightened us for public health reasons. A standout
example is the 'Don't die of ignorance' campaign about AIDS
in 1986. It was a powerfully chilling television and leaflet
campaign, and still haunts our memories.

According to the campaign, AIDS had an 'explosive
infection rate' and it was predicted that millions of Britons
would become infected.[1] Sound familiar? In another parallel
with Covid-19, the media coverage was a cacophony of doom.
Fear and death sell.

The Chief Medical Officer, Donald Acheson, and the
Health Minister, Norman Fowler, pushed to create a hard-
hitting campaign that would convey that everyone was at risk,
rather than particular groups being more at risk. Similarly,
our government has done very little to explain that risk from
Covid-19 varies according to age and co-morbidity, and as we
know there was an intention to increase our 'perceived level of
threat'.

In the early days of the AIDS campaign, the message
was given that anal sex carried the highest risk and should
be avoided altogether, which was an unrealistic and overly-
prescriptive expectation. That message was soon replaced by
the advice to use condoms for safe sex. Advice which doesn't
take human nature into account is harder to follow.

The focus on death aimed to frighten people into changing
their behaviour. People still remember the ad and the feelings

it conjured. I know I do. As a 13-year-old the haunting campaign imprinted on me that 'something' was very, very dangerous. Three years earlier, I'd had to pretend to the cool kids in primary school that I understood the lyrics to the Frankie Goes to Hollywood song, *Relax Don't Do It*. I didn't quite understand this campaign either, but it was frightening.

Rather like the messaging on Covid, the AIDS advertising elevated fear but did not provide balance. People with HIV had to live with the disease, and still do, and the campaign did nothing to calm their fears. I imagine it must have been frightening to see the tombstone and loaded messages for those who were living with a positive diagnosis. Perhaps it drove the fear and social ostracism which people with HIV experienced. The British TV series *It's a Sin* about the AIDS epidemic in the 1980s has provoked people to write about the terrible fear that they felt at the time. One nurse recalled the 'fear, the isolation on the wards, gowns, masks and gloves to enter a patient's room.'[2]

I spoke to doctor and public health expert Jackie Cassell about her recollections of the AIDS campaign. 'The fear was controversial at the time,' she told me 'People in public health generally thought they were terrible adverts. But they seemed to have an impact and it changed what politicians would talk about, such as condoms and sex. There was a sense that it was a success, but we didn't like the fear.'

Similarly, how many people have been terrified by the thought of Covid, even though for the vast majority it is not very dangerous? As a reminder, Patrick Vallance told the nation on 13 March 2020 that 'the vast majority of people get a mild illness',[3] but just 10 days later, Boris Johnson warned of 'the devastating impact of this invisible killer'.[4] The messaging mutated faster than the virus or the scientific evidence.

Research showed that the AIDS campaign changed people's behaviour and the government considered it a success. However, some critics felt that it created panic rather than a proper understanding of risk and that it was actually grassroots organisations, such as the Terence Higgins Trust, which did more to slow the spread of infection among the impacted groups of people. As Cassell told me, 'What really made a difference to the people at highest risk was the gay community action and activism. The government's big success was needle exchanges for drug users.'

Is it ethical to use fear if it is in our best interests? For the sake of our health? Some would say so. As the Behavioural Insights Team report, *MINDSPACE Influencing behaviour through public policy*,[5] says, 'If we can establish that the behaviours do reduce wellbeing, the case for nudges is compelling', while also acknowledging that it is 'controversial'. In other words, the ends justify the means, even if the public wouldn't like it if they understood they were being hoodwinked. And does the government claim credit for its own campaigns rather than honestly attributing credit where it is due? Normal Fowler said of the AIDS campaign: 'There was no time to think about whether it might offend one or two people. And history shows we were right – people took care and HIV cases went down.'[6] What about the Terence Higgins Trust or other grassroots organisations? Might a different sort of campaign also have encouraged people to take care without scaring everyone witless?

Since the AIDS campaign, the use of behavioural psychology has become more formalised and deeply embedded in government. The Behavioural Insights team has a couple of handy acronyms to detail its methods: EAST (Easy, Attractive, Social and Timely) and MINDSPACE. I'm going to zoom in on the effects described in the MINDSPACE[7] document, as it offers more detail.

MESSENGER
We are heavily influenced by who communicates information, including their perceived authority, our relationship to them and how we feel about them. If the messengers are perceived as possessing high levels of authority, or to be worthy of admiration, people will be more likely to believe them and follow their advice and directives. Think of NHS frontline medics relaying the importance of staying home to protect the NHS.

INCENTIVES

Our responses to incentives are shaped by predictable mental shortcuts such as strongly avoiding losses. Incentives are not just financial (although they can be, such as fines) but can be the costs and benefits of behaving certain ways.

NORMS

We are strongly influenced by what others do. The power of norms comes from the social penalties for non-compliance, or the social benefit that comes from conforming. Being 'deviant' can feel highly uncomfortable. Would you rather be a Covid hero or a 'covidiot'? The government has repeatedly used normative pressure throughout the coronavirus crisis to gain the public's compliance with their escalating restrictions.

DEFAULTS

We 'go with the flow' of pre-set options – we stand on the dot in the supermarket.

SALIENCE

Our attention is drawn to what is novel and what seems relevant to us, from flashing roadside signs reminding us not to travel (too late!) to relatable data and statistics, such as risk of deaths.

PRIMING

Our acts are often influenced by sub-conscious cues such as sights (for example, face coverings), words ('Hands, Face, Space') and sensations (again, wearing face coverings), causing us to be behave differently. This is one of the least understood of the MINDSPACE effects, and 'has led to considerable controversy, not least to the slightly sinister idea that advertisers – or even governments – might be able to manipulate us into buying or do things that we didn't really want to buy or do.'[8] That indictment is from the behavioural scientists themselves!

AFFECT

Our emotional associations can powerfully shape our actions. Our emotional state significantly influences our mental processes and behaviour. This 'mood congruence effect' will result in a person selectively noticing and remembering information that is consistent with an existing mood. When happy, you are more likely to remember past successes, to notice the positives and develop optimistic beliefs about the future. When sad, you are more likely to remember failure and loss, notice the negatives and subsequently harbour pessimistic beliefs about yourself and the world. When fearful, your memory will be skewed in favour of past scary events, your attention will selectively focus on potential dangers in your current environment, and your mind will be swamped with thoughts about future threats and potential disasters. This recalibration of our minds towards the fear mode has been exploited by the government and the behavioural psychologists to ensure mass compliance with the emergency laws and rules.

COMMITMENTS

We seek to be consistent with our public promises, and reciprocate acts, agreeing to commit to a goal or commitment if someone else does.

EGO

We act in ways that make us feel better about ourselves. We all strive to maintain a positive view of ourselves and, in so doing, exhibit cognitive biases in the way we make sense of the world. For example, to preserve a virtuous self-image, each of us routinely displays what psychologists refer to as a 'fundamental attribution error', whereby we take the credit for good outcomes while blaming others for bad ones. This inherent drive to protect our ego, to act and think in ways that make us feel better about ourselves, has been comprehensively exploited to make us conform with coronavirus restrictions.

These effects can be seen in many of the campaigns

and strategies employed by the UK government this year. I interviewed psychologist Gary Sidley, who has also authored an excellent article about MINDSPACE[9], and behavioural scientists Patrick Fagan and Richard Shotton, and Dr Ashley Frawley, senior lecturer in sociology and social policy at Swansea University in Wales, to discuss the government messaging.

A central tenet of this book is that the use of fear to create compliance is ethically dubious and, at the very least, warrants public debate. In a short window of time, behavioural psychology has become core to how the UK government does business and these days it's the business of fear. The psychologists 'are operating in ethically murky waters in implementing their nudges, without our consent, to promote mass acceptance of infringements on our basic human freedoms,' said Gary Sidley. The ethics of nudging deserve their own consultation but are even more worthy of scrutiny 'when one considers the ongoing carnage associated with the elevated fear levels'. (See Chapter 16, 'Terrifying impacts', for more on the 'carnage'.) Frawley told me that she believes the deliberate manipulation of our emotions 'affects our deepest existential questions. The ability to manage our emotional lives is not entrusted to us.'

Behavioural scientist Richard Shotton, author of *The Choice Factory*, was more sanguine about nudging. I asked him to talk me through some of the highs and lows of the behavioural science approach during the Covid epidemic. Overall, he argued that behavioural insights are an effective tool to shape communications; as you have to choose how to communicate, you may as well do it in a way that will engineer the desired results.

Shotton offered the example of 'social proof' which is the 'norms' effect. He told me that people can be seen as 'slightly silly' for following these biases, but if they were misleading or useless we wouldn't follow them. In essence, 'social proof is a remarkably useful tactic', and has helped humans stay alive in our evolutionary past. These days, for example, you can't weigh up every single purchase in the supermarket. It would take a phenomenal amount of time and be an illogical approach. Social proof, simply doing what most other people do, is a faster way of making choices. As Edward Bernays put it, 'It would be ideal if all of us could make up our minds independently by evaluating all pertinent facts objectively. That, however, is not possible.'[10]

Likewise, Patrick Fagan, author of *Hooked* and former lead psychologist at Cambridge Analytica, told me, 'Most people can't deal with the facts. We have limited brain power, we can only think about so much. So rational appeals to the general public are less effective than nudging. Talking in concrete emotional terms is more effective.' Hmm – so, did he think the government's nudging had been ethical? 'I'm talking about my own profession here, but behavioural science has become egregious. At the moment it is about fundamentally changing how people live and taking away their freedoms. The nudge unit have appointed themselves as the Ministry of Choice and have decided to do the deciding for everyone else. In David Halpern's book, *Inside the Nudge Unit*, when he considers the ethics of this he says you don't ask children if they want to learn to read and write, you just teach them to do it. I think it shows he thinks of the population as being like children.'

I asked Fagan if he thought the government were relying on fear when other forms of persuasion were possible. He agreed that 'there are many ways to nudge. You can appeal to duty. You can use reciprocity – the older generation did this for you, you can do something in return. And fear has been overplayed. But emotion is the steam in the engine that drives behaviour and fear is the oldest and strongest emotion.'

How is fear confected? How exactly have our minds been nudged to influence our behaviour? Here are some examples from the myriad UK government mind-control campaigns.

FRIGHT NIGHT

The behavioural psychologists advised that the sense of personal threat had to be ramped up at the end of March. The prime minister's doomsday speech was scripted to do just that, by inducing fear and evoking war and authoritarianism.

Chapter 1, 'Fright night', details this. From that point onwards, the risk of death was energetically amplified, particularly during the 6pm and 10pm news broadcasts and on newspaper front pages. The Downing Street briefings were characterised by authority figures in suits on raised podiums and yellow and black chevroned signage warning danger, danger, danger.

While the number of deaths in the UK to date is sobering, the British people have vastly over-estimated the risk to themselves from Covid-19, the country has been locked down or under restrictions one way or another for most of a year, and it was Boris Johnson's speech that first set the framework for that miscalculation.

HEROES, COVIDIOTS AND SLOGANS

The media resounded with a dialectical theme of 'heroes' and 'covidiots' during the epidemic. 'Heroes' was used repeatedly to praise people following the rules, inspiring community activists, and frontline workers. Praising heroes is laudable, but what is determined to be heroism is key, and heroism consisted mainly of following the rules and following a nascent creed of safetyism and collectivism. A BBC film on 25 December celebrated 'London's 2020 pandemic heroes'.[11]

Slogans on government and NHS advertising appealed to heroic altruism:

'Stay home, protect the NHS, save lives'
'Protect your loved ones'
'I wash my hands to protect my Nan'
'I wash my hands to protect my family'
'I wear a face covering to protect my mates'
'I make space to protect you'

Heroism and altruism appeal to 'norms', as we all want to be in the right crowd. 'Ego' is affected as the terms and framing equate compliance with virtue. The slogans themselves work through 'salience' as they are simple and catchy. We're hardwired to notice what is distinctive. Roadside signs commanded us to 'Stay Alert'. This was distinctive for a while.

To start with I noticed my local illuminated 'Stay Alert' sign each time I drove past it, although I'm sure I wasn't alone in wondering what I was supposed to be alert to exactly while driving my car. After a couple of months I felt irritated by the relentlessly glowing 'Stay Alert' signage. After another couple of months it was no more than roadside wallpaper. It had lost salience.

Instructional slogans also came in triadic structures, because of the 'power of three'. Rhyme and repetition are proven to increase believability. They 'afford statements an enhancement in processing fluency that can be misattributed to heightened conviction about their truthfulness'.[12]

The term 'covidiot' emerged early on to describe people behaving 'stupidly' or irresponsibly. Or you can swap 'covidiot' for 'selfish moron', or 'granny killer'. The *Urban Dictionary* website has a selection of definitions, including this dour piety: 'an individual who in the face of dire circumstances for all, acts selfishly toward others instead of in solidarity and with generosity.' Through 'affect' people will not want to be in the disliked deviant group. The negative labelling ensures that the altruistic majority who are openly conforming with the rules will blame any subsequent increase in coronavirus cases or deaths on those who didn't comply, while themselves taking the credit for any positive change in the statistics. The covidiots and 'lockdown sceptics' become responsible for the virus being a hard-to-control virus, or the ineffectiveness of unproven non-pharmaceutical interventions. Scapegoating is 'convenient'.

As I explained in Chapter 4, 'Fear is a page of the government playbook', the use of 'othering' and dehumanising language can go on to have tragic consequences. Patrick Fagan told me that in an analysis of the Rwandan genocide, one of the first linguistic predictors was the tendency to look backwards, to blame, and to focus on past wrongs and injustices, and he had noticed similar precursors in the language of blame during the Covid epidemic. This sounds extreme, but it's important to at least be aware of these linguistic signposts – they have always led us down the ugliest roads in human history.

When pubs reopened in the summer, 4 July 2020 was characterised as 'Independence Day', implying an entitlement to excess and conveying disapproval. Pubgoers were derided in the media as wanton and selfish – the classic covidiots. Even if no rules had been broken, the sight of people enjoying a convivial drink was heavily criticised by pious 'lockdown zealots'.

It's worth noting that when we are influenced by 'norms' and coalesce into a group – a herd – we are easier to govern. It isn't a stated aim of the behavioural psychologists but it's an undeniable effect. And it makes spotting the dissenters all the easier.

Scary slogans also used the effects of 'incentives' and 'affect' to deter rule-breaking:

'If you go out you can spread it. People will die'
'Don't kill granny'
'Coronavirus. Anyone can get it. Anyone can spread it'
'Don't let a coffee cost lives'

I felt a whiplash of shock when I first saw the 'Don't kill granny' campaign. It was simultaneously insensitive to the youngsters who have lost grandparents, and placed a jaw-slackening burden on the others. I felt a visceral maternal need to reassure my children that they were not responsible for the deaths of the elderly. One son told me in response that a teacher at school had shouted at non-mask-wearers in the corridor that they were 'killing people'. Killing people would warrant calling the police, would it not? In fact, teenagers were merely making their way from one lesson to the next. Has this kind of hysterical and accusatory attitude towards our children been fuelled by government-initiated campaigns?

I contacted Professor Ellen Townsend, who heads up the Self-Harm Research Group within the School of Psychology at the University of Nottingham about the granny-killing catchphrase. After a long pause – I sensed she had a lot to say and was composing herself – she responded: 'It is an unethical

and morally repugnant slogan that compassionate, holistic
public health researchers would never endorse. Using fear
to psychologically manipulate people, especially children, is
unlikely to engender trust in science or future public health
messaging.'

To maximise the impact of scary slogans, the posters
displaying dire warnings have often been accompanied by
images of emergency personnel wearing medical masks and
visors, stark black and white imagery and bold typefaces. The
use of red and especially yellow and black have been typical of
the scary advertising, as they suggest danger and threat. Yellow
and black chevron-edged images remind us of painful wasp
stings as well as disaster area cordons. Beware, do not cross
(the rules), for on the other side of this chevron lies pain.

Patrick Fagan observed that some of the language used
in the slogans might also be intended to bamboozle us. The
term 'social distancing' is oxymoronic; distance is not social.
In Australia, the advice was even more Orwellian: 'Staying
apart keeps us together'. The confusion aroused by this type of
bamboozlement means you are more likely to be compliant to
the command.

CAUTIONARY TALES AND CASE STUDIES
The media focused on case studies which serve as cautionary
tales: stray from the rules and all will not go well.

> 'Patient in Wales makes coronavirus plea – "I didn't
> believe it was this bad"' *Sky News*, 26 January 2020
> 'Man who believed virus was hoax loses wife to Covid-19'
> BBC, 24 August 2020
> 'Mum who didn't believe in Covid-19 struggles to breathe
> after 22 days in hospital' *Mirror*, 20 October 2020

Clapping your hands and shouting you believe in Tinkerbell
doesn't keep fairies alive, and simply believing Covid is a
dangerous respiratory disease doesn't keep you alive either.
Of course, people needed to take sensible precautions and
follow the law and guidance, but if being frightened enough to

follow all the rules was enough to keep people safe, far fewer would have died. These lurid headlines and cautionary tales are designed to frighten people into following the rules – look at what happens to those who didn't believe hard enough.

But do the media do this at the express bidding of the government? In Chapter 2, 'Fear spread in the media like an airborne virus', I explored the complex and inter-connected relationship between the media and the government. In addition, do the behavioural scientists have a direct line to some journalists?

During a Public Administration and Constitutional Affairs Committee on 19 January 2021,[13] MPs put questions to David Halpern of BIT and Stephen Reicher, Professor of Social Psychology, both of whom sit on SPI-B. Reicher referenced a relationship with the media a few times. He mentioned a specific and early case in the media: 'a nurse crying in distress in the first wave was immensely important in getting us to understand the realities on the front line… I have been arguing for the need for more of these, including stories of compliance.' He reiterated later that he wanted 'more stories of their [the public's] compliance'. He said he had argued on Radio 4's *Today* programme that they needed more such stories and 'to be fair to the *Today* programme over the next few days they had stories of everyday heroic compliance'. Reicher seems to exert some influence.

FINES

We can't credit the nudgers with the invention of punitive fines. We've always had them. Although, without exaggeration, the Covid fines are the worst this country has seen since the Weregild or 'blood money' of the Dark Ages.[14] In fact, the behavioural scientists seem to prefer carrot to stick, although fines would fall under the heading of 'coercion'[15] in the recommendations from SPI-B. The problem is that laws to compel compliance must of necessity involve punishments for non-compliance. And Halpern believes that 'it does matter that egregious examples are enforced'.

32,329[16] FPNs (fixed penalty notice fines) were issued

under the *Health Protection (Coronavirus, Restrictions) Regulations, England and Wales* and handed out by police between 27 March and 21 December 2020.

SEEDING, THE OVERTON WINDOW, A FOOT IN THE DOOR AND BOILING FROGS

Seeding is the art of planting an idea like a seed, to let it grow – later your audience is ready for the sale, or the next Covid restrictions, as the case may be. Leading on from that is the foot in the door technique: once someone has agreed to one request it is harder to refuse the next bigger request, as a precedent for acquiescence and acceptance has been established. Both seeding and foot in the door are tools which can manipulate what is known as the Overton window. This is the model for a framework which can shift and expand the policies that a government can follow without alienating their electorate.

Once the idea is seeded, and the foot is in the door, it means you can be boiled like frogs. The boiling frog metaphor was famously used in *The Handmaid's Tale* by Margaret Atwood: 'Nothing changes instantaneously: in a gradually heating bathtub you'd be boiled to death before you knew it.'

In the biggest example of how these terms have played out in the Covid epidemic, we started with a single lockdown for three weeks to 'flatten the curve', which itself transformed into many weeks and, one way or another, we lived under restrictions for over a year by the time of publication. Currently we are in a lockdown which has no guaranteed end date or exit strategy. Whether through bumbling incompetence and lack of planning, or through a covert foot in the door agenda, or combination of all of it, the fact is that a three-week lockdown was the seed for a much longer-term and more drastic arrangement.

We were told that masks didn't work, and that they were even a bad idea, because you 'trap' the virus and breathe it in, and that they can also increase transmission.[17] We were told they would not be introduced. But even saying that we wouldn't have to wear masks planted the seed of an idea about mask-wearing. Then, despite no new conclusive evidence in their favour, masks were mandated on public transport, then in shops. Just before this mandate there were seemingly coordinated (or oddly coincidental?) calls from politicians and scientists. The Royal Society issued a report[18] and press release urging the adoption of masks, although it concentrated on behavioural psychology and messaging rather than hard evidence. In fact, it had to note that uptake had been depressed by a lack of evidence-based medicine in favour of masks. Sadiq Khan asked for masks to be legally required. Once mandated, Matt Hancock said the mask policy would be rolled out 'in chunks'.[19] This was a rare explicit glimpse of the government's considered foot in the door strategising.

The prospect of vaccine passports was also floated, withdrawn, and mentioned again. On 12 January 2021, the Vaccine Minister, Nadhim Zahawi, pledged that there were no plans to introduce vaccine passports. Yet on 24 January the *Daily Mail*[20] reported that eight companies were in receipt of government funding to develop vaccine passports. Has a seed been planted? What will happen to the ministerial promise? Let's see what grows.

KEEPING FEAR IN OUR FACES

Face coverings, or masks, appeal to 'norms' and social conformity. The behavioural psychologists love masks. They absolutely love them. They believe they promote collectivism, the feeling that we are all 'in it together'. This attitude, clearly gleaned from my interviews with the SPI-B advisors, was confirmed when David Halpern answered MPs' questions and said, 'It took a long time to get people in masks. Our view early on was that masks are effective, not least because of the signal they create and of course the underlying evidence.' So, he believed there was evidence in favour of masks, but note that 'signal' comes before 'evidence'. Behavioural scientists pushed for masks because they create a 'signal', when in fact not a single Randomised controlled trial can demonstrate the value of mask-wearing outside clinical settings.

How does the signal work? Normative pressure is enhanced and sustained when we wear masks in public. They are a visible indicator that there is danger present all around, in the air we breathe and in the people we meet. Masked faces prime you to think of danger. We become walking billboards for disease and danger. They keep fear in our faces. Literally. They also distinguish the compliant from the rebels, although of course there are many valid reasons, and non-exhaustive legal exemptions, for not wearing a mask.

And what of the evidence? At the beginning of the epidemic, politicians and public health leaders around the world told us masks were not effective in the community. England's Chief Medical Officer, Professor Chris Whitty, said, 'In terms of wearing a mask, our advice is clear: that wearing a mask if you don't have an infection reduces the risk almost not at all. So we do not advise that.'[21] In the US, Dr Anthony Fauci was clear on 8 March 2020 that 'People should not be walking around with masks.'[22] He went on to say that a mask might make people feel better and it might even prevent 'a droplet', but doesn't give the protection people think and can even increase transmission. But although there was no new hard evidence, policies changed country by country. In England, masks were legally mandated on public transport on 15 June 2020 and then on 24 July in shops, in Scotland on public transport on 22 June and in shops on 10 July, Wales on public transport on 27 July and in shops on 14 September.

In a speech on 3 August 2020 WHO Director-General Dr Tedros Adhanom Ghebreyesus said 'the mask has come to represent solidarity'. What he did not mention was any new evidence behind the policy change. In fact, the WHO's guide, Mask use in the context of Covid-19,[23] published on 1 December 2020, said, 'At present there is only limited and inconsistent scientific evidence to support the effectiveness of masking of healthy people in the community to prevent infection with respiratory viruses, including SARS-CoV-2.' The European Centre for Disease Prevention and Control (ECDC) concurs that 'evidence regarding the effectiveness of non-medical face masks for the prevention of COVID-19 is scarce'.[24] Matt Hancock said that masks 'give people more confidence to shop safely and enhance protections for those who work in shops'.[25] The UK government website does not offer the facts and figures behind the 'science', it just says that the 'best available scientific evidence' is that face coverings 'may reduce the spread of coronavirus droplets in certain circumstances, helping to protect others'.[26]

An MP told me off the record that the Health Minister had told him that masks were introduced because the economic bounce-back was not strong enough after the first lockdown in 2020. It was felt that masks would make people feel safe enough to go shopping. Masks were supposed to serve as an economic stimulus. However, once we were wearing masks it became about social control, because it turned out they reinforced a feeling of abnormal threat and stimulated fear. The reason for wearing masks became inverted.

When I spoke to Robert Dingwall (a Professor of Sociology who advises the government) he told me he was convinced that masks had been introduced partly because they are 'a symbolic reminder that people are dangerous, the world is dangerous, and you might feel safer at home. They create a sense of threat and danger, and that social interaction might be something to be anxious about. So mandating masks can feed the fear.' He agreed that there was little 'scientific basis' for masks and that, in his view, they were designed to 'make people compliant'. I asked about the ethics of that tactic and he retorted that 'the ethics of it stink. The BPS [British Psychological Society] should be taking a look at it. I'm disappointed that the psychologists have not taken this up.' Well, the problem is that at least some of the psychologists wanted us in masks precisely because of the fear signal...

A recent large-scale randomised controlled trial in Denmark, *Effectiveness of Adding a Mask Recommendation to Other Public Health Measures to Prevent SARS-CoV-2 Infection in Danish Mask Wearers*,[27] found no conclusive evidence that masks protect the wearer, although the study was not designed to test whether others could be protected.

A doctor wrote about the sobering reality of caring for critically-ill Covid patients for news website Unherd. What she said about masks leapt out at me: 'I then put on my PPE (FFP3 mask, hairnet, long-sleeved gown, gloves, visor) and enter the bay to examine the patients. I feel lucky to have this level of protection – my colleagues outside of the HDU only have surgical masks, which offer little protection against an airborne virus.'[28] And there is the acknowledgement – from a doctor – that a surgical mask (also known as a 'spit-stopper') does little to protect against viruses.

I also quizzed Shotton about masks. Even though he is a behavioural psychologist and understands how the subliminal pressure operates, he admitted that 'if I walked into a shop wearing a mask and no one else was, I'd be embarrassed. If I wasn't wearing a mask and everyone else was, I'd feel embarrassed.' It's difficult to be deviant.

People who are obeying the rules often don't like to see others break them. There have been harrowing accounts of people with PTSD or disabilities feeling unable to go about their lives in public unmasked because of aggressive questioning, or the fear that it will happen, despite their legal exemption. Halpern referred to the desirability of this citizen policing when he commented that, 'Most of the heavy-lifting is done by the public, frowning at people who aren't wearing masks. The British are particularly good at doing this.' The nudgers want us to monitor each other. In an astonishing public admission, Metropolitan Police commissioner Dame Cressida Dick said she hoped that people would be shamed into complying by other members of the public.[29] She hoped we would shame each other, even though no one can know by looking at another, what their reason is for not wearing a mask.

In addition to face masks there are other visible symbols in public which do their part to help prevent transmission, but also prime our behaviour in a broader way. Shotton brought up the example of the dots in the supermarket. He told me he likes the dots, 'because they remove the social ambiguity. You follow prearranged signs.' I told him I dislike the dots, and I don't enjoy abundant signage telling me what to do. It feels infantilising and bossy. 'Behavioural science doesn't measure whether we like the dots or not, just whether we follow them,' he said. I had another one of my breakthroughs: behavioural science isn't about how we feel, it's not about making us happy, it's not about our attitude, it's about behaviour. The clue was in the name all along.

LIES, DAMNED LIES AND STATISTICS

Numbers, data, statistics and graphs can all, if done well, appeal to 'salience'. They catch our attention if relevant to our personal circumstances and concerns. Simplicity is important because our attention is much more likely to be drawn to things that we can understand.

An example of doing this well was when NHS Chief Executive, Simon Stevens, revealed that the UK's health service had prepared the equivalent of 50 hospitals to be ready for people suffering severely from the epidemic.[30] It conveyed scale in a relatable (and reassuring) way.

But Simon Stevens doesn't always use this relatable and salient way of helping us visualise the scale of infection. Nosocomial Covid infections (hospital-acquired infections) have been a problem for the NHS and care homes during the epidemic. Hospitals are built like little cities, a far cry from the fever hospitals of yore, and an infectious respiratory disease can spread easily. The NHS has not been transparent about the scale of hospital-acquired infections. I had access to privileged information in mid-January 2021 and wrote for the *Daily Mail*[31] that since the start of the the second wave alone, 25,000 patients had caught Covid while in hospital. That is a staggering number. It's the equivalent of 50 hospitals worth of people.

Deaths, hospitalisations and cases were the main metrics discussed in press briefings and in the media. These were not placed in context with recoveries and discharges. Without providing that balance, the overall impression would be that you catch Covid and die, creating more fear.

There is so much to say about the use of numbers, percentages and steep-lined graphs that there is a whole chapter devoted to them: Chapter 10, 'The metrics of fear'.

THE NEW VARIANT, U-TURNS AND THE CHRISTMAS THAT NEVER WAS

Professor Hugh Pennington of the University of Aberdeen accused the Government of waging a 'propaganda campaign' to get the public scared enough to follow lockdown measures. He said: 'It is all very frustrating. In my heart of hearts I believe there is a propaganda campaign to get the public very scared.'[32]

In mid-December 2020 Matt Hancock warned that the new variant was 70% more infectious and behind a surge in cases in London and the south-east. Various scientists urged calm, reiterated that viruses do mutate, and that there was no evidence yet that this particular variant was more transmissible or deadly. On 16 December the government performed a U-turn and changed the rules for Christmas, reducing the number of households that could meet from three to two.

Pennington confessed he thought the new variant had become 'a very handy excuse for cancelling Christmas as rates were rising – in fact it is extremely hard to prove transmissibility without infecting people with the virus, which would be unethical.'

If the Kentish Covid variant was indeed used to justify changing the rules for Christmas, this is an example of 'placebic information', another behavioural psychology tool. New strains provide a psychological justification for actions the government may wish to take anyway. Worryingly, the virus will always mutate and produce new variants, which can justify action before the new variants are fully understood. A government could keep new variant bait and switch policies going for as long as there are viruses. That's forever, by the way.

U-turns were typical during the epidemic. This can be very reasonably explained and justified by the twists and turns of following the science during a new epidemic. But uncertainty is also a form of bamboozlement and is akin to the tactics used in psychological warfare. On 5 November 2020, Boris Johnson said, 'These rules will expire on 2 December,' about the second lockdown. But on 16 November, Matt Hancock said, 'It's too early to say.' This flip-flopping and good cop, bad cop routine was a feature of the government messaging.

I talked to the UK's leading disaster and recovery specialist, Lucy Easthope. She's a senior lecturer on disaster recovery and mass fatalities and has advised the government on Covid-19, as well as Grenfell, the Salisbury Novichok poisoning and the Manchester bombing. She told me 'this is some of the worst psychological torture I have seen. Christmas is on, it's off, it's on. It's not unusual in disaster recovery to go back and forth. In disaster recovery we say the kindest thing you can do is make one decision early. The government are making one of the big classic disaster recovery mistakes.'

It's not possible to know whether there was a lack of coordination between ministers, a lack of planning, or a deliberate plan to confuse. Regardless, it had the effect of creating a level of uncertainty which was bad for business and bad for mental health. We house some of the most advanced behavioural science in the world in our government – surely the comparison to psychological torture would not be missed? The lack of certainty about lockdown finish lines could arguably be said to create a more stressed and therefore compliant population. It is probably reasonable to assume the UK government's Covid U-turns were due at different times to both a lack of planning and psychological manipulation.

On 11 February 2020, Matt Hancock said that 'the clinical advice about the risk to the public has not changed and remains moderate'.[33] Of course, we all know about the U-turn that followed on 23 March. Did he and the government respond to the 'science', but also to public opinion, polling and media pressure?

SOME OF THE WORST DOOM-MONGERING ADS

We have endured a year of fear thanks to the government's Covid advertising campaign. Extreme, visceral and deliberately frightening TV, radio, poster and print advertising were designed to elevate your sense of threat and risk and encourage obedience to the rules.

Using fear in advertising is controversial because it can be distressing and harmful. The Advertising Standards Authority states in its Advertising Codes that advertising must minimise the risk of causing harm or serious or widespread offence. There are specific guidelines regarding fear:

> '4.2. Marketing communications must not cause fear or distress without justifiable reason; if it can be justified, the fear or distress should not be excessive. Marketers must not use a shocking claim or image merely to attract attention.'[34]

Some of the government's advertising is flagrantly in breach of the ASA code, as you will see in some of the worst doom-mongering ads I noted throughout the year.

Sociologist Dr Ashley Frawley conducted a brief semiotic analysis of the government's advertising and described its trajectory to me: 'The first hard-hitting campaign showed yellow and red caution tape and a healthcare worker in a mask which looks like a gas mask. This is trying to tell you that this is very serious indeed. There is a horror movie dystopian quality to it. In another campaign they used a raspy, stern male voice, telling you, "people will die!" By the summer the advertising is using a woman's voice, the tone is upbeat, there's whistling, you're being told to enjoy summer. Then in September, October, we were back to a more stern actor, signalling the tension and the risk are building again. It's like an abusive relationship – uh-oh something is about to happen. In January, the stern, raspy voice man is back.'

As Frawley said, a dominant tactic of the campaign was not just to say that you are at risk, but more importantly, you are *a* risk. It is dark messaging indeed to tell us we are responsible for killing other people, including our loved ones.

> 'George left the pub… and went home to kill his dad.
>
>   Sasha had a great night out at her friend's house… and popped in to kill her nan on the way home.
>
>   Once Ade's finished keeping fit… he'll go home to kill his mum over dinner.
>
>   Stop.
>
>   Horrified? Of course.

But would you feel different if their weapon of choice was Covid-19?

Coronavirus is killing people every day.

Not adhering to public health guidelines is a principal cause of the spread of Coronavirus.

Covid kills. And you don't have to have symptoms to spread it.

Protect the lives of friends, family, neighbours, and the community.

Don't bring Covid home this Christmas.'

This is the wording from a sensationalised video[35] produced for social media and shared by a councillor at Haringey Council.

'Someone jogging, walking their dog or working out in the park is highly likely to have Covid-19. This is a national health emergency. Around one in three people have no symptoms and are spreading it without knowing. So exercise locally… If you bend the rules, people will die…'

This government radio advertisement was withdrawn after complaints to the Advertising Standards Authority as the claims were misleading and could not be substantiated.[36] However, no apology or correction was ever issued. Many millions of people might still think these false claims are true and be unnecessarily frightened or concerned.

Santa lies unconscious in hospital, surrounded by NHS staff. He is saved, thereby Christmas itself is saved, and he rewards a nurse with a surprise Christmas present.

The Santa ad created for NHS Charities was incredibly divisive. Some people found it moving, while others felt it was insensitive and would disturb children. Surely it's misleading, as Santa is magical and therefore can't get ill or die? Hmm. Anyway, it was withdrawn to avoid further controversy.

'Don't let a coffee cost lives'

Hyperbole on a double-shot of caffeine. Meeting a friend for a walk with a takeaway coffee has never been illegal and has been some people's lifeline during long lockdowns. This advertisement could have frightened and deterred people from a helpful act of socialisation. The exaggeration might not help engender long-term trust in the government.

'Look him in the eyes
And tell him you always keep a safe distance'
'Look her in the eyes
And tell her you never bend the rules'
'Look him in the eyes
And tell him the risk isn't real'

A poster, print and broadcast campaign shows people wearing oxygen masks looking straight into camera. The tight close-up and the eye contact are designed to take you straight into their predicament. The grainy processing is evocative of horror, like an upscale *Blair Witch Project*. This campaign didn't just leverage fear, but also guilt and shame, pitting the sick against the 'perpetrator'. 'Othering' the offensive disease-spreaders could create ill-will and conflict. And maybe it was no one's fault. Maybe he got Covid while in hospital for a hernia operation. Maybe she caught Covid while working in a care home.

Grassroots campaigners against lockdown, Recovery, commissioned an independent poll from market research company Yonder and found that 15% of respondents reported depression, anxiety, or fear as a direct result of government pandemic advertising.[37] A further 7% reported that the advertising has made an existing mental health condition worse: that's almost 12 million people around the country whose mental health has been damaged by an unprecedented government advertising campaign designed to create fear. And 3% said that the advertising has brought on an entirely new mental health condition requiring treatment.

ANONYMOUS

I have several disabilities, physical and psychological. I am unable to wear a face mask because I have PTSD from sexual trauma as a young teen. I'm sorry for TMI but it's relevant. I was raped and penetrated in my mouth too. Due to this, nothing can cover my mouth, it's an instant panic attack.

I had to attend the minor injuries unit at hospital yesterday. When I approached the desk to book in, I was instantly ordered to put on a mask. One was offered to me, and I replied I was unable to do so due to a mental health condition. The receptionist fetched a nurse who asked why I was refusing to wear one and said that if I did not, then I would be removed from the unit. This area is very open and very public, with other patients being seen at the side of me. I asked for a private area, and this was refused. I was also wearing a sunflower lanyard.

I was becoming extremely anxious at this point and explained that I have PTSD. They wanted details. I was essentially railroaded into detailing what happened as a teen. I was told to wait and then taken into a room with a doctor and another nurse. I again had to explain in detail my PTSD. I was then offered a visor type mask which I found very claustrophobic and in all honesty unbearable, but was left in no doubt non-compliance would lead to my being asked to leave.

I was then triaged, assessed and treated. In total I explained everything three times. I had an hour-long major panic attack in the car afterwards. I had two more overnight. Since then I have been very on edge and I can't sleep.

8. CONTROLLED SPONTANEITY AND PROPAGANDA

'Controlled religious and political ceremonies are welcomed, however, by those in authority, since they provide 'opportunities for planting suggestions in minds which have momentarily ceased to be capable of reason or free will.'

From *Battle for the Mind*, William Sargant

If you liked me thus far, this might be the point at which you change your mind, because this is when I admit I didn't like Clap for Carers. The nationwide sensation left me cold. It's not that I'm naturally curmudgeonly, but something about the weekly ritual felt performative, forced and, well, a bit Stalinist. I appreciated the NHS but it didn't feel authentic for me to demonstrate that in the streets on Thursday evenings. I skulked indoors for the first one, but on the second Thursday night I found myself outside, watering my hanging basket, as the entire street stepped outside at 8pm and started clapping, cheering and banging pots and pans. It felt impossible to do anything except slap my watering can with my free hand and sheepishly beam at the neighbours. Yes, I was in thrall to 'norms' and maybe a bit of 'ego'.

If I'm honest, it actually felt quite nice to be joining with my neighbours in a collective act of appreciation. I didn't do it again because, for me, it was reminiscent of the innocent animals performing 'Beasts of Britain' in *Animal Farm* by George Orwell, or perhaps the conch in *Lord of the Flies* by William Golding – it felt like a ritual designed to give people a sense of purpose and unity. The underlying feeling of obligation created by the intense media coverage of the clap felt pressured and concerned me.

Extending the *Animal Farm* metaphor, it seemed to me that the NHS was playing the part of Boxer, the strong farm horse, faithful and fêted. But after being worked to the bone, would the NHS also be sent to the knacker's yard, like poor Boxer? It was blindingly obvious that lockdown would devastate the economy, and I wondered about the NHS's future in a poorer nation. There is no health without wealth. My skin prickled with warning.

Clap for Carers pulled people together so quickly and definitively, yet it made me uncomfortable. It spectacularly embodied the classic propaganda attributes of 'euphoria' and 'flag-waving'. My creative nature leads me to confront the points of tension. I've always been fascinated by our inner workings, the taboo, the stuff we push to the back of the darkest closet. So, as I said in Chapter 6, 'The SPI-B advisors', I decided to approach Annemarie Plas, the founder of the UK's Clap for Carers, for an interview and to take her portrait. I wanted to understand the person behind this positive campaign, how she made it happen and, of course, make an interesting article out of it.

On social media I had come across rumours that the campaign was secretly powered by the government. I asked Plas about this and she denied the rumours were true. I liked her a lot and believe she had nothing but good intentions when she started Clap for Carers. Her charming flat was the lair of a boho chic metropolitan yoga-practising upwardly-mobile professional, not a sleeper agent. Her back story was very interesting. With no humility, I have to tell you I got a great story out of her, alongside some beautiful portraits. Yet I felt unable to pitch the piece, because she let slip she had a friend who worked at Number 10. Considering the runaway success of Clap for Carers, this seemed too much of a coincidence. My initial story idea was derailed.

The very first Clap for Carers was covered in the national media and supported by high-profile figures including the Duke and Duchess of Cambridge, the prime minister and the

Beckhams. How many truly grassroots campaigns have the support of royalty, the PM and major celebrities in the first few days? It's understandable that the media would support a positive campaign in dark times, but this was an astonishingly fast and resounding public relations success. Friends with someone at Number 10, you say?

I checked in with Annemarie again, to ask her directly if she had knowingly worked in concert with the government. She told me, 'my friend was so busy with her job at Number 10 that she did not have the time to even think of Clap for Carers. It was the first days of lockdown. But yes, it is amazing how the world shared it so quickly, given that I made an image on Friday night (with a spelling mistake and no permission to use the NHS logo) and it was picked up by the Beckhams and royalty within the span of 24 hours.' Did her friend whisper in the right person's ear? Annemarie seemed vague. I asked outright if she knew whether Number 10 had at least sprinkled PR magic behind the scenes. She said she had no idea. I didn't think she would, to be honest. It's not how it works.

Clap for Carers ran for 10 weeks. There was a muted attempt to revive it in early January. Annemarie Plas received a deluge of negative responses on social media and distanced herself from the campaign. ITV News managed to find a few lone people clapping on their middle-class doorsteps on a drizzly January evening. Then it fizzled out.

Number 10 tried to revive the clap once more, in honour of the passing of Captain Tom, the 100-year-old veteran who had raised money for NHS charities in 2020 by famously doing laps of his garden, aided by a walking frame. As much as Captain Tom deserved admiration and honour, the idea of being told to step outside and clap by Boris Johnson felt forced and exploitative to many. When did the state start telling people how to grieve and that they should mark respect for a stranger? A state funeral was even suggested. Clap for Carers had evoked a propagandist feeling of deification of the NHS. Clapping for one individual took it a step further. Throughout history, leaders have exploited the propaganda tool of 'apotheosis' – elevating someone to divine levels. We weren't told to bow down and worship, we were told to stand outside and clap, but the exhortation and effect is similar. Boris Johnson was creating a cult of personality by proxy.

I checked in with my very well-connected anonymous scientist who did nothing to smooth my rising hackles. They told me that in their opinion the clap had felt 'fast, slick, ready to go. This isn't how disasters happen. Authentic responses are messy. I'd say this was engineered. If it was a genuine idea then the government engineered it by amplifying the media and celebs involved.' These suspicions had been shared by one of the anonymous SPI-B advisors I talked to.

The scientist suggested I put some FOIs (Freedom of Information requests) into various government departments. The first response I received to an FOI said my request would take longer than 3.5 days, the maximum limit. This is a common basis for refusal. Fair enough. I streamlined my request. The second response said there was no communication to share with me as they assumed I only wanted 'Treat Official and Ministerial Correspondence'. No, no, I wanted all communication, so asked for an internal review of that decision, which was upheld. It is surprising that there is no communication between Annemarie Plas and Number 10 or the Cabinet Office, not least because she was invited to a party at Number 10 for the NHS. At the time of going to print my ongoing FOIs are lost in the back and forth of civil service goop. A civil servant contact who is in and out of Number 10 tells me it looks like I am being fobbed off at politician level and that I shouldn't expect answers.

Speculation about Clap for Carers might appear cynical or ungracious. I don't want to be. It is also not possible to know what happened, at least at this stage. I can't write a book about these times, while we are in these times, without a dose of speculation. The whistleblowers, the uncovered documents, the testimonies all come later. I must envisage character motivations before waiting for the plot twists to be neatly tied up. However, the government does have form for either initiating or super-charging propaganda to create the 'desired' emotional responses in the population. Breaking stories like this often relies on the anonymous sources, the whistleblowers, not official FOI channels, which is why it's useful to look at propaganda campaigns in our recent past.

After the terror attacks on London Bridge in 2017, there were bunches of flowers and graffiti messages of solidarity behind the cordons at the scene of the attack. On social media there were outpourings of support and positively-themed hashtags, such as #TurnToLove, #ForLondon and #LoveWillWin. The media resounded with comments from faith leaders and politicians. You probably thought all of this was spontaneous. Some of the flowers might have been – the British public is generous and demonstrative – but much of the response was reportedly pre-planned by the UK government.

Middle East Eye has broken some important stories about the UK government's staged campaigns to manage the public response to terror attacks, through RICU, the government counter-terror psyops unit, and Breakthrough Media, an agency which has undertaken various campaigns on RICU's behalf. All of the tactics are guided by the government's desire for 'controlled spontaneity'[1] to facilitate recovery and to prevent civil unrest in response to terror attacks.

Disaster and recovery planner Lucy Easthope wrote for *The Guardian* that 'the "I heart"' messages that appear in cities in the wake of a terrorist attack are not always spontaneous' but 'carefully planned in advance'.[2] We spoke a few times during the course of researching this book. She told me she herself has penned the pre-emptive plans which include staged displays of positive emotion and resilience. However, after the Manchester bombing, she had a change of heart about the level of guided response when she realised that people needed a window of raw grief: 'I was wrong to insist in my training that the first message should be "we will overcome" as if the enemy was on the beaches and weakness would be letting someone or something win. Yesterday I realised that the fight rhetoric has gone too far and instead what we need to do is to admit how much this hurts.'

In our recent history, propaganda efforts have so far been largely turned towards attitudinal and behavioural change among Muslims – in other words, changing the way that British Muslims think and act. But perhaps there has been a redirection of efforts towards all of us because the government feared that totalitarian lockdowns would cause riots, as we know from SPI-B papers dedicated to the subject. Is it such a leap of imagination to think that the government either instigated a ritual of 'controlled spontaneity' to support the NHS we were purportedly saving, or that it heard of an idea (through a friend of a friend who works at Number 10, say?) and pushed it along with behind the scenes PR help?

Posters and a website were produced by a creative agency pro bono in a generous act of support. As you know, the media lapped up the Clap for Carers story. Very, very few grassroots campaigns go so well, so quickly, unaided. I approached the agency to talk about their involvement but I was triaged and denied an interview. That, in itself, is a little suspicious.

Fortuitously, I managed to track down someone who had worked on multiple propaganda campaigns for RICU. Again, this contributor has to be anonymous to protect their reputation and new career, but also because they signed the Official Secrets Act.

According to my source, propaganda is outsourced from RICU to external agencies who then work with other parties. This enables the government to stay distanced from the propaganda and deny direct involvement. It also means that the parties involved and the people they are trying to influence, who might otherwise be suspicious of the government, are more easily hoodwinked.

My source confirmed the tactics described in the *Middle East Eye* article. They knew about the bunches of flowers which were organised for the terror scene and the graffiti inside the cordon. They worked on the propaganda hashtags and the videos with positive messaging made by grassroots organisations, who had no idea they were working just one step away from the UK government. 'How many times can you say #Lovewins?', they mused, 'before it starts to lose all meaning?' They told me that they would be 'very surprised if the government wasn't involved in Clap for Carers and putting rainbows in our windows'.

I posed my constant question: was it right for the government to use fear and behavioural psychology techniques to encourage compliance? 'I think it's wrong for the government to try and change how we think and feel,' they said.

My source was keen to stress that all of this propaganda work came out of a well-intentioned government desire – fuelled by pressure from the public and the media – to do something about radicalisation and extremism after the war on terror. However, the efforts became 'bloated' and the unit and agency were producing campaigns to 'justify their existence'. This is the ratchet effect described by Robert Higgs. My source was reluctant to name agencies or individuals they had worked with – even just to satisfy my curiosity and not for the book – because they are 'good people' trying to do good work. Also, there's that Official Secrets Act.

Over time though, my source said the work felt dishonest: 'Even if the political project is "nice" it's political and it's trying to change the way people think. And it's paid for from government money.' Hang on a minute, government money? You mean our money – this is funded by the taxpayers, isn't it? They concurred. When you think about it, it's quite amazing that we're paying to be subconsciously manipulated by our own government.

Adil Ray, a British actor and presenter, launched a video[3] to promote vaccine take-up in ethnic minorities on 25 January 2021. It was rapturously received and shared by celebrities, politicians and the media. The video made strong claims about the vaccine. It also followed on the back of two relevant SPI-B papers that I had just read.

There are issues with the take up of vaccines among ethnic communities in Britain and the video obviously aimed to dispel myths and encourage confidence. According to a government paper, *Factors influencing COVID-19 vaccine uptake among minority ethnic groups*,[4] published on 17 December 2020, 'white groups' are 70% likely to take various vaccines, whereas only 50% of 'Black African and Black Caribbean groups'[5] are likely to be vaccinated.

The paper suggested 'culturally tailored communication, shared by trusted sources', such as 'educational videos' to 'increase awareness' and 'address misperceptions'. Importantly, such communications should not be 'affiliated with government or formal healthcare services' in order to be 'more trusted by some groups'. The report also recommended providing immunisations in community-based settings and religious sites. Robert Jenrick, the Secretary of State for Housing, Communities & Local Government, also talked about the importance of this as he visited the UK's first vaccination centre in a mosque[6] – the plan clearly put into action. As Dr Daisy Fancourt had told me, it 'mustn't look like it's propaganda. It needs to come from… influencers'. The key word is 'look' – it mustn't look like propaganda, even if it is.

A report, *Role of Community Champions networks to increase engagement in context of COVID-19: evidence and best practice*,[7] published on 22 October 2020, recommended the use of community champions in health contexts where trust is low. Since that report, over £23 million of funding has been allocated to 60 councils and voluntary groups across England to expand work to support those most at risk from Covid-19 and boost vaccine take-up.[8]

Was Adil Ray's video part of a government-initiated campaign to increase trust and confidence in the vaccination programme? It seemed to tick SPI-B's boxes. The video finished with an end credit saying that it was 'recorded independently from the government'. The word 'recorded' is telling. Could it have been conceived by the government, or scripted by the government, or given PR support by the government? And if not the government, could an intermediary agency employed by a unit like RICU at the Home Office have kickstarted it? If it was created at an arm's length from the government, the people involved with the video might have no idea there was any government connection at all.

As with Clap for Carers, I don't want to denigrate the intentions of the campaign or the people involved, but to draw attention to possible covert psychological manipulation, which I believe deserves public scrutiny.

Like Clap for Carers, the video was also instantly and positively shared by celebrities, the media and politicians, which indicates helpful hands behind the scenes, although it's possible that the famous faces in the video may have propelled it into the spotlight on their own. But as with Clap for Carers, I found obtaining answers difficult, which is suspicious. And I'm told by those on the inside that this is one of the hallmarks of a government propaganda campaign.

I tweeted Ray to say I was going to write about the video and that I had some questions. I asked if it had been produced independently or by an agency, and he said 'we produced it with lots of help, but no agency'. Nevertheless, when I said I had questions, he passed me on to an agency – Samir Ahmed, founder of Media Hive agency. On the agency website it says Ahmed has worked with 'Bollywood stars and YouTube sensations to UK politicians and global philanthropists'. (Politicians?) Ahmed said he couldn't help with my questions either.

I tried to fact-check the claims in the video with the NHS, MHRA (Medicines and Healthcare products Regulatory Agency), Public Health England and the Department of Health and Social Care. They aren't the easiest press teams to deal with, but in a really poor show, I only received opaque responses to my fact-checking questions from the MHRA – the others ignored my emails and calls. The Cabinet Office did reply to tell me that the video was 'not part of a government campaign'.

As I was finding it hard to make headway, I contacted the anonymous scientist for an opinion. 'Ah yes, this video is Nudge 101,' they sagely observed, 'and the fact that no one is answering you and you are being fobbed off means it's come out of the government.' I called the ex-government propaganda contact: 'I only had to watch the first few seconds to see it's come out of a government department. It's an openly discussed problem that the Muslims don't trust the government and this is their solution. Put it this way, white people sit around in a room saying brown people are the problem, then they use brown people to fix the problem. It's not sophisticated. If you approached the people who made it and they bounced it around and wouldn't answer you, that's typical of something that's been done with government in the background. It's the kind of thing we used to do when I worked at the agency.'

I emailed Samir Ahmed at the agency in 'one last try' as my book manuscript deadline was looming. His reply was interesting: 'Hi Laura, I believe you've been in touch with Cabinet Office comms etc as well so you should be able to get something from them. Unfortunately I'm just not the best person to direct questions to as I've mentioned before. Thanks, Samir.' I'd been told by Adil Ray that the film was not produced by an agency, but he'd referred me to an agency for answers. According to the end credit the film was 'recorded independently' from the government, but the person at the agency knew I'd been in communication with the Cabinet Office. Hmm. I hadn't mentioned that to him. If nothing else, this was a breadcrumb trail of communication between the video creators and the Cabinet Office. We might call it circumstantial evidence. And these breadcrumbs might lead us towards a heftier collaboration.

I understand the need to improve trust in vaccines in ethnic minority communities, but if this film has been created at arm's length by the government through the filter of RICU, or an agency or a 'community champion', does that ultimately deal with the real issues and improve trust? Call me a crazy idealist, but surely the best way to improve trust in the government is for the government not to use covert propaganda? Richard Shotton concludes his book *The Choice Factory* by saying that 'if a nudge doesn't help the long-term health of your brand it is worth reconsidering using it.' What is the government doing to its own brand by trying to manipulate us? There will always be whistleblowers even if they are anonymous. Eventually, the truth will out. As my contact said, he left the agency because the work was 'fundamentally wrong'.

I was also worried about what the strength of the claims in the video might do to engender long-term trust in government, healthcare and vaccines. Here are some of the claims:

'Soon we will be reunited with our friends and family

provided we do one simple thing. Take the vaccine.'
'How can you save someone's life? Take the vaccine.'
'There are no cases of significant side-effects among the
millions of people who have received this vaccine.'
'The vaccine does not include pork or any material of foetal
or animal origin.'

There were several exhortations to 'take the vaccine' in order
to be reunited with people. Emotional manipulation could be
seen to interfere with someone's ability to provide informed
consent, which is an ethical bedrock of medicine. This type of
messaging was literally promoted by the NHS in a document
entitled *Optimising Vaccination Roll Out – Dos and Don'ts for
all messaging, documents and "communications" in the widest
sense*,[9] published in December 2020. It advises healthcare
workers on using messaging such as 'normality can only return
for you and others, with your vaccination' and 'this vaccine
is effective in your age group and will allow you to return to
normality, which means freedom to do what you enjoy, such as
group classes, swimming, seeing friends and family, and getting
your life back'. Behavioural psychology seems to have left
reflective consideration about influencing informed consent
in the pre-pandemic golden days of medical ethics. I talk more
about this in Chapter 18, 'Happy endings are not written in the
language of coercive control'.

How can you save someone's life by taking the vaccine?
And which vaccine did the video mean? At the time the video
came out, there were two vaccines being used in the UK, from
Pfizer and AstraZeneca. At the time of releasing this video it
would not be possible to definitively prove that the vaccines
interrupt transmission, which would help others. Therefore
this was an unsubstantiated claim as well as emotionally
manipulative. It was reported on 24 January that Israel had
seen a 60% reduction in hospitalisations in over 60-year-olds,[10]
but firstly this was not proof of interruption of transmission,
and secondly it could not have been factored into the video,
which was released on 25 January. I asked the NHS, Public
Health England, the MHRA and the Department of Health and

Social Care if this claim is accurate, but they didn't reply. I have a feeling that if I had asked the various press offices about a video which was negative about vaccines they would have been much more responsive.

I was surprised by the claim that there have been 'no cases of significant side-effects'. There are always side-effects with vaccines and it's essential to be honest about risks for ethical informed consent. For example, according to Pfizer's patient information safety leaflet, the vaccine may cause 'temporary one-sided facial drooping' (Bell's palsy) in up to one in 1,000, and 'events of anaphylaxis have been reported'.

The MHRA's Yellow Card reporting system provides data on adverse effects. When I contacted the MHRA for their comment about the claim made in the film, the press team responded: 'The general safety profiles of the COVID-19 vaccines authorised in the UK are similar to other types of routinely used vaccines. As previously stated, the MHRA will publish details of all suspected reactions reported in association with available COVID-19 vaccines, along with our assessment of the data on a regular basis. We will inform you as soon as this has been published.' This was opaque, but of course they cannot say 'there are no significant side-effects among the millions of people who have received this vaccine therefore the claim in this video is wrong', without risking the credibility of the video and disrupting trust in the vaccine. The first month of Yellow Card data[11] for both vaccines showed there were some significant side-effects, even if they occurred in relatively small numbers, just as you would expect, including anaphylaxis, Bell's palsy, and many more.

I would have felt more comfortable fact-checking all of these claims through the NHS, the government or the MHRA; I wish they had responded to me. Another of the claims that niggled at me was 'the vaccine does not include pork or any material of foetal or animal origin.' Well, again, which vaccine? And what does the video mean by 'include'? According to fact-checking website Fullfact, the AstraZeneca Covid-19 vaccine was developed using cells which have been replicated from the kidney cells of an aborted foetus called HEK 293. Put simply, 'While human-derived cells are used to manufacture the vaccine, they are filtered out of the final product.'[12] So, the vaccine does not include foetal material, but was developed using it. Don't people of faith deserve the complete truth for informed consent? The British Medical Islamic Association does cover this in its own Q&A on the AstraZeneca vaccine: 'While the key recombinant protein is made in cells descended from human embryonic cells, the original and descended cells are not present in the final vaccine.' Faith groups don't advise against the AstraZeneca vaccine, although it is a very controversial area and I suggest individuals should be fully informed in order to make up their own minds.

I interviewed Calvin Robinson, educationalist, political advisor and commentator on race issues, about the video for a sanity-check and a different perspective. Broadly speaking, he was sanguine about the aims and benefits: 'As much as I hate propaganda, I think things like this are necessary. I've seen a lot of anti-vax content shared on social media. I have concerns about lockdown and civil liberties but I'm not an anti-vaxxer. If this video is going to help encourage people to trust the vaccine, then I am for it.'

I explained my concerns about the unsubstantiated and bold claims made in the video, and he agreed that 'individual statements in the video are worrying, and I don't think we should combat misinformation with misinformation. I don't like the idea of manipulation.'

One reason I wanted Calvin's perspective is that as well as being known for his incisiveness, he is from an ethnic minority. I asked him if he could imagine this video being made by white people for white people. He laughed and said he couldn't. I said I thought that despite its obviously good intentions, it felt infantilising and racist. He agreed.

On 18 February a re-shot version was aired on ITV, Channel 4, Channel 5 and Sky. Boris Johnson and the Prince of Wales tweeted the film on 19 February. This is a phenomenal level of support.

I couldn't quite get to the bottom of how the film was made, but the reluctance of everyone to answer my questions was in itself suspicious. I offered the right to reply numerous times to Samir Ahmed and the Cabinet Office. Eventually I eked sparse responses from the Cabinet Office which seemed designed to close down the questions rather than deny involvement.

I asked the Cabinet Office some specific questions:

- Samir Ahmed at Media Hive told me he knew I had been in touch with the Cabinet Office. As you are communicating with each other, please can you tell me more about the level of collaboration between the Cabinet Office (or a different government department) and the creators of the video?
- Did the UK government, a government unit, or an agency employed by the government collaborate on the video in terms of conception, script, direction, public relations?
- Was the UK government involved in fact-checking the video to ensure accuracy about the vaccine?
- The video states: 'Soon we will be reunited with our friends and family provided we do one simple thing. Take the vaccine' and 'Not only will you be saving your life, but you will be saving other lives too.' Would you agree that this statement, alongside a few similar ones in the video, could be seen as emotional manipulation? And do you think this could interfere with someone's ability to make a decision based on informed consent?
- The video states: 'How can you save someone's life? Take the vaccine.' How will you be saving someone else's life by taking the vaccine?
- The video states: 'There are no cases of significant side-effects among the millions of people who have received this vaccine.' The video does not make it clear which vaccine it is talking about. Is the statement correct?'

The Cabinet Office press officer replied that 'the video by Adil Ray is not part of a Government campaign and was made independently.' I pointed out that 'made independently' could refer simply to the recording (as the end screen of the video stated), but allowed room for collaboration between government and the agency and Adil Ray over inception, scripting, fact-checking and publicity, for example. There had obviously been some collaboration as Samir Ahmed at Media Hive knew I had been in touch with the Cabinet Office. I pressed again for answers to my specific questions. The reply was: 'We have nothing further to add to the below.'

The unwillingness of government departments to comment on the accuracy of the vaccine claims, the media support, the dovetailing of the film with SPI-B's recommendations and other resulting actions, the fact that the Cabinet Office and agency were communicating behind the scenes, and social media support from the PM and Prince of Wales do suggest a level of collaboration.

I asked Lucy Easthope about the video. She said: 'In disaster and recovery planning we make "safe" lists of people who can deliver the messages for us, act as 'interpreters' for us. One of my concerns was sitting in meetings where psychologists come up with the lists of celebrities who will best sell messages to different communities. I'm afraid I can see how this would have been done. It's a reductionist approach to use people for their ethnicity.' On one hand, it's understandable to use 'community champions'. But on the other hand it feels grossly offensive to recruit people based on their ethnicity. According to Easthope, she has been told by ethnic minorities that they are aware of being racially targeted which leads to cynicism. She cited an example of black youths laughing with her about videos that targeted them being set in 'chicken shops'.

An article[13] in the *BMJ* summed up the issues of informed consent around the Covid vaccine: 'it is important to ensure that information communicated to the public be truthful, transparent and accurate. This is best communicated by experienced professionals. Risk should be disclosed in terms of both known risks, including common side-effects, and potentially unknown risk.'

It looks like the government is using all the behavioural insights techniques at its disposal to encourage people to take the vaccine. Many will think the ends justify the means if the vaccine ends lockdown. Stephen Reicher, SPI-B advisor, commented to MPs, 'I used to say until we get a vaccine, all the things we can do to contain an epidemic are behavioural. I was completely wrong, the vaccine itself raises many issues. The vaccine solves nothing, it's people getting vaccinated that solves things.' But are covert tactics and emotional manipulation ethical?

Sometimes celebrities are used more obviously than this. Earlier in the year, TV celebrity Amanda Holden tweeted, 'I've downloaded the #NHSCOVID19app to help protect my family, who are my everything. ad. #HaveYouDownloaded covid19. nhs.uk'. The word 'ad' should have had a hashtag before it, but its use indicated that this was a paid promotion. I wonder how paid promotions like this helped the app? Personally, I see it and I think, hang on, if it's so good, why did you need to be paid to promote it? Richard Shotton told me that 'having a celebrity associated with your product can be seen as "costly signalling". People rate products as better quality if the manufacturer sponsors a major TV programme. Celebrities can have a flatter effect. People who like the celebrity may rate a product better, but people who don't like the celebrity might like the product less.' A risky strategy then?

A company called Main Street One in the US contacted celebrities, offering to pay them to promote vaccines: 'I'm reaching out to share a paid partnership opportunity to share your voice about what the COVID vaccine means to you… Can you use a personal story to explain why you're blocking out misinformation around the COVID vaccine and prioritising the health of your community? Why are you confident that vaccines are both safe AND effective?'

I don't know if companies would pay people to promote vaccines in the UK. Again, it is ethically dubious. (I don't for a moment think the people involved with Ray's video were paid, by the way, they were clearly involved in good faith.) The Main Street One pitch is an insight into the origins of the kinds of messages we see endorsed on global social media. As Main Street One says, they are about 'messages people are ready to believe, delivered by messengers they already trust.'

Breakthrough Media, which works with RICU, is now rebranded as Zinc Network. This is how they describe their mission on their website: 'At the centre of our work are people and communities. To reach and influence them, we work with a network of grassroots partners – those closest to the issues we tackle. We design behavioural science informed interventions that change attitudes and actions for the better.' They are more upfront now about 'countering extremism and radicalisation' and working with government. As well as radicalisation they also focus on 'preventing online harms'.

On 19 November 2020 there was a coordinated campaign of over 300 tweets, comprised of accounts which looked genuine and some which appeared to be bots, to promote the Online Harms Bill. The tweet said: 'More and more people are scared of getting #vaccinated after reading anti-vax #fakenews online. We finally need a law to rein in the #socialmedia giants @BorisJohnson #onlineharms'.

The tweet campaign was initiated by SumOfUs, but the use of obvious bots indicated that it was being amplified beyond their own dedicated followers. I wondered who initiated the campaign and who deployed these accounts to push for online censorship? I spoke to Silkie Carlo, who had also noticed the campaign. She told me that campaigns run by her organisation Big Brother Watch had also been artificially boosted in the past, and you could never get to the bottom of who did it and why. We agreed it made Twitter a deceptive and toxic environment for most unwitting users on the platform.

Also on 19 November, MP Damian Collins took part in a debate about online harms in the House of Commons, pushing for a strong bill. (Interestingly, Collins is the co-founder of Infotagian, a Covid fact-checking service.) Furthermore, Met Police Assistant Commissioner Neil Basu called for a debate on 19 November on the introduction of new laws to punish people who spread anti-vaccination conspiracy theories. So, 19 November was a day when there were different types of public calls for an online harms bill – was this coordinated?

I approached SumOfUs and exchanged emails with an employee. She said she was not aware of how their campaign had been co-opted and she said they hadn't worked with the government. I also approached Zinc Network to see if they were involved or had suggestions but did not receive a reply.

Twitter abounds with shady tweet campaigns. The potential deliberate amplification of the SumOfUs campaign is one of many. At the end of January there was a series of tweets all proclaiming 'Boris we love you and stand by you, your [sic] doing a great job, keep working hard and doing as your [sic] doing! My prime minister [heart emoji]' As the tweets were identical, I'm afraid it can't be a natural and spontaneous outpouring of love for Boris Johnson. Paid 'promotion'? If so, it was very, very badly done. People playing a prank? The opposition? It's hard to second guess such a clumsy campaign.

Another facet to Twitter propaganda is the use of troll accounts to discredit people. You will notice that a common retort to trolls in the UK is that they are '77th' – operatives in the UK army's 77th Brigade. It is impossible to know if these individuals are genuine people, or paid trolls, or who employs them, let alone whether they are part of the 77th Brigade, but this does reveal the suspicion raised by nasty tweets and the sense of 'organisation' behind it. It also reveals a sizeable contingent of people who don't trust their own government. I spoke to former footballer and sports commentator Matt le Tissier, who has come under fire for being outspoken against lockdown, and he showed me reams of examples of trolls he'd had to block. They can be characterised by names with numbers, 'egg' profiles, and taking a 'one note' approach to certain issues. These trolls en masse create a sense of disapproval which the individual experiences on their timeline, as well as sending a signal to the rest of the world. The intention is clearly to discredit the individual, which can have real-world implications for their mental health, participation in social media and also for careers with public profiles.

If we're talking about online harms, what about the harm caused by shady actors buying Twitter campaigns for covert purposes? Who amplifies tweet campaigns that coordinate with political debates and why? A transparent investigation is needed.

DAVE, HOSPITAL DOCTOR

I want to share three examples that illustrate the breadth of the impacts of our country's response to Covid.

W e treated a young man who had advanced cancer. He was scared to access healthcare last spring. When he did try and get help, he wasn't able to see someone in person and he had a video appointment. He felt they didn't take him as seriously as maybe they should have done. By the time we saw him, it was inoperable. We gave him palliative surgery and intervention. Might he have been saved? Almost certainly. He had a wife and a family. He is almost certainly now deceased.

We are treating a woman at the moment. She is younger than me and has children. She has made a very serious suicide attempt. Her life is still in the balance and she's suffered irreversible brain damage. She had no previous history of mental ill-health and self-harm, but she is in financial ruin and couldn't see a way out. She's not the only one. We've seen many others. There is no way of recording this, no way of coding data that someone suffered extreme mental harm as a result of lockdown. It is intuitive the restrictions have caused harms, but how will this be measured?

A woman in her late 60s had been gradually deteriorating and suffering chest pains over many months. She didn't want to make a fuss and overwhelm the health system, and she was scared of catching Covid in hospital. Eventually, she presented with end-stage heart failure. Had she not been fearful and gone to her GP, she could have had treatment and continued to care for her children.

9. COERCION

'Those who consciously justify torture, and are not candid enough to state that they use it to defend their own power and privilege, rely essentially on the philosophic argument of a lesser evil for a greater good. They reinforce this with an appeal to the doctrine of necessity – the existential situation forces them to make a choice between two evils.'

From *Report on Torture*, Amnesty International, 1973

S ocial psychologist Albert Biderman investigated and reported on how Chinese and Korean interrogators 'brainwashed' prisoners of war in the 1956 paper *Communist attempts to elicit false confessions from Air Force prisoners of war*. His studies resulted in a framework, Biderman's *Chart of Coercion*, which has since been used in other contexts, such as domestic abuse, to understand coercive techniques. While not as extreme, lockdown and social distancing measures bear more than a passing resemblance to the tactics featured in Biderman's Chart of Coercion.

Dr Harrie Bunker-Smith, a psychologist, also compared some of the government's tactics to psychological abuse. She told me that 'there is a parallel with an abusive relationship, which I noticed because I am trained in domestic abuse. The phrases were the same. A few months in we saw that mistakes had been made. A paper came out that said lockdowns cause more harm than good in the summer. And fair enough, mistakes happen. But they kept on happening. Like people working in care homes could go in and out, but family couldn't visit their loved ones. Social isolation can kill people, it's a serious risk to be considered alongside infection with Covid. Abusers will say they won't do something again but then they keep doing it. Abuse is not constant, it's not bad all the time, you have periods of extreme abuse followed by the honeymoon period, where you get flowers and apologies and promises and then things deteriorate again.'

She told me she believes people are getting used to being controlled by the government in a similar way. We have gone between lockdown (the extreme abuse) and more freedom (the honeymoon period) but that freedom has become controlled and authorised. The control crept in and the goalposts were moved, again like domestic abuse: 'Freedom becomes conditional. You wait to be told you are allowed it. And it can be removed from you. The British public are in a coercive control relationship with the government. Most people will say they are not; in fact they will defend the "relationship". People in an abusive relationship can get very angry when they are called out, if they are not ready to hear what's going on.'

See if you think Biderman's *Chart of Coercion* can be applied to the government's policies.

BIDERMAN'S CHART OF COERCION

TOOL	EFFECT	LOCKDOWN EFFECT
Isolation	Deprives victim of all social supports and of his ability to resist. Develops an intense concern with self. Makes victim dependent upon interrogator. Solitary confinement and isolation.	'Stay at home orders', self-isolation, social distancing, isolation from loved ones.

Monopolisation of perception	Fixes attention upon immediate predicament, fosters introspection. Eliminates stimuli competing with those controlled by captor. Frustrates all actions not consistent with compliance. Physical isolation. Darkness or bright light. Barren environment. Restricted movement. Monotonous food.	The monopolisation of the 24/7 news cycle, social media flooded with government and public health advertising and messaging, censorship of alternative viewpoints. The closure of social, cultural, artistic and leisure venues and events.
Induced debility and exhaustion	Weakens mental and physical ability to resist. Semi-starvation. Exposure. Exploitation of wounds. Induced illness. Sleep deprivation. Prolonged interrogation. Forced writing. Over-exertion.	Isolation and loneliness affect sleep and physical health. Being forced to stay at home and closure of sports affect fitness and health.
Threats	Cultivates anxiety and despair. Threats of death. Threats of non-return. Threats of endless interrogation and isolation. Threats against family. Vague threats. Mysterious changes of treatment.	Fines threatened for activities which were previously normal, like working, travelling, seeing friends and family, dating, worship etc. Vague threats of mandated vaccines and vaccine passports create stress. Threats of repeated lockdowns if measures don't work and compliance is not high enough.
Occasional indulgences	Provides positive motivation. Occasional favours. Fluctuations of interrogation attitudes.	Reopening of some social and sporting activities and civic functions at certain points, then taken away again.

Demonstrating 'omnipotence'	Suggests futility of resistance. Demonstrating complete control over victim's fate. Confrontation. Pretending cooperation taken for granted.	The previously unimaginable situation of basic rights being withdrawn. Claiming omnipotent scientific and medical authority, by 'following the science'. Proclaiming that we must not act on basic human instincts such as hugging family. Repeating and assuming adherence to the values of collectivism and solidarity and showing you care.
Degradation	Makes cost of resistance appear more damaging to self-esteem than capitulation. Reduces prisoner to 'animal level' concerns. Personal hygiene prevented. Filthy, infested surroundings. Demeaning punishments. Insults and taunts. Denial of privacy.	Shaming people for struggling with or refusing to wear masks, which may be impossible with a disability, or feel dehumanising.
Enforcing trivial demands	Develops habit of compliance. Forced writing. Enforcement of minute rules.	Standing on dots in shops and public spaces, queuing, following illogical rules such as entering a restaurant with a mask on, taking it off when seated, but putting it on to go to the toilet.

MAVIS, 35

We can't do what we normally do. I'm too afraid to even go to the park, I keep my son indoors all the time. We do the Joe Wicks exercise every day and reading. That's how we manage the lockdown.

I t's better to stay indoors than go outside and catch the virus, but I don't know how long this can go on. I pray for it to be over soon.

We have lived here for one year. We have one room, we sleep together in the same single bed, there is a cooking area and a fridge. There is no window and no ventilation. There is a cooker hood but it doesn't suck up the smoke and steam. We have our own bathroom at least. I do my best to make my home nice, but it's not easy. There is damp and some things are broken. The landlady says she can't fix things, it will cost too much money.

There is no space for my son to play. If I cook, he is under my feet, I tread on his toys. We have to squeeze around each other. It's not easy. Sometimes I tread on his feet or something, and he starts crying, and I say, 'Mummy is so sorry, so sorry, I didn't mean it.'

My son is three, so normally he goes to nursery. He misses his friends. I miss it too, because I do my shopping and jobs when he is at nursery. He cries a lot at the moment.

I don't know how online shopping works, but I know a Sainsbury's delivery man from church and I tell him what I need and he buys it for me, delivers it, and I pay him.

I pray that we will be released quickly from lockdown. Summer is coming and this room gets very hot with no ventilation.

10. THE METRICS OF FEAR

'Like dreams, statistics are a form of wish fulfilment.'
Jean Baudrillard

Logic is slow and fear is fast. Understanding numbers requires logic and sound reasoning. Politicians and the media very often use fear to circumvent our logic, because it slows our thinking. We can be dazzled and alarmed by a big number, or a steep line on a graph, and then we're less likely to question the nuance and more likely to be suggestible. From the beginning of the epidemic, the government and media reported the daily death tolls with a macabre dedication and, as I have said before, without context, such as comparisons with deaths from other causes, or total deaths, or recovery figures.

Humans can't sustain fear indefinitely: we get bored, we relax or, some might say, we become complacent. Covid didn't impact our lives in the ways the Chinese social media videos promised. People didn't fall over in the streets, to be instantly surrounded by medics in hazmat suits. The weight of rational evidence and experience could have started to outweigh fearful imaginings, and then people's sense of 'personal threat' – as SPI-B put it – might have relaxed. How was the government to sustain the belief in the necessity of restrictions to our lives over the months? One method seemingly favoured by the government was the choice of metrics.

Daily death tolls dominated government press briefings and media reports until they stopped 'surging' and were perhaps too low to report, or didn't seem newsworthy. At that point the focus switched to the reproduction number (R) and then cases. However, hovering just above or below 1, the R is not a very attention-grabbing number, whereas cases have seized headlines, because the absolute totals are large.

I spoke to David Paton, Professor of Industrial Economics at Nottingham University, who has taken a keen interest in the reporting of data during the epidemic. One of his worst data moments came in mid-April 2020 when 'it was clear deaths were going down, but Chris Whitty, the Chief Medical Officer, said we hadn't seen the peak yet. That was a big one for me. He was downplaying the downward trend in deaths. I think there were obviously deliberate policy decisions to make people take it seriously, but the data should be presented factually and then interpreted.'

Fear is a depreciating asset and we found ourselves in a time of short selling. Cases which don't translate into deaths can't sustain the fear, which is perhaps why Chris Whitty and Patrick Vallance delivered a 'shock and awe' presentation on 21 September 2020 about cases and hospitalisations. Metrics selected for maximum impact gave way to fantasy. A red chunk of predicted-but-not-predicted cases loomed like a child's red crayon drawing of a monster – the mythical monster a rather bad parent might scare their children with if they don't behave.

Apparently, their decision to present 50,000 cases by mid-October as a possibility was taken carefully, but it was widely suspected that the decision was made because the bigger the number, the greater the fear, and the more compliant the adherence by the population. The anonymous scientist who works within Whitehall told me, 'You can't do a pandemic without honesty and trust, but the problem is people don't trust the government anymore. The Whitty and Vallance press briefing was the ultimate psyop. Even really intelligent people had so much cortisol flooding through them that they couldn't think rationally. I know people who believed the fantasy graph. Now they're sold on more lockdown.'

While death tolls and cases dominated the headlines, other metrics were quieter casualties. Discussion of all impacted metrics is essential for people to make cost-benefit analyses. Yet Covid deaths were not balanced against unemployment, the lengthening NHS waiting list, missed cancer screenings, national debt, business closures, or calls to suicide helplines. As Paton told me, 'There is a lack of critical thinking about parallels. We don't say no one is allowed to drive a car to prevent all road traffic accidents. We can have different value judgements, but it's not unhealthy or wrong to discuss tradeoffs and take a cost-benefit approach.'

What is the result of all this fear-mongering? The messaging that was initially designed to help us stay safe by scaring us has been so effective that Britain quickly became the most frightened nation in Europe.[1] People significantly over-estimated[2] the spread and fatality rate of the disease. The British public thought 6–7% of people had died from coronavirus – around 100 times the actual death rate based on official figures. I tested this out on a neighbour and asked her what percentage of the British people had died. She said 10%. That would have been a very noticeable 6.6 million corpses.

Did using the metrics of fear work? Did it create more compliance in the British public? Whether you think people followed the rules or not will depend on your own experience and attitudes. I asked a dear friend if he and his partner had been compliant. He told me that they had followed the rules very strictly to start with, and they had always followed them in general. It transpired they had had people over to their house, but only a couple at a time and only for drinks, not for dinner, so that was alright in their eyes. Of course for a long time people couldn't enjoy a drink in a pub without ordering a substantial meal so, although he had the best intentions, my friend was negligent in omitting the life-saving food. I expect most people followed the rules, but they broke them in small ways when it suited them.

One study[3] in September set out to investigate adherence to 'Test, Trace and Isolate' as it was considered 'one of the cornerstones' of the recovery strategy. It found that only 18% of people self-isolated after developing symptoms and only 11% quarantined after being contacted by Test and Trace. People's reported behaviour fell short of their intended behaviour, but this seems a very unsurprising insight into human nature.

The government and media whipped people into a

sustained and at times hysterical fear. Then frightened people voted for harder lockdown measures in public opinion polls. Government then obliged the people with more restrictions. The restrictions didn't allow the fear to subside, then people voted for more restrictions, and so on in a self-perpetuating doom-loop. Public health policy became a sick dog chasing its own tail.

There is another reason that the government focused on particular metrics during the epidemic. Key Performance Indicators (KPIs) are to civil servants what the Ten Commandments were to Moses.

KPIs enshrine the work of all professionals in a department towards improving those goals and evidencing how they are doing so. For Covid, the KPIs were 'cases' (positive PCR test results), hospitalisations and deaths. Once established, the KPIs would have superseded the metrics for the economy, or other aspects of public health, or anything else. Staggeringly, the Treasury revealed it did not forecast the economic impact of the second lockdown.[4]

The clearer and more easily measurable the KPI, the more powerful it is in rallying activity and obscuring contexts outside the KPI. These KPIs overtly act to blind the government and all civil society to anything else, and then effectively confuse journalists and the public, which in turn creates more fear. The Covid KPIs sit like greedy little gods on thrones made of skulls, demanding obsequious worship.

It gets worse. The Covid KPIs are not reported as they are actually defined. I noticed throughout 2020 that journalists, doctors and politicians would misuse them. For instance, 'Patients admitted' actually includes 'people admitted to hospital who tested positive for COVID-19 in the 14 days prior to admission, and those who tested positive in hospital after admission. Inpatients diagnosed with COVID-19 after admission are reported as being admitted on the day prior to their diagnosis.'[5] So, patients admitted with Covid aren't just patients admitted with Covid – which is what anyone would assume unless they have read the small print – they are also patients who were admitted for something completely different, but tested positive routinely for Covid, as well as patients who were infected with Covid while in hospital. The overall total will be a useful measure when planning how to manage wards and healthcare, but as a public-facing metric it is misleading, and as a KPI it cannot solely respond to restrictions designed to reduce community transmission, when it is also driven by nosocomial infection.

Similarly, deaths were frequently reported using the figure that the UK government dashboard pushes to the top: death 'by date reported'. Due to time lags in death registration those figures could be lumpy, subject to sharp ups and downs. There was always a dip on a Monday (after weekend delays) and then a higher figure on a Tuesday. On a day with a big number you could guarantee certain MPs and journalists would grimly tell us that 'x' people died today, when in fact they didn't die 'today', they died at some point over the recent days and weeks. On 30 December there were 981 deaths by date reported. This figure was bandied around the media and social media, with the incorrect interpretation that the people had died that day. However, the figure included a lag of death registrations over Christmas. In fact 588 people died on 30 December, which was not confirmed until 6 January. (That total will continue to rise over time as late death registrations are added.)

These people all died, so it does it matter how and when the deaths are reported? Am I splitting hairs? Lumpy data produces 'hot spot' days, creating panic and driving (or maybe justifying?) policy decisions. And maybe that is the plan. After all, the low days were not reported the same way.

The government's cost-benefit analysis of lockdown published on 30 November didn't include the use of QALYs (Quality Adjusted Life Years). This was a strange omission, as they are the bread and butter metric of the NHS. The average age of death with Covid is 82.3 years[6] – one year more than the average life expectancy in Britain. The NHS normally allows up to £30,000 for each QALY that a treatment could save. Depending on how many QALYs lockdown saved, the cost is £96,000 to £1.97 million per QALY according to a report by Civitas.[7] And that's quite generous because it might be that lockdown saved no lives at all.

The precautionary principle behind lockdown has been ideological and may be proven, in the end, to be more harmful than doing nothing, because the cost-benefit analysis didn't contain the numbers.

Here are some examples of the dodgy data and mendacious metrics wielded during the Covid epidemic.

THE IMPERIAL COLLEGE MODEL

Neil Ferguson's Imperial model predicted that there would be over 500,000 deaths in the UK and 2.2 million deaths in the US if there were no measures to suppress the virus. Described in an article in *The Telegraph* as 'the most devastating software mistake of all time',[8] the modelling used outdated code. However, that insight was not gained easily. At a time when there had probably never been such a need for scrutiny, there was remarkably little. The paper by Imperial was not peer-reviewed and calls by scientists to inspect the code were ignored for weeks. When the code was released it was not the original, but had been modified by teams from Microsoft and Github. The delay was unacceptable given the level of public importance and interest.

The doom-laden modelling grabbed headlines around the world and is credited with some of the responsibility for shifting policies on lockdown.

Aside from the dismal coding, was it robust? Models based on assumptions in the absence of data can be over-speculative and open to over-interpretation. Professor John Ioannidis of Stanford University issued a strong warning[9] to disease modellers to recognise the severe deficiencies in reliable data about Covid-19, including assumptions about its transmission and its essentially unknown fatality rates. For instance, the model assumed no existing immunity to Covid. Since then, six studies have shown T-cell reactivity (which gives protection) from previous coronaviruses in 20% to 50% of people with no known exposure to Covid.[10]

In 2000 Ferguson predicted there would be up to 136,000[11] cases of Creutzfeldt-Jakob disease in the UK. In fact there were 178 over 20 years.[12] In 2001, Ferguson's modelling led to the policy of 'contagious culling' (culling healthy animals on neighbouring farms) which led to 6.5 million cattle, sheep and pigs being slaughtered, economically devastating Britain's farmers. A report entitled *Use and abuse of mathematical models: an illustration from the 2001 foot and mouth disease epidemic in the United Kingdom*[13] strongly concluded that 'the slaughter that took place was grossly excessive' and that 'the rift between the models and the practical reality of implementation may be so huge as to make the models irrelevant'. In 2005, Ferguson said that up to 200 million people could die worldwide from bird flu. They didn't.

MP Esther McVey neatly argued that the Imperial modelling should not be considered infallible by pointing out that 2,700 prisoners were predicted to catch Covid and die, yet only 47 did. As she said in January 2021: 'There is no better example of the scaremongering to drive government policy they wanted to see from the so-called experts than the predictions on prisoner deaths. I appreciate that these estimates aren't an exact science but the difference between a prediction of 2,700 to the reality of 47 is embarrassing to say the least.'[14]

At the time of publication the modellers on SPI-M have predicted a 'pessimistic but plausible' third wave in the summer of 2021, resulting in a further 59,000 deaths.[15] Models are only as good as their ingested data and this model reportedly under-estimated vaccine efficacy, herd immunity and did not allow for the seasonality of a respiratory virus. So, what is the point?

Model reliability doesn't seem to need to be proven. There are no penalties for being over-cautious and getting it wildly wrong. And despite his track record, Ferguson et al are still producing models for the UK government, terrifying people and unleashing dire consequences on the way.

PUBLIC HEALTH ENGLAND DEATH DATA
Under Public Health England's original system, a Covid death was anyone who tested positive for Covid and then died of anything at any time. So, if someone was run over by a bus,

their death would be counted as a 'Covid death' if they had tested positive for Covid at any point in the past. No further explanation is needed about how wrong that is, and how it would inflate the death figures.

The team at the Oxford Centre for Evidence-Based Medicine pointed out the anomaly and Matt Hancock, the Health Secretary, ordered an inquiry. Dangerously poor-quality data from Public Health England was misleading the government. Were Public Health England innocent of such a misleading mistake?

The new system counted deaths within 28 days of a positive Covid-19 test. This would still include people who died from other causes – not all of these deaths were 'from' Covid either – but it was an improvement and resulted in the immediate removal of 4,149 deaths from the 15 July death count.

As David Paton said, 'The metrics always seem to err on the side of maximising numbers and it takes time to undo that, like with the Public Health England death counting. The BBC continued to report PHE death data even though the government had officially suspended it, so that had the effect of people thinking deaths were higher than they were. There is also a case for saying we don't report daily cases and deaths for flu, so just reporting by day is damaging in itself.'

And on a stronger note, the anonymous scientist who advises at Whitehall told me, 'The higher the death toll, the more draconian the measures you can bring in. The plan would be to go with the big numbers and then say there was a problem with the figures.'

THE BMA AND MASKS

Some data has crumbled like icing sugar at the merest whiff of a challenge. Sadiq Khan quoted some quite astonishing figures: that someone not wearing a face covering had a 70% risk of transmitting the virus, but by wearing a mask the risk was reduced to 5%, dropping to 1.5% if both parties were wearing masks.[16] The source was the British Medical Association (BMA). I contacted the BMA, which claimed that their Medical Academic Staff Committee and Public Health Medicine Committee had produced the calculations. Seven emails, two tweets and one phone call later, it turned out these figures had not been calculated by the BMA, but were 'based on a presentation by Chinese infectious disease specialist Professor Wenhong Xhang in March'.[17]

The BMA withdrew its claims, but by then the figures had been published on national broadcast and print media and in Twitter memes shared by Sadiq Khan, and are all still in circulation now. Associated Press Factcheck came to the same conclusion as me and labelled the claims 'partially false'.[18] The strange thing is that memes were circulating in other languages at around the same time and earlier, making BMA's claim to have produced the calculations even more spurious.

The effort to counter misinformation online has certainly seemed one-sided.

HOSPITALISATIONS

Sir Simon Stevens, the Chief Executive of the NHS, said on 29 December 2020 that 20,426 people were being treated for Covid in hospitals in England, which was higher than the previous peak of about 19,000 in April.

Comparing two absolute numbers was problematic. During the winter we always have more patients than we do in April. Numerically there were more patients in December, but just presenting that as a crude statistic is disingenuous because we also had more beds nationally overall than we did in April and without the occupancy figures as a percentage it's impossible for anyone to understand what the inpatient numbers mean. Further breaking down occupancy into overall total, ICU, beds with oxygen and mechanical ventilation beds for Covid and non-Covid would provide more insight.

In April 2020, all the Covid patients were there because they were truly ill with Covid. Later, we were routinely testing people in hospitals regardless of why they were admitted, which was a sensible measure for infectious control, but meant some people were classed as Covid patients in the government dashboard figures but were actually in hospital for different reasons. The absolute number of 20,426 includes those admitted with Covid and diagnosed with Covid in a hospital setting. So, what was the total split by people who go into hospital because they had Covid, nosocomial infections (acquired in hospital) and those who were routinely tested when they were in for something else and had a positive test result? Answers to those questions would have revealed how much of a problem community versus nosocomial infection was and helped guide decisions about the value of restricting liberties in the community.

An NHS England data scientist who must remain nameless for the sake of their job, shared some confidential information with me. We looked at the data for the south-east and London when I was writing to my MP about the tier restrictions at the time. At that point my MP told me that local hospitals were overwhelmed with Covid admissions. In fact, in mid-December in the south-east and London only 20% of the total hospital admissions were patients actually admitted with Covid. About 25% of 'hospital admissions' had caught Covid in hospital. And the remaining 55% had been tested while in for another matter and found to be positive. By January 2021 the government had admitted (albeit in a very low key no-fanfare way) that test results could be positive 'long after' someone is infectious.[19] Which means that of those 55%, an unspecified but significant number will be 'false positives'. All this paints a different picture. In addition, approximately 30% of the most recent admissions were from care homes, therefore also nosocomial infections, as they were acquired in a care setting.

Another important consideration is staffing levels. Talking about absolute numbers of in-patients requires the context of occupancy percentages and also staff available to look after them.

A responsible government and NHS would be providing this context. The use of absolutes was not untruthful, but it obscured more important facts. It seemed like a false flag, designed to create alarm and therefore soften us up for the next tranche of emergency restrictions. A BBC article[20] reporting on Stevens's statement only gave a modicum of context and led straight into a scientist's call for more lockdown, in what had become a familiar government-media lockstep.

The use of alarmist data is, well, alarmist, and the elision of detailed data is suspicious. Combined, this erodes trust in leaders and the media.

I emailed NHS England's media team with a request for all of this data. I followed up with emails, phone conversations and tweets. I did not receive the data.

By March 2021, Covid hospitalisations were at the same levels as October 2020. Strangely, Simon Stevens did not provide an update to the nation. As usual, numbers were used to scare, but not to reassure.

THE WHITTY AND VALLANCE 'SHOCK AND AWE' PRESENTATION

Chief Medical Officer Chris Whitty and Chief Scientific Adviser Sir Patrick Vallance warned on 21 September that there could be 4,000 Covid deaths per day in the autumn. Nothing like that total was ever reached. The Vallance chart showed infections hitting 50,000 cases a day by 13 October without action. When this day arrived, the moving average was 16,228.

Former Prime Minister Theresa May criticised the government's approach, remarking that 'for many people it looks as though the figures are being chosen to support the policy, rather than the policy being based on the figures'. Even *The Guardian*, which in general took a pro-lockdown approach during the epidemic, commented that the 'data was selective… determined to cause alarm'.[21] In a highly unusual move, the UK Statistics Authority also voiced concerns that the graphs presented to the public were out of date and over-estimated deaths.

THE SECOND WAVE

Public Health England said that more people died in the 'second wave' compared to the first wave of the epidemic.[22] Yet according to the Continuous Mortality Investigation, set up by the Institute and Faculty of Actuaries, there were 72,900 excess deaths from March to the end of December. 60,800 of those occurred in the first wave, but just 12,100 in the second.[23] It means that, unlike the first wave, huge numbers of people included in the coronavirus death figures would have been expected to die of other causes in those final few months of the year. It seems unlikely – impossible even – that Public Health England would not know this.

THE MOST DEADLY INFECTIOUS DISEASE IN A CENTURY

To mark the anniversary of a year of restrictions, the ONS produced a report which declared Covid-19 to be the most deadly infectious disease to hit Britain for over a century. Naturally this led to lurid doom-laden newspaper headlines such as 'Coronavirus is the deadliest pandemic to hit Britain since the Spanish flu in 1918 and has caused the worst recession in 300 years – but house prices KEPT going up',[24] 'COVID-19 most deadly infectious disease in UK in 100 years'[25] and 'Devastating UK Covid data lays bare impact of virus on lives, jobs and society in 2020'.[26]

But according Covid the accolade of causing 'more deaths in 2020 than other infectious diseases caused for over a century' was only possible with a disorientating twisting of truths. The ONS categorised Covid as an 'infectious and parasitic disease', putting it in a different category to other respiratory diseases including influenza. In this surprising category, Covid wasn't even keeping company with sepsis, as David Livermore, Professor of Medical Microbiology at the University of East Anglia, wrote for the Lockdown Sceptics website. As he pointed out, the ONS's graph 'wildly underestimates infection deaths' such as for bacterial sepsis and flu, which falsely elevated the deadliness of Covid.

Lockdown Sceptics asked 'What was the ONS thinking producing such a misleading graph and report, knowing full well it would grab lurid headlines and feed the hysteria that has characterised the last 12 months?'[27] This was a disheartening report from the ONS, but it was at least in keeping with marking a year of the 'metrics of fear'.

THE PCR TEST

'We have a simple message for all countries: test, test, test,' said Dr Tedros Adhanom Ghebreyesus, Director General of the World Health Organization, on 16 March 2020.[28]

How would countries test? Using the PCR (polymerase chain reaction) test.

On 14 December 2020, the WHO issued an Information Notice for IVD Users 'to ensure users of certain nucleic acid testing technologies are aware of certain aspects of the instructions for use for all products'.[29]

As many doctors and scientists had pointed out, the PCR test can produce false positives as well as false negatives. One problem is that when run at a high cycle threshold (Ct), the test can create a false positive, or pick up that someone had an infection weeks earlier. It is not a definitive test of infection or infectiousness.

As the notice says, 'when specimens return a high Ct value, it means that many cycles were required to detect virus. In some circumstances, the distinction between background noise and actual presence of the target virus is difficult to ascertain... the cut-off should be manually adjusted to ensure that specimens with high Ct values are not incorrectly assigned SARS-CoV-2 detected due to background noise.'

In Portugal, judges ruled that a single positive PCR test cannot be used as an effective diagnosis of infection for the purpose of quarantining someone. [30] Did the WHO issue the notice because of concern about legal action? When only a small proportion of people being tested have the virus, the operational false positive rate becomes important – think how many people might have had to quarantine unnecessarily, missing work, or an urgent medical exam, or to the detriment of their mental health, for example. For some people, being told they were positive with a disease that has been described 'the greatest threat in peacetime' could have been very stressful. Lockdowns and restrictions were based on the number of 'cases'. And absolute totals of cases were used to scare people into complying with the rules.

The Ct in the UK appears to be set at 45. As Professor Carl Heneghan said when he gave evidence in the House of Commons to the Science and Technology Committee on 17 September 2020, 'A cycle threshold above 35 generally involves people who are not infectious, yet NHS England documentation that has not been updated since January runs cycle thresholds to 45 that identify people who are not infectious.'

Heneghan was asked about introducing random testing – mass testing – as Professor Alan McNally of Birmingham University had recommended. This was his answer: 'In effect, you are saying that random tests will pick up people, potentially with dead virus. Remember, it picks up an RNA strand that is 220 nucleotides long. That degrades much slower than the actual infection when you have it on board. After eight days, we cannot isolate live virus, but for up to 90 days you can isolate the RNA fragments and pick them up when you test, so, if you randomly go into schools, you might as well shut them down right now. It is not a process that I have recognised in 20 years' experience of being a clinician, as a GP, or a process that is aligned with evidence-based medicine. If we are to go down those routes, we have to think of the wider context of what harms they introduce, what the social consequences are and what the plan is.' The UK government rolled out mass testing and proposed mass testing in schools. Although, when mass testing was introduced in schools in March 2021, the less sensitive lateral flow test was used.

POSITIVE TESTS, CASES AND PATIENTS

This is an example of scary semantics rather than dodgy data. People who tested positive were called 'cases' and in one case I noted the word 'patient'[31] was used. Both 'case' and 'patient' imply illness and symptoms, whereas many of the positive test results were asymptomatic or post-infectious. A medical diagnosis of 'case' would normally involve symptoms plus a positive test, not a test on its own.

DEATH STATISTICS

I was flung into my armchair death-expert status by the whiplash of an epidemic and lockdown. The next chapter explains how changes to the death registration process mean there are now serious problems with counting the dead.

EMILY, 45, NURSE

A colleague who does the bookings emailed me to say, 'You've got a patient coming in for an overdue blood test this afternoon, she's really nervous and she's been shielding since March. Can you meet her from the car to make sure she attends?'

t's not unusual to have a nervous patient – needle phobia is certainly not uncommon! The appointment time came, but I was busy finishing off with another patient so I hadn't made it out to the car park. As I completed some forms I suddenly heard shouting and screaming coming from the reception area. I rushed out and saw a lady, obviously very distressed, walking with two sticks and wearing a mask and visor, supported by a man. She was incomprehensibly sobbing, shaking and flushed, as she staggered down the corridor.

I rushed over (obviously in standard mask and apron) and tried to calm her down and ascertain what was wrong, encouraging her to come into the blood test room to sit down.

She continued to cry and hyperventilate. It was difficult to comprehend anything that she was saying. I was worried that she was becoming increasingly short of breath, so I encouraged her to remove her mask but her husband said she wouldn't take it off because she was 'too scared of the virus'.

I asked her if she was nervous about the blood test but she continued to cry in a distressed manner, saying over again, 'I don't want to die, I'm so frightened, I don't want to die, I'll die of anything but not that virus.' I managed to get her to slow her breathing and stop moving long enough to get the sample. Her husband told me that this was only the second time she'd left the house since March.

11. COUNTING THE DEAD

We humans keep dying. We always have. We always will. In 2019, approximately 57,000,000 people died globally, and 600,000 people in the UK, which equates to 1,600 people per day. As the only real certainty of life is that we are all going to die, we should be better at the death business by now.

It's important to count the dead. We count the big numbers and compare them annually – excess deaths are a barometer that 'something is happening'. But we also need to know and record how people die, for public health management, planning NHS resources in the future, to inform government policy, for legal and jurisprudence reasons, and to provide certainty and alleviate the concerns and grief of the bereaved's family.

While death and disease dominated the headlines in the UK for most of 2020, we're not as good at considering our own demise. Perhaps the potent blend of death tolls in the headlines and our intrinsic fear of death blunted the nation's ability to scrutinise exactly what these totals actually meant.

The UK's emergency legislation in response to Covid-19 radically changed how deaths were registered. If the Imperial modelling that predicted 500,000 deaths came to pass, it would be essential to fast-track the registering and disposal of bodies. The UK did not want an Italy or Ecuador situation with bodies piling up. But this came with costs: at a time when it is crucial to understand why people are dying, we have less clarity due to the changes in registration and recording.

'Unprecedented' is a word that has been horribly over-used during the epidemic, but it should not equal 'unplanned'. Ministers claimed not to have read the 2016 Exercise Cygnus pandemic planning report. Before Cygnus there was 2007's Exercise Winter Willow, as well as detailed debriefs of SARS, MERS, H1N1 and even Ebola. Plans should have been robust and flexible, but the NHS and Public Health England were ill-prepared in terms of surge capacity and PPE stocks.

'Unprecedented' is no excuse when pandemics are the basic bread and butter of disaster planning. Lucy Easthope, disaster planner, has a special interest in pre-emptive pandemic and recovery planning. She is the visible representation of the depth and detail of the UK's disaster preparation and puts the lie to the so-called lack of planning. She said, 'The media and the government have sold the idea that no one could have expected this, but a pandemic is the most likely national risk, and very well prepared for in the Home Office and the Cabinet.'

Easthope is involved in planning for excess death and told me, 'For every Covid death we would estimate another four deaths over two to five years, and that is how we plan body storage. You see extra deaths for domestic violence and obstetrics, delayed or missed oncology diagnosis, no admission to A&E, sepsis and suicide.'

I was surprised by Easthope's foreknowledge of non-Covid excess deaths and asked if it's seen as inevitable: 'The disruption that a pandemic causes means that people who would have died over the next five years will be brought forward. This has been made worse by a vigorous and long lockdown.' So, should we have locked down? She was cautious, and said, 'The virus is nasty and it must be respected. Some social changes would be essential, but otherwise I would advocate business as usual. The idea that essential civil function and hospitals would shut is incredible. In a pandemic you plan to keep as much open as possible.'

Although lockdowns seem to be accepted by the government officials, the media, and therefore the wider public as orthodoxy, the shocking truth is that they are not orthodox. They were specifically not recommended in the UK or the WHO's pandemic plans prior to 2020. There is more on this in the essay 'Lockdowns don't work' in Appendix 2.

I spoke to a coroner (who did not wish to be named) who confirmed that the UK quickly increased mortuary capacity. They thought the lockdown and changes to death registrations were necessary when knowledge was scant and the system was threatened by having to house and process 500,000 bodies. As it turned out 'the epidemic was essentially the sort of pressure we get over a normal winter. It was way less than what we had planned for.'

The anonymous special scientific advisor also told me they warned at SPAD and senior civil service level that there would be severe consequences for excess deaths if the country locked down. 'Lockdown was not the way to go,' they said. 'Bluntly, you should try and power through an epidemic. Lockdown was obviously going to tank the economy. We have never trained for a lockdown like this. You don't do it for a coronavirus. I've been through all my papers. It's just not something we do.'

Except we did. The difficulty now is that although death totals are confidently asserted, the relaxation of the death registration in order to cope with the worst case scenario means we don't really know how many people have died of Covid.

Where once a doctor had to have seen the deceased within 14 days of death to sign off a death certificate, now it is 28 days, although according to the coroner both are arbitrary numbers. And in a time of social distancing, what does 'seeing' actually mean? It might be a Zoom appointment or telephone call. The coroner told me an apocryphal story about a family holding a dead body up to a window so the doctor had 'seen' the body. He wasn't entirely sure whether the story was a joke or not.

Also, if the deceased's doctor is not available, then any doctor can issue the death certificate. The doctor need not see the body, but can speak to people who have seen the deceased and use the medical notes. Remote verification of the body is even possible by someone who is not a medical professional,[1] although they should usually be independent of family members. The coroner told me that in his view 'it was entirely the right decision to make based on the information we had and would work if backed by a functioning Medical Examiner system.'

The problem is the UK does not have a functioning Medical Examiner system. It was being rolled out in England

and Wales to add a safeguarding scrutiny to non-coronial deaths and improve the quality of death certification. A second, more senior doctor should agree the proposed cause of death. This would mean some arbitrary rules like 28 days or 14 days since seeing the deceased could be relaxed, and it should also safeguard against another Harold Shipman. The implementation varies across different hospital trusts, there is no software yet to manage it nationwide, and the senior doctors who should act as Medical Examiners were called to frontline work during the epidemic. Worryingly, according to the coroner, 'At the moment we are not set up to prevent another Harold Shipman.'

The anonymous scientific advisor was frank about the result: 'We have no idea how many people died because of this disease, or poor clinical decision-making in the early days, or neglect in care homes.'

Easthope told me that 'death scientists noted immediately that the Coronavirus Act had been framed to take away all the problems we found in exercises like Cygnus, but by doing that also stripped a load of safeguards and protections for the dead and for death data. We have a crisis in death recording. For the first time in 50 years of slowly improving death registration we've lost our ability to differentiate the cause of death. It surprised me that the "no confirmatory death certificate'" was in the Coronavirus Act. I think that should only have been enacted at a certain threshold. In other plans that we'd done, the idea that death scrutiny would be one of the first sacrifices was an anathema.'

24,709[2] deaths occurred in care homes in England and Wales in 2020 and up till 22 January 2021, nearly a quarter of the total Covid deaths, and approximately another 4,810[3] care home residents died with Covid after being transferred to hospital up to 20 June 2020. Another 1,419 have died in hospices. It's hard to see how deaths in hospices can be attributed to Covid, and there is uncertainty about some care home 'Covid deaths' actually being due to Covid.

I spoke to a care home worker in the north of England confidentially to discuss this problem. They had cases where

Covid had been inaccurately put on the death certificate as the cause of death or an underlying cause of death. One resident, well into her 80s, tested positive for Covid at the end of March 2020, when she had mild symptoms. She recovered, but went on to die in August. A covering doctor who had never met the resident, or seen the body, insisted that Covid must have been a cause of death. The care home worker told me 'she actually died of old age, quite peacefully and contentedly. Old age isn't supposed to be used on death certificates, but sometimes it's what it is. There wasn't really anything wrong with her, people do wear out. That's why people come here. Before, old age would go on death certificates occasionally if there were no other underlying issues, but it would not go on a death certificate now.'

How many times did this happen in care homes across the country? There is an abundance of anecdotal stories on social media from families or care home workers who say Covid has been incorrectly put as a cause of death on the certificate.

The coroner had a similar story. They were called by a doctor they know personally, asking for advice about 'an old boy who'd had multiple kidney infections and died eight hours later in hospital.' Against her better judgement, the doctor agreed to do a Covid swab, although she knew he'd died because of his kidneys. It was positive and she had to put Covid on the death certificate. I asked the coroner if they think this will be a common tale. 'We have no idea,' they retorted.

There are a number of dangers. The Covid death total is probably inflated, because Covid has been used too liberally on death certificates. Early on, when testing was not routine, it would have been an easy mistake due to the uncertainty around symptoms common to Covid and also other coronaviruses, flu and respiratory diseases. But even a positive test doesn't mean Covid was truly influential in death. Many residents in care homes did not see doctors for months, testing was not routine, and families were largely unable to visit and check on their relatives' health or be able to form an opinion about their condition in the lead up to death. As all of my interviewees said, we have no idea how often it has happened, and now we never will. If, in the most horrible of circumstances, a resident was neglected or suffered some grave misfortune, it could be passed off as Covid. Before 2020, a care home or hospital might have been sued for poor treatment or negligence. That is much harder without the same oversight and with minimal forensics.

Lockdown itself caused a horrifying number of excess deaths, just as Easthope warned. A SAGE report[4] predicted that the overall death toll would be 222,000, but over 100,000 deaths would be non-Covid deaths caused by lockdown and other impacts. There were nearly 30,000[5] excess non-Covid deaths at home between 21 March 2020 and 15 January 2021, and 2,937 in care homes. These might be due to delays in treatment or a reluctance to seek treatment, or 'missed' Covid deaths, or other causes like suicide. Non-Covid deaths in private homes, and deaths from conditions which can quickly become fatal if not treated in time, are well above the five-year average. You could say there was an 'epidemic' of people needlessly dying at home because they were reluctant, or unable, to seek medical help.

Frontline mental health professionals were concerned about the impact of lockdown. Suicide is the biggest killer of young people in the UK.[6] Some children were on lengthy waiting lists for mental health treatment in 2020. Ged Flynn, CEO of suicide charity Papyrus, said, 'This is scandalous. Saving young lives is no longer a national priority and we must change that.' While suicide must never be attributed to a single cause, nine out of 10 calls to Papyrus during the first lockdown reflected the impact of Covid and lockdown, with many concerned about a loss of income, reduction in service provision, domestic violence and abuse, and the potential to become infected with Covid-19. Ged warned of the 'longer-term problem of emotional distress' for young people as the impact of lockdown continues and mental health services are stretched.

A report *Suicide in England since the COVID-19 pandemic – early figures from real-time surveillance*[7] claimed that suicide had not increased in the first lockdown. I was surprised and asked Easthope why suicide had not increased, because I thought the isolation and impact on income would have been detrimental to people already struggling with mental health. She responded by telling me that disaster literature says that suicides only tend to increase from six to nine months into a disaster. The first months don't normally reveal it. She also urged caution about early reports as only a coronial inquest can determine suicide.

The report *Traumatic Stress and Suicide After Disasters*[8] details the phases after a disaster and, while you would not expect to see increased suicides or ideation in the immediate 'impact', 'heroic' and 'honeymoon' phases, they could come later during 'disillusionment' and 'reconstruction'. This is a long-running disaster, so the 'impact' point for one person might be the beginning of lockdown, for another it might be a few months later when they lost a relative they couldn't say goodbye to, or for yet another it might be when they lose their job when furlough ends.

Lockdown is a new experiment in response to an epidemic, Covid is a new disease, and fear has been leveraged in new ways. The impact of lockdown will be felt in economic and social ripples for many years. Of course people want to believe that lockdown hasn't caused an increase in suicide. No one wants to see suicides increase, that would be horrific, and this pressure is probably felt even more acutely by the policymakers and those around them.

A generous interpretation of *Suicide in England since the COVID-19 pandemic – early figures from real-time surveillance* would be that it sought to evaluate the most disturbing impact of lockdown too early. A cynical interpretation would be that it was conducted early to placate people, before the impact on suicide could be known.

Easthope also told me that she worried that 'we've done something incredibly traumatising to the families that is potentially bigger than the bereavement itself. In any disaster you should still allow people to see the dead. It is a gross inhumanity of bad planning that people couldn't visit the sick, view the deceased's bodies, or attend funerals. Had we had a more liberal PPE stockpile we could have done this. PPE is about accessing your loved ones and dead ones, it is not just about medical professionals.' She said previous plans had flooded resources into death registration and management, not taken them away. It was recognised that overwhelm was an issue, but just removing the safeguards should not have been the answer. 'This is the sort of thing that I had expected us to be doing in January and February,' she said, 'but a sort of paralysis set in.'

Good planning was cast aside. We were not equipped to process the Covid dead, and we'll never be able to properly count them. In decades to come, when the inevitable reports and studies into the Covid dead are published, they will be littered with asterisks and freighted with footnotes. Or worse, taken dangerously at face value.

Beyond counting the dead, how do we count the cost to ourselves socially? Dying alone in a hospice, last rites delivered in full PPE, no family beside the bed. People unable to visit elderly relatives in care homes for months. Funerals limited to 10 people. The young calling suicide helplines, bewildered and traumatised. The uncertainty over cause of deaths, the lack of closure. How do you count the cost of dying alone at home, too scared to go to hospital, or without holding someone's hand? For this, we need the ultimate inquest and then the birth of better ways to count the dead.

ROSIE, 13, BY HER MOTHER

We were really scared with all the images we'd seen in the media. We put ourselves in isolation a week before lockdown because the kids had coughs. When we officially went into lockdown on the 23 March we stuck to the rules. We stayed inside 100% for a good three months, except for a dog walk once a day.

We got to the stage where it was obvious my 13-year-old daughter, Rosie, was scared to go out. So at that stage, even though it wasn't technically allowed, we thought we had to start encouraging her to go out with her friends.

When you are 13 the world should open up to you. It's really sad to think of teenagers having so many restrictions placed on them. I worry it will stunt their emotional growth.

She has to use hand sanitiser before each lesson at school and her hands hurt. She has been sent out of class for coughing, but she coughed because of the sanitiser fumes in the air. They have a mask monitor who screams at them if they don't have their masks on. Our daughter complains about the constant eyes on her and telling her what to do. It's a tyranny over them.

My daughter started having panic attacks. They happen more often at school, and I think that's because of the rules and restrictions. I have to pick her up from school if it happens. The first time, I genuinely thought something was seriously wrong with her. Her body went into overdrive.

She feels dizzy and weak when she has one. She feels like her neck can't hold the weight of her head and has shooting pains in her head. After the huge rush of adrenalin she starts to shake. She couldn't walk after the first one.

When she had the first one, apparently the teacher wouldn't come near her. I couldn't believe a teacher wouldn't stop her falling, or help her, because she was so scared of touching another human.

Some of her friends are experiencing anxiety in their own ways too. It's made me think about how young girls are going to cope. Hysteria and feelings do pass especially between young girls.

She is on a waiting list for a counsellor at the school who probably won't be available till January. It feels like we don't have anywhere to go. We feel cut off from the world. I feel angry. It's where we are headed as a society that worries me.

We don't make our daughter stick to the rules anymore, She has enough to deal with in school with these measures. She needs normality at the weekend, so we let her see friends and family. Grandparents hug her. We won't have people tell us we can't hug.

12. THE ILLUSION OF CONTROL

D uring the epidemic we were told repeatedly that mass gatherings and the loosening of lockdown screws would result in more Covid cases, more deaths, a surge, another wave, a tsunami, a worst-case scenario. Disaster was always around the corner, or in 'two weeks'. By the time we were around the corner, or the fortnight had elapsed, we were onto the next crisis.

Here are nine times that the doom-mongering modellers and the pessimistic politicians and pundits told the people of the UK that they would cause disaster and death during 2020.

8 MAY – VE DAY

Despite being urged to stay at home, people held socially-distant street gatherings for VE Day, braving the UK media's disapprobation. Villagers in Grappenhall were described as 'breathtakingly stupid' for performing a socially-distanced conga holding a rope marked at two-metre intervals. A local journalist commented that 'the best thing the Grappenhall conga line could have done was to keep on dancing all the way down Knutsford Road to Warrington Hospital'. Yet they must have found their way home, as there were no Covid deaths in the local hospital over the next several weeks.

26 MAY – BANK HOLIDAY

Tourism bosses and local authorities, panicked by the beautiful weather forecasts, warned people to stay at home for the bank holiday. Merseyside employed a charming 'Wish You Weren't Here!' campaign. Perhaps the high temperatures and fresh air weren't conducive to disease transmission; no spike in deaths followed.

16 MAY ONWARDS – ANTI-LOCKDOWN PROTESTS

Anti-lockdown protests inspired outrage. People who attended were labelled 'idiots' and 'selfish anti-lockdown morons' who would 'put everyone at risk'. The mayor of London, Sadiq Khan, branded anti-lockdown protests 'unacceptable'. There was no discernible impact on deaths.

31 MAY ONWARDS – 'BLACK LIVES MATTER' PROTESTS

Many thousands took to the streets in a series of protests over the death of George Floyd and in support of Black Lives Matter. This time, politicians, the police and media were fairly quiet about the risk of spreading Covid. Sadiq Khan said, 'To the thousands of Londoners who protested peacefully today: I stand with you.' An article in *The Guardian* claimed that the mobility of crowds and mask-wearing reduced risk. One study, reported in *The Independent*, went further and said the protests helped increase social distancing behaviours. However, the science must have changed, as Priti Patel, Home Secretary, said in November that she would like to ban protests of more than two people.

25 JUNE – BOURNEMOUTH BEACH

A 'major incident' was declared at Bournemouth beach on 25 June. There were half a million visitors in Dorset, roads were gridlocked and the beaches were full. Local MP Tobias Ellwood said that people were 'being selfish and also acting dangerously'. Chief Medical Officer Chris Whitty responded to the beach scenes by saying that Covid cases would 'rise again'. They didn't. Eventually, by mid-February 2021, Mark Woolhouse, Professor of Infectious Disease Epidemiology at the University of Edinburgh, told the Science and Technology Committee in the House of Commons[1] that no outbreaks of Covid had been linked to a beach so far.

4 JULY – 'SUPER SATURDAY'

Dubbed 'UK's Independence Day' or 'Super Saturday', 4 July was the day that pubs reopened in Britain. Places of worship opened too, but people seemed more cross about the pubs.

Predictably, news stories on 5 July contained photographs of crowded streets of 'drunken idiots'. While most of Britain probably celebrated sensibly, one police officer claimed to have dealt with 'naked men, happy drunks, angry drunks, fights and more drunks'. Saturday night then. 'Welcome to the second wave' one furious commentator said. There was no impact on cases or deaths associated with 'Super Saturday'.

SEPTEMBER – BACK TO SCHOOL AND UNIVERSITY

Academics and unions warned that students preparing to return to university were risking a 'public health crisis' and that we were 'weeks away' from 'sleepwalking into a disaster'. They also grumbled that plans to make schools 'Covid secure' were 'unviable'. In line with fresher's flu and back to school sniffles, cases of Covid undeniably rose in September although deaths remained low.

CHRISTMAS

Neil Ferguson of Imperial College warned that households mixing 'risks some transmission and there will be consequences of that. Some people will die because of getting infected on that day.' Happy Christmas to you too, Neil. Susan Michie said, 'If we really want to keep our loved ones safe, the best thing is not to see them.' And Anouchka Grose wrote in *The Guardian* that, 'Anybody with any kind of conscience is beating their brain, calculating all eventualities that may result from showing up for lunch in a week's time – one of

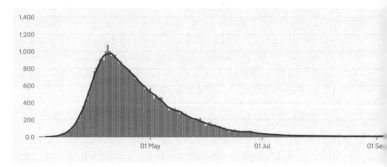

UK deaths within 28 days of positive test by date of death[2]

which involves inadvertently killing your aged parents.'

Just a couple of weeks after Ferguson's predictions, the UK government changed its plans to relax social restrictions for Christmas due to a new infectious and rapid-spreading strain which was 'was out of control'.[3]

According to the Office for National Statistics,[4] around half of the people who were allowed to meet for Christmas did so. There was a spike in infections at Christmas, but unrelated to Christmas itself. Paul Hunter, a professor at the University of East Anglia's medical school, said, 'I actually can't see any convincing evidence that Christmas actually did anything to make things worse at all,' in an analysis for the BBC.[5]

BACK TO SCHOOL AGAIN

By now you know the script. Some experts were worried that when pupils returned to school, Covid cases would go up. It was almost as though all their previous predictions had been true rather than false, such was the confidence. Also, it was as though the UK had not rolled out a successful vaccination programme, and that spring was in the air. Professor John Edmunds of SAGE warned that 'it looks as if it would be touch and go' and that 'if we opened secondary schools and primary schools both at the same time, I suspect we would be lucky to keep the reproduction number below one'.[6] There was a slowdown in the fall in cases attributed to the return to school, although this was thought to be due to the increased mass

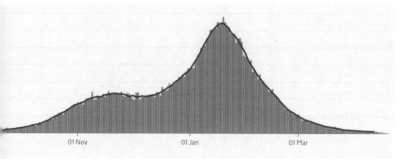

LFT testing in schools. Once again, there was no catastrophic effect on cases, deaths or R.

In a twist on the game 'pin the tail on the donkey', see if you can locate the super-spreader events on the graph of Covid deaths and discern any impact. Then see if you can pinpoint the following interventions: lockdown 1.0, masks on transport, masks in shops, rule of 6, lockdown 2.0, tier restrictions or lockdown 3.0.

Has the illusion of control exaggerated our belief that we can control the course of a virus?

The attitudes towards people who would gather and mingle are definitely not illusory. Journalists, politicians and the public condemned and sneered at ordinary people they described as 'Covidiots' and 'selfish'. This created social division, shame, anger and more fear. People are more likely to assume responsibility when things go right, and less responsibility when things go wrong, so perhaps they simply need scapegoats lined up for the crisis around the corner.

MARK, 44

I did feel a sigh of relief when the second lockdown was announced. We've been having a trial thing of going back to the office one week out of every three. I felt really uncomfortable leaving the house and my village. I found it very peculiar. So to be honest, I am looking forward to the next four weeks.

E ven though the journey time is only half an hour by car I didn't enjoy the commute and found it difficult. I feel like I have lost driving and navigating skills, and I felt very tired when I got there. I'd arrive and wonder why I was there. The sanitised environment of the workplace, the smell of bleach, wearing masks in the corridors, it all felt so unnatural. Being inside my village and especially inside the house feels more normal, welcoming and calming than being outside.

I have genuinely wondered if I am developing agoraphobia. On the few occasions when I have been to the supermarket, I have not enjoyed being around other people. I find being around masked people really odd. You can't smile at people any more so I'd rather not go out.

I'm most worried now about social cohesion. The regionalised lockdowns have almost been finger-pointing at the people of Leicester or Manchester. I think we could end up in a position where the mask-wearers and the non-mask-wearers and the lockdowners and the anti-lockdowners feel very different to each other. On a smaller level I have seen it in my village. On our village Facebook group some people have said they won't do this lockdown, and they don't see why our pub has to close.

I don't like not being aware of society, not meeting people, not really knowing how people are feeling. I haven't met anybody in the last six months who I didn't already know. I am becoming more introverted.

It's a paradox that I am developing agoraphobia, but I am also frightened of being cut off from the world.

13. THE CLIMATE OF FEAR

'Scapegoating worked in practice while it still had religious powers behind it. You loaded the sins of the city on to the goat's back and drove it out, and the city was cleansed. It worked because everyone knew how to read the ritual, including the gods. Then the gods died, and all of a sudden you had to cleanse the city without divine help. Real actions were demanded instead of symbolism. The censor was born, in the Roman sense. Watchfulness became the watchword: the watchfulness of all over all. Purgation was replaced by the purge.'

From *Disgrace* by J.M. Coetzee

The scapegoat is an ancient religious and ritualistic practice and, these days, a metaphor for social exclusion. In the Bible, the scapegoat was one of two kid goats. One would be sacrificed, and the living one, the 'scapegoat', was sent into the wilderness, symbolically carrying sins and impurities with it. Scapegoating is not just to be found in the Bible though; it is one of the enduring human archetypes found across cultures and times.

The ancient Greeks practised scapegoating rituals during 'extraordinary circumstances such as famine, drought, or plague'[1] in order to save the whole community. While the Israelites and the Hittites used animals, the ancient Greeks used humans. Being 'civilised' does not necessarily mean being more humane.

Death was not essential, but expulsion from the community was key, one way or another. The scapegoat might be banished, or stoned or burned to death – there is a comparison with the hysterical 'burning times', during the centuries when witches were tried and executed, accused of all the 'sins' and troubles of their communities.

Who is scapegoated in the time of Covid and who are the high priests and inquisitors? We might like to believe we are above such superstitious and archaic behaviour, but where is the evidence that human beings have changed? In fact, can we observe the early warning behavioural signs and symbols of a nascent religion?

It looks like the NHS co-opted the rainbow from the Pride movement, but it's also an ancient religious symbol, integral to the Bible's flood story and in Graeco-Roman mythology it was a path between earth and heaven. Fans of the *Avengers* films will remember the rainbow Bifrost, which links Midgard and Asgard. Rainbows in windows ostensibly honour the NHS and its workers but, because they represent our health service, perhaps at an unconscious level they also serve a talismanic role in warding away disease and bad luck, just like other amulets and home adornments such as the Hamsa, the Green Man, the Nazar, a lucky horseshoe or the Romans' flying pottery penises. There is mixed evidence that community mask-wearing protects us from viruses, but we wear masks anyway, as the vesture of the faithful and the obedient. Hand-sanitising baptises us daily into the new religion of health and safetyism. As valued government advisors, the priest caste has been replaced by a scientist caste. Churches closed their doors at the behest of modellers and behavioural scientists with scarcely a murmur of resistance. Vaccines are modern medical miracles, but they also evoke a modern biosecurity incarnation of transubstantiation – especially when delivered in cathedrals with organ music playing, in an intersection of the old religion and the new religion. In this new creed, what is to be done with the impious and the heretics? As always, they are scapegoated.

As Coetzee wrote in *Disgrace*, in modern times scapegoating has transmogrified into censorship. There is a discernible blend of scapegoating and censorship among the self-appointed keepers-of-truth during the Covid epidemic. These days, no one is to be burnt at the stake or ritually sacrificed, just metaphorically cast into a desert, professionally shamed, no-platformed, unpublished, removed from the modern-day public fora of Twitter and YouTube. Silenced and banished. In this way the scapegoat can take on the sins of society, as well as serve as a warning to other potential dissenters. Speak up, and you are next. The media, Big Tech social media giants, politicians, scientists and perhaps all of us, the 'mob', have enforced a climate of fear through scapegoating.

MP Neil O'Brien appointed himself inquisitor of 'covid sceptics'. Alongside other volunteers, he created a fact-checking website as well as regularly denouncing dissenters in Twitter threads. He was praised for his efforts by fellow MP Jacob Rees-Mogg, who said he was doing 'a fantastic job',[2] leading some to believe that O'Brien was acting unofficially on the government's behalf. The website contained 'lists' of people as well as general claims that he deemed wrong and misleading. Some saw this as an important service in combatting 'disinformation', such as Rees-Mogg. Some were troubled that an MP, both a public servant and someone holding a position of authority, created lists of British citizens in order to pillory them and digitally 'cast them out'.

The lists are also one-sided. They only include people who have made mistakes that go against the government narrative. The government, its ministers and SAGE advisors have also made mistakes during the epidemic but they are not included on the lists. A one-sided presentation of mistakes betrays the intention to silence particular voices and views. Mistakes will be made, and they should be accounted for. We all make mistakes. The danger is when mistakes are weaponised to intimidate and stifle debate.

The website Anti-Virus: The Covid-19 FAQ may even make mistakes of its own. After all, how can all the Covid science be definitely settled? How can the website creators be confident that they arbitrate the absolute truth? One of the refutations caught my eye. The website asserts that 'suicide rates have not risen during lockdowns, either in the UK or worldwide'. A report[3] from the University of Manchester looked at 'real-time surveillance' and claimed there was no evidence of a rise of post-lockdown suicides. As I explained in Chapter 11, 'Counting the dead', it is too soon to be certain about UK suicides, and I expect the same is true internationally.

Neil O'Brien's Twitter attacks felt dogged and personal. Journalists with strong personalities were better able to weather the slings and arrows. The distinguished scientists were probably more discomfited by their placement on the lists, including two from the UK's Oxford University: Professor Sunetra Gupta, a highly regarded Professor of Theoretical Epidemiology, and Dr Carl Heneghan, a GP, clinical epidemiologist and a Fellow of Kellogg College, the director of the University of Oxford's Centre for Evidence-Based Medicine and Editor-in-Chief of *BMJ Evidence-Based Medicine*. Dr Clare Craig, a diagnostic pathologist, also came under fire for asking controversial questions about the PCR testing. She described the attacks by O'Brien as 'bullying' and responded on Twitter: 'Almost none of Neil O'Brien's tweets about me offered evidence to prove me wrong. I believe his intention is to deter me and other people from speaking out. I am concerned that a Government representative would behave this way about good faith scientific discussion.'[4]

Public execration has a silencing effect. When dissent is framed as mistaken, irresponsible and 'dangerous'[5] it creates serious personal, public and professional consequences for the individuals and beyond. Speaking out during the epidemic felt akin to questioning the Church, rather than contributing to an ongoing scientific debate or discussing the political decisions made in a democracy. That is not a healthy situation for journalism, science or public debate. Democracy requires a free press and free speech.

But is scapegoating simply driven by individuals, such as O'Brien, or do we have to accept something about human nature? It might be a natural human tendency to scapegoat from a position of assumed moral high ground. A study, *Moralisation of Covid-19 health response: Asymmetry in tolerance for human costs*,[6] found that during Covid 'health-minded approaches have been moralised, even to the point of a sacred value' and that 'merely questioning sacred values led to moral cleansing'. Defending lockdowns and restrictions was seen as moral, and questioning them seen as immoral. As a consequence, the human costs of the restrictions were under-acknowledged, de-prioritised and granted less moral weight. The report warned this could lead to 'deaths of despair' among those human costs. As we have seen, proponents of lockdowns might wish (even unconsciously) to underplay these in order to remain comfortable on the moral high ground.

The *Behavioural Government* series by the Behavioural Insights Team talked about how we reject ideas from another group, even if they are good ideas: 'If another party does not think the same way, then our preferred reaction is not to reassess our own opinions. Instead, we try to come up with ways of denigrating the opposition. This happens because we find it hard to maintain both a positive image of ourselves and a positive image of someone who disagrees with us… we decide that those who think differently are biased, through ideology, self-interest, malice or stubbornness. While we have considered the issue carefully, they are just proceeding from dogma. This perception of bias makes conflict and division escalate further… This process happens most clearly between competing interest groups, where it has been called the 'devil shift': seeing your opponents as more extreme and more 'evil' than they actually are.'[7]

This goes some way towards explaining the viciousness towards opposite views in the Covid epidemic. Someone can happily justify their 'inquisitor' status when the 'devil shift' has occurred. You would think that, as this explanation emanated from behavioural scientists embedded in government, the government would learn from it, rather than permit or encourage an MP to denigrate people with opposing views. This perspective from BIT could also explain why people on the left did not oppose lockdown even though it disproportionately harmed the poor and vulnerable, because they did not think it was possible that they could share the same perspective as those on the right, or libertarian, side. Oppositional group thinking creates tribalism and closes minds to different points of view. Response to lockdown was hyper-partisan.

People who questioned the use of lockdown were sometimes labelled 'lockdown sceptics'. Being sceptical can be seen as a positive attribute, which is probably why the terminology shifted to 'Covid denier'. This reframing made people seem silly rather than sceptical, as though they denied the existence of the virus, rather than questioned public health policies. The word 'denier' conjures the callousness of Holocaust deniers. Anyone with any concern or question could be given the umbrella term 'denier' – who on earth wants to be on that team? Another label was 'conspiracy theorist', which again no one wants to be called. (Some conspiracy theory predictions actually came to pass, but more on that in Chapter 14, 'Cults, conspiracy and psychic epidemics'.) People with concerns about the vaccines were 'anti-vax'. One study[8] labelled people who didn't want to wear masks psychopaths. All these labels contribute to a climate of fear which makes people timid about expressing their opinions.

These reports chimed with the on-the-ground views of Professor Ellen Townsend of Nottingham University, a psychologist and specialist in suicide and self-harm, who told me that 'the culture of suppression and scapegoating of dissenting academic voices in this crisis has been dreadful. Leading experts have been cast as outliers by those in power because their theories and evidence do not fit the official Covid narrative.' She was also alert to the personal costs, telling me that there were people who might never speak to her again, but she also received emails from people thanking her for speaking up.

Townsend and fellow academics set up Reachwell, a group which focuses on the impacts of lockdown and restrictions on young people, because 'the refusal to name and account for the harms of restrictions is one of the biggest scientific errors of all time – especially in relation to children and the disadvantaged.' She told me she had been very concerned about the exploitation of 'a fear campaign' to 'raise the sense of threat and imminent danger of death', which had left people frightened and bewildered.

I came across Professor Townsend on Twitter. Sadly, during the epidemic she decided to withdraw from the platform. 'I've always had a love-hate relationship with Twitter but during the dark days of 2020–21, I witnessed reprehensible behaviour by some academics,' she told me. 'People who I previously admired have behaved in dreadful ways and said absolutely vicious things about other academics that were completely unwarranted. Science, or at least scientific debate, has died in these times. I decided to leave the toxicity of Twitter and focus my energies on other ways of communicating that permit dialogue and nuance.'

Two more psychologists, Dr Gary Sidley and Dr Harrie Bunker-Smith, wrote to the British Psychological Society in December 2020 regarding their concerns about the ethics of the government's use of covert behavioural psychology. Sidley said that it was hard to get co-signatories to the letter because 'many psychologists working in the NHS are twitchy about their jobs, and the ones in the private sector are nervous because they interact with the NHS. The brainwashing has been so effective that I can understand it – being in a minority is uncomfortable.'

Bunker-Smith, a co-author of the letter, had experienced this discomfort. She said 'it felt incredibly risky to question the data and the measures' when she posted on a clinical psychology forum about her ethical concerns. The post had a lot of likes and she received personal messages from people who said they were too scared to like her post or comment. But there were some 'challenging replies' and 'some people were very aggressive, considering it was a professional forum.' She was called a conspiracy theorist and 'accused of not caring about the people who died of Covid'. No one wants to be seen as uncaring and these public accusations inhibit professional debate. 'People told me about personal stories, people they knew who died of Covid,' she said, 'and I was told I should join Covid frontline support groups to understand the PTSD they feel. This became very black and white. Psychologists should be able to sit in the grey.' She has been told she should be struck off from the Health and Care Professions Council and felt she had to be willing to lose her career just to raise questions.

Sidley had hoped more psychologists would be shocked and angry about the policies around lockdown, masks and restrictions that have caused distress to people, but had been in a minority. He expected more to care about the mental health impact. While he thought 'some would like to speak out about the behavioural science techniques but they are nervous about putting their head above the parapet', he also thought some 'think the world might be better after all this for some reason, because they are socialist or worried about the environment', and yet more were 'driven by their own fear of death'. Echoing SPI One in a previous chapter he believes psychologists are particularly 'prone to being more neurotic'.

On 23 March 2021 Sidley received a reply from Dr Roger Paxton, the Chair of BPS's Ethics Committee, to his letter. It said that although he had intended to raise the ethical concerns voiced in Sidley's letter at their Ethics Committee meeting in March, the agenda was too full. He promised to raise the concerns at the next meeting in June. We must deduce that the BPS didn't find the ethical considerations of fear messaging to be troubling or pressing.

Dr Knut Wittkowski, former Head of Biostatistics, Epidemiology and Research Design at Rockefeller University, also experienced troubles online. He was fiercely critical of lockdown measures in an interview on YouTube in the spring of 2020, which garnered nearly 1.5 million views before being removed. The only explanation for its removal was that it 'violated' community standards. Susan Wojcicki, CEO of YouTube, warned that the platform would remove any information about the virus it regarded as 'problematic': 'Anything that would go against World Health Organization recommendations would be a violation of our policy.'[9]

Wittkowski seemed bemused when I asked him about the reaction to his views. He told me 'the reaction generally is good. I don't come across as somebody who has weird conspiracy theories. I base what I say on data.' I remembered my own reaction to his views. Back in the early, innocent days of the epidemic when I was vacuuming up as much virus information as possible online, I found Wittkowski. His credentials, experience and views about Covid were interesting and reassuring. Maybe I gravitated to the reassurance at a time when others were feeling panicked, but I liked his interview on YouTube. I remember one of his central points was that there was no reason to believe Covid would be significantly different to all the other respiratory diseases the world had ever known. Extremist views of the pandemic rose to the top of public consciousness, pushed by the media's helping hands, while his brand of perspective and rationale sank and was drowned by arbitrary censorship decisions.

This wasn't the first time Wittkowski had been opposed to a fear-mongering 'constellation of journalists, politicians and doctors', as he put it. He recalled that during the AIDS scare 'they said children would be infected by toys. That was one of the images they used to scare people. At that time I stood up and said – correct as it turned out – that it would never spread among Caucasian German heterosexuals. And it did not, of course.' He perceives a similar programme of fear in play around Covid, which he said is actually 'not the end of the world'.

Wittkowski had an interesting take on why the video was removed. He said that people were commenting and he was engaging with them in the comments under the video. 'Interaction is not currently wanted,' he observed, 'and that may be another reason YouTube took it down. If people interact they start forming their own opinions.'

I wondered what he thought the solution to this censorship was and he identified the scope of the problem more broadly: firstly, the scale of fear and, secondly, the loss of independent science. He told me that in his view 'politicians and media are spreading fear. It goes far beyond what the situation would justify. The media makes money by selling fear. People 'buy' fear, they listen, they get emotional, they spend more time looking at commercials. For more than 20 years I read the *New York Times* every morning. Then I cancelled it. I couldn't stand it anymore. It used to separate reporting and opinion. Not any more. The front page says the numbers are "surging". That is an opinion. If they said "increasing" that would be reporting.'

What was Wittkowski afraid of? 'My fear was that one evening I couldn't go and have dinner any more! But more seriously, giving the government information about who is meeting whom and for how long, tracking us… It is becoming dangerously close to 1984. And like in 1984, it is fear which keeps people in a state where they follow the government. It's not Oceania and Eurasia anymore, it's Covid. It doesn't matter what the fear is. If there is fear you can control the people.'

Of course, I agreed that the media had, regrettably, peddled fear, and the government might be exploiting it. I was keen to know what he meant about the loss of independence in science. He told me the main problem is the way science is funded: 'When I started my career at university you were fully funded with a salary from the university. People had independence. That is now gone. Virtually all scientists in the field of epidemiology and medicine have university positions where they get a desk and access to a library. In the US the funding comes from the NIH (National Institutes of Health). You don't want to bite the hand that feeds you.' I asked how he was able to speak up and he told me 'the people who have spoken up are retired and so they have independence' but that when he was at Rockefeller University, he 'would not have dared to say what I did or I would have compromised the funding'.

I asked how he thought some of the 'leading' voices in the pandemic might have been influenced. I was specifically interested in Neil Ferguson, whose modelling was considered partially responsible for triggering lockdowns. He didn't take the question too seriously because 'among scientists, Neil Ferguson does not have any credibility because his predictions are always wrong.'

Another scientist who experienced the glare of a controversial public reaction was Henrik Ullum. He was one of the researchers and authors of the Danmask study *Effectiveness of Adding a Mask Recommendation to Other Public Health Measures to Prevent SARS-CoV-2 Infection in Danish Mask Wearers*.[10]

At the time of the presidential election Ullum wrote a tweet saying that the researchers were sorry that the publication of the study was delayed, and people inferred that the delay was political. He told me, 'a lot of people in Denmark and on social media were pissed that we wouldn't release the data. People thought we were influencing the presidential election.'

As one of Denmark's social public health scientists, his inbox is always full. He told me that in one day he received three emails which exemplified the reaction to him: 'One person emailed me asking me to lock the country down and make young people behave well. One person asked me not to be the mouthpiece of the press. Another person accused me of being on an axis of evil with Bill Gates and the Danish prime minister. That's three emails in one day from one interview on Danish radio.' As he said, he has 'received fear and madness in all directions' during the Covid epidemic.

So, what was so controversial about the mask study? Masks have been mandated around the world despite very little evidence that they are effective. The study was designed to investigate whether the mask-wearer was protected. According to Henrik, the results were 'weak and insignificant' and 'not conclusive'. In both the write-up of the study and in talking with me on the phone, Ullum was careful to say that he didn't want the data 'to disturb public health policy'. In fact, since the very muted publication of the study, Ullum has been appointed Director of the Statens Serum Institut, the Danish equivalent of Public Health England. I presume that it wouldn't do, in his position, to publicly undermine his country's mask laws.

I asked Ullum why the study did take so long to be published, given that masks were such a controversial and un-evidenced imposition on people around the world? He was evasive: 'your guess is as good as mine'. Maybe it's just not the done thing for scientists to criticise the publications which publish them? You don't want to bite the hand that feeds your future credibility. Maybe there's an embarrassment that the study didn't produce the positive results the team were looking for. Ullum was so keen not to blame the publications he even suggested that 'maybe they thought the science is not good enough'. Really? His science wasn't good enough? But it was peer-reviewed and published. He qualified: 'If you look at the confidence limit of our results they were quite wide. No statistical difference means there could be major effects hidden because the sample size is not big enough.'

I asked outright if the difficulty in finding a publication was, in fact, political. Was the study a hot potato? 'No,' he said, 'there was tension about masks but I don't think it was politically motivated.' He did concede that 'the editors don't want their publication to upset the handling of an epidemic on a global scale. Almost all health authorities are promoting mask-wearing, we don't want our paper to disturb that. There was no evidence to support not wearing masks. There was slight data in favour of mask-wearing. As a researcher I also don't want our data to disturb public health policy.'

I asked if the delays, the controversy and criticism from both sides of the mask debate would be bad for science: would it put scientists off taking risks? 'I've been a researcher for 30 years and I have not experienced anything like it,' Ullum said. 'This experience was because Covid is so high on our political agenda at the moment. We'll go back to normal. Vaccines and warm weather in the spring will bring normality.'

I agreed that I hoped normality would return in the spring, after a long year. I wondered what he thought of the level of fear people feel about Covid, and he said 'we haven't managed the fear well enough. There has been too much fear. This is a serious epidemic, and we need to do the right things, but it's not an apocalypse.'

Censorship was evident across science, journalism and politics. Lucy Easthope is used to being seen as a 'wild card' in government advisory meetings. She told me the UK didn't follow existing science and pandemic planning during the Covid epidemic. Lockdown went against previous protocol and there was 'a cost to that'. Lockdown is 'now ingrained deeply into our psyche. People made choices to not see loved ones, they made decisions they have to live with, it's going to be very difficult to admit it was a mistake.' I asked if she thinks people will be able to admit mistakes, or see there were other paths to follow?' 'They will fight us like weasels in a bag.'

Part of the fight is pre-emptive censorship. I talked about the inhibiting effects of Ofcom's guidelines in Chapter 2, 'Fear spreads in the media like an airborne virus'. The Big Tech platforms also developed policies designed to counter 'disinformation'. We saw interviews with established scientists removed from YouTube, and articles published on Facebook from sources as respected as *The Spectator* and Unherd were flagged as containing 'potentially false' information for including the wrong views from the wrong people; where 'wrong' means counter to government or WHO advice. A video interview with Professor Karol Sikora, a world-leading oncology expert and a former Chief of the Cancer Program of the WHO, was removed from Facebook for 'violating guidelines'. An article by Professor Carl Heneghan about the landmark Danish mask RCT was labelled as containing 'false information' on Facebook. Google appeared to shadow ban (whereby the search results are suppressed) the Great Barrington Declaration,[11] a website and letter written by respected scientists recommending an approach called 'focused protection', in opposition to many countries' policies of lockdown. Google claimed this was not deliberate, but people were suspicious that the effect was seemingly switched on and then off after there was a fuss.

In traditional media, journalists mocked and discredited the 'wrong' scientists. Professor Sikora's 'positive' and 'balanced' views were described as 'dangerous' in *The Guardian*.[12] *The Guardian* had particular form for criticising dissenting scientists, also describing the authors of the Great Barrington Declaration as creating a rift which was a 'dangerous distraction'.[13]

The 'devil shift' was seen all the more clearly through the metaphors used by Paul Mason, who wrote in the *New Statesman* that 'like Dante's inferno, Covid denialism is structured in concentric circles', and said the innermost circle of hell is reserved for 'prominent lockdown sceptics such as Toby Young, Allison Pearson, Laurence Fox, Julia Hartley-Brewer and Peter Hitchens'. All bar one are journalists, specifically, in Mason's view, 'a bunch of rich, well-connected Conservative journalists' and their views are 'dangerous'. The inter-group opposition between leftwing and rightwing journalists seems to have obscured from Mason that all have voiced concerns about the impact of lockdown on the disadvantaged. And so, journalists seek to stifle not just scientists, but also other journalists. Opposite and different views were described as 'dangerous' so many times.

In the course of researching this book I was told variously that I was probably under surveillance, that I might not be published again, that I should do a Freedom of Information request to see if there was 'a file' on me because I'd put so many awkward questions into the government (incidentally, I never got a reply to that FOI), and that there would probably be a campaign to smear and discredit me before the book was published. So, if any unpleasant rumours emerge, don't necessarily believe them.

The Covid epidemic has produced scapegoating on a mass scale. Professionals and academics were 'cast out' of approving professional circles. But were we all scapegoated in some way?

The government imposed many restrictions on the population to control the spread of Covid and used fear, among other tactics, to encourage compliance. Yet one of the chief ways people caught Covid was in hospitals, which is beyond the responsibility of the population. A SAGE paper[14] claimed that a staggering 40.5% of Covid infections in the first wave were caught in hospital. Between the beginning of the 'second wave' in September 2020 and 13 January 2021, over 25,000 people[15] caught Covid while in hospital, but this may be an under-estimate due to the limitations of the data available. The NHS was resolutely tight-lipped about hospital-acquired infections.

Many people would have been discharged before receiving a diagnosis (I anecdotally heard of a number through interviews with nurses and doctors) who would then have spread Covid among their families and the community. We don't know the scale of nosocomial and the respective secondary infections, but the NHS's withholding of the data most likely speaks to the volume of it.

In January 2021, Keir Starmer called for tougher measures including the closure of zoos.[16] All the animals in the zoos, the visitors, the staff, the very notion of fun itself, were scapegoated while hospital-acquired infections were ignored, to save the hallowed NHS from being criticised. Of course, if you believe that legally mandated restrictions and lockdowns are the way to go, you might as well throw in zoos, I'm not making a special point about them, except that the idea they are a big problem is farcical. But still, none of this addresses hospital-acquired infections, about which we heard very little from the Minister of Health, NHS spokespeople, or the media.

Nosocomial infections are higher when community prevalence is higher, probably because of increased 'traffic' in hospitals,[17] so lockdowns do make some sense in helping to suppress hospital-acquired infections. But otherwise, creating fear in the population and locking everyone down did nothing about the problem of nosocomial infection. There also wasn't enough PPE (personal protective equipment) at the outset of the epidemic. Did we all have to carry the sins of an inadequately prepared government and ill-equipped NHS? Instead of being 'cast out' into the desert, did our scapegoating take the form of restrictions and confinement?

The ultimate scapegoats in the Covid epidemic and lockdown might have been children and the young. As Ellen Townsend told me, 'Their needs were subjugated. The legacy that we are creating for the young people of this country is horrendous. There are austere times ahead for them. They lived through a time when they were virtually ignored. In all actions people in power should be doing things for the benefit of children. Why are we not putting them first in everything?'

Scapegoating is an enduring human practice. Imagine trying to explain to the Mayans that they did not need to throw live children to their watery graves in Cenotes in order to ensure the rain fell? Perhaps our children were Covid's sacrificial lambs.

JIMMY, 32, BY HIS MOTHER

I found my son after he tried to kill himself.

We normally message a lot as a family. One day he left a message saying 'I bloody love you lot.' He told us he'd changed his phone number and then he left the group. Twenty-four hours later I still hadn't heard anything else, which is not like him. I messaged his girlfriend and she said she thought he was with us because he'd said he needed a few days away. So I knew something was wrong. We found him at a hotel. His voice was very flat when I spoke to him. Then I got a very strange message saying 'Don't ring me.'

We rushed there and the hotel had to help us break into his room because the chain was on the door. He'd tried to kill himself. We called an ambulance.

We've talked a lot since he's been at home. Before lockdown I think we could have helped before things got this bad because we'd have been seeing him in person. Life's been harder without the normal things you can do in life like going out, going to the gym, even just sitting on a bench if you take a walk with someone. There's no joy in life anymore and there's nothing to look forward to. There's no end point to this lockdown.

When he first came round he didn't know where he was or why he was there. He said all he could see was people in masks and it looked like they were all angry. Normally you'd have seen the nurse's face and they would probably say everything will be OK, but he said they looked like robots and he couldn't see any kindness or concern. He said it freaked him out. You'd have thought they would know when he came round he would be like that.

He has said he's sorry, but the last thing I want is for him to feel guilt. I don't want anyone who has thought about killing themselves to feel guilty if they read this. People can't help it. A lot of us are feeling very bleak.

I have a rage bubbling away. I am so angry about the way we have had this fear-mongering going on for such a long time. People think the BBC would never lie and the government wouldn't be trying to frighten us, but it's all about trying to scare people and all the time they are doing this, it is impacting people's stress and health.

14. CULTS, CONSPIRACY AND PSYCHIC EPIDEMICS

'I want to touch you, move you and inspire you' said a friend to me during an out-of-the-blue phone call, over a decade ago. He told me about an incredible self-development course he was taking and asked me to come along and see what it was about for myself. Inquisitive, I asked questions about why he thought this course would be good for me. Was he telling everyone about it or just me? If just me, then why? How would it move and inspire me? Although he raved about it, he couldn't actually describe the course content clearly or explain why it would benefit me. It wasn't enough to convince me to part with a few hundred pounds and risk falling into this brand of inarticulate euphoria. My then-husband decided to sign up for it though.

'I want to touch you, move you and inspire you,' said my husband when he came home, late, the first evening of the course. Oh dear. Same words. Same euphoria. Same inability to describe why it was so good and why I should do it. Extremely unnerved, I was now absolutely certain I should not do the course, but research it instead.

In the end, my husband and a few friends all took the Landmark Forum 'human potential' course. It's a 'Large Group Awareness Training' programme which has polarised people around the world. Some claim it has miraculously changed their lives. Some warn it is both a pyramid-selling scheme and a dangerous cult.

I learnt that Landmark Forum used some very particular techniques: the training room had no natural daylight or clocks so participants felt disorientated, and therefore more suggestible; specific vocabulary that needs explaining to the outside world, such as 'racket', which is your state of being; very specific and limited break times so participants were hungry, thirsty, and needed the loo, making them feel physically uncomfortable but also infantilised and disempowered; emotional manipulation; hard selling to get new members; long hours and homework, so the rest of life is just crowded out, making the experience more intense. I became interested in how cults work in general.

When I told my husband I thought he had been 'brainwashed' he was shocked and deflated. There was a feeling I had ruined this for him. He completed the course but, to my relief, didn't take the next level.

When we locked down in March 2020, I noticed that aspects of the situation, how we were 'managed' by our leaders, and people's responses matched elements of cult programming. I wasn't alone. In July, Peter Hitchens wrote in his *Mail on Sunday* blog:

> 'When this madness began, I behaved as if a new and fanatical religion was spreading among us. Be polite and tolerant, I thought. It may be crazy and damaging but in time it will go away. Now it is clear that a new faith, based on fear of the invisible and quite immune to reason, has all but taken over the country. And it turns out to be one of those faiths that doesn't have much tolerance for those who don't share it.'[1]

There are close parallels between cult induction, religious conversion and political propaganda. The similarity in techniques is the subject of *Battle for the Mind*, by William Sargant. As he said, 'Religious conversion techniques… often approximate so closely to modern political techniques of brain-washing and thought control that each throws light on the mechanics of the others.' He noticed that Chinese Communist Party experiments on mass excitation and reconditioning of groups were comparable not just with religious conversion, but also group psychotherapeutic treatments. The politician, priest, police officer and psychologist all have much to learn from each other.

As with the Landmark Forum, we all had to learn a new language at the outset of the Covid epidemic: social distancing; flatten the curve; self-isolate; build back better. We were captive indoors and although our curtains could open, the days soon blended and we lost sense of time. Extreme emotional manipulation was standard fare from politicians and through the media. We were denied relationships, dating, to go out to work, to decide the minutiae of our lives – we were infantilised and disempowered. People gleamed with the heady fervour of cult novitiates.

I am not suggesting that an overarching sinister cabal deliberately inducted us into a cult, or that Boris Johnson is a cult leader. But there are some parallels with cult leadership and induction. Perhaps it is simply the case that these techniques are naturally employed by particular types of leader who wish to command their subjects.

Dr Margaret Thaler Singer, author of *Cults in Our Midst: The Continuing Fight Against Their Hidden Menace* was an expert in the steps required to 'brainwash' people into joining cults. She described a thought reform programme, whereby a person or an organisation puts into place a coordinated programme of coercive influence and behaviour control. The novitiate puts their old value system aside and makes decisions based on what the cult leader wants and will reward, and stopping the behaviour that will get them in trouble.

Cults tend to be totalitarian. The leader has the power and decision-making. Our government ruled via ministerial diktat from March 2020. Questioning, doubt and dissent are discouraged in the cult, and cult leaders use feelings of shame and guilt in order to influence members. Often this is done through peer pressure and subtle forms of persuasion below the level of consciousness. This book has explored the tactics that were used on the British public.

Contrary to popular opinion, you don't have to be a vulnerable or damaged person to be recruited to a cult. Anyone can join a cult! The recruiter will narrow your attention in a controlled situation and create an experience which leaves you panicky or disorientated. Remember Fright Night? That's when it began with a big bang, but it really began with little fizzles when you read doom-mongering headlines or watched China's 'Stunt Covid' videos. You are most susceptible to the cult when you are stressed and emotionally vulnerable.

Next comes the love-bombing. While you are emotionally vulnerable you are flooded with affection and validation. A mere four days after Fright Night, most of the nation was clapping appreciatively in common purpose for the NHS. We flicked in a flash from fear to adulation. The media covered stories of death and the dangers of Covid (creating fear and vulnerability) as well as Covid heroes (love-bombing, feel-good stories and aspirational behaviour).

Cults need to get hold of a good deal of a person's time, especially their thinking time, so they don't dwell on what's happening and don't think too critically about it – so they are split off from their friends and dependency is encouraged. The media and government press briefings took care of that. We have never been so socially atomised.

Cults also use dependency and dread, creating a sense of powerlessness, anxiety and fear. Natural events are reframed to encourage obedience in members. Cult leaders almost always say that if you follow their rules it will help change the world and make it perfect. If followers leave the cult, they are told terrible disasters will befall them, they will die, or they won't have good karma, or some such flannel. The outside world, and the people in it, are presented as very dangerous. Does any of this sound familiar? In the case of the 'Covid Cult', the ultimate consequence is death, because if you don't comply the virus will get you, or you'll be fined or shamed if you go out without a reasonable excuse.

The novitiate's conscience is dimmed to accommodate new cult behaviour and attitudes. Desensitisation is important in cults, through seeing things done to other people. We became desensitised to things that would have been unacceptable to our conscience before. During the epidemic we were encouraged to snitch on neighbours, we grew nonchalant about the idea of life-destroying fines for breaches of rules (remember that two students were fined £10,000 each for arranging a snowball fight!) and we tolerated the transfer of infected elderly patients in hospital to care homes where they were like a spark to dry tinder, to give just a few examples of a relaxation of conscience.

The leaders maintain a closed system of logic and restricting criticism. Management is always right, you are always wrong. Failed prophecies are reframed to maintain the authority of the cult leader, no matter what. If the prophecy did not come true, it's because the followers didn't follow the rules. Then the prophecy date gets moved forward. The UK's lockdowns couldn't offer a more apt example. We were told we must obey the rules for them to work. 'Covidiots' were derided and blamed for failures in the media and social media. The finger was never pointed at hospital-acquired infections, for example, or the seasonality of the virus: it was our fault and we were easy scapegoats. And so, the lockdowns were extended and repeated. The 'prophecy date' for ending lockdown ever-shifting.

The book *When Prophecy Fails: A Social and Psychological Study of a Modern Group That Predicted the Destruction of the World*, is the true story of a cult which believed in the coming apocalypse and that the cult followers would be rescued by aliens in a flying saucer. Several rescue dates were announced, but each passed without disaster or spacecraft. Through the medium of 'automatic writing' one of the members was told that earth's apocalypse had been cancelled because the cult had waited patiently all night. The disappointments didn't shake their faith. Cult followers can double-down on their beliefs to resolve the intense discomfort cognitive dissonance creates. Sometimes it just feels easier to stay wedded to false beliefs than to face the truth.

The book's authors concluded that if someone was to remain a fervent believer in the face of such disappointment then they must truly commit themselves firstly by taking difficult actions, and also by being part of a social group who are all committed. It is easy to draw a comparison with supporters of tough Covid restrictions, despite the lack of convincing evidence that they work. The commitment to the lockdown, our 'new normal', has been life-changing and immense for the country.

People have held strong convictions during the epidemic. They have over-estimated danger, placed enormous faith in un-evidenced measures, and accepted vast social and personal changes. In a time of huge uncertainty it has felt more comforting to cling to conviction. I expect I am guilty too. We will need more distance to understand the social experiment we have endured and where convictions were misplaced. How will people de-programme from 'cult' thinking? This might be especially difficult for those who stand to lose professionally, such as scientists, journalists and politicians who expressed convictions and enacted policies publicly. By March 2021, Boris Johnson said 'lockdown came too late',[2] furthering the narrative that lockdown should have been earlier, harder, longer, sounding more like his 'opposition' in the House of Commons, rather than acknowledging the empirical evidence against lockdowns. The 'confession' served to endorse the role of lockdowns, therefore diverting attention from the collateral damage they caused and their ineffectiveness.

I felt discombobulated by the early strong convictions held by others about Covid and lockdown. It was as though everyone had gone on a Large Group Awareness Training Course for Covid and I'd missed the invite. I perceived a gap between rationality and reality. There were people who solely relied on the BBC and Number 10 press briefings, and then others who had ferreted around for alternative perspectives, such as the interview with Dr Knut Wittkowski which was removed from YouTube, or read one of Dr John Ioannidis's articles. A broad range of media offered balance, allowed room for doubt and nuance and, in so doing, calmed the fear.

Regardless, there was a certain amount of fear in the air and it was catching. With messages designed to elevate your sense of threat, if you weren't frightened of the virus, did your fear switch direction? I was frightened of authoritarianism and the consequences of lockdown for our country. I observed the fear around me, I felt my own, and it led me to research and write this book.

What do people do when they perceive a gap between reality and rationality? When their fear roams away from the path laid out by the state? If your rational mind looks at the evidence and says, well, this might be really bad, but it isn't going to be the plague, or even Spanish flu, and yet you are told it is the greatest threat in peacetime, what do you make of the panic? If you are told it is best for everyone to quarantine, including the sick, the potentially infectious and the healthy, even though that has never happened before, and you foresee economic devastation, what are you to make of the government using such a destructive policy without precedent or evidence?

What if it feels like everyone around you is being inducted into a cult, using brand new language you don't relate to, the emotions flicking disorientatingly between fear and love-bombing, and punishments for dissent are mandated, rewards for compliance seep into society, but you were impervious to the programming?

People look for answers. Some people grow 'conspiracy theory' in this gap between rationality and reality. A conspiracy theory is a theory about a plot which is carried out in secret, with a sinister end goal. The term has a negative connotation, the implication being that the conspiracy is based on insufficient evidence, or prejudice, or stupidity. Generally, it's considered that decent journalism, state-sponsored inquiries, whistleblowers and Freedom of Information requests are the bedrock of uncovering conspiracies. Until they are proven, they are 'conspiracy theories'. State-sponsored inquiries are slow. Whistleblowers don't always come forward. And when they do, the media don't always want to go near them. It was *Middle East Eye*, not the broadsheets, which reported the extraordinary stories of government propaganda through RICU and external agencies employed by the unit. And Freedom of Information requests are sadly not a reliable way to extract information. In my own experience they go unanswered or responses can be avoidant.

Investigation and verifying claims is not straightforward. Absence of evidence could indicate that a theory is just a 'conspiracy theory', or it could mean the evidence is obscured for the time being. Although conspiracy theories have a bad reputation, some conspiracies turn out to be true, and people in power at the highest levels try and cover up what they are doing. In our own recent history in the UK there are weapons of mass destruction used to justify an invasion of Iraq in 2003, and the lies perpetrated by South Yorkshire Police after the Hillsborough disaster.

Actor Sean Ward was surprised to find out that he might feature in a BBC documentary 'about people who have lost, or are losing loved ones down the conspiracy rabbit hole' and families 'ripped apart… by harmful conspiratorial belief'. A BBC TV researcher contacted Ward's sister through her personal Facebook account and her work email.

Ward has been vocal about opposition to lockdown and also talked about vaccine concerns through his popular social media channels. The BBC researcher may perhaps characterise him as an 'anti-vaxxer' and conspiracy theorist. He also received 'bad press' – in his words – for attending anti-lockdown protests in London. But he feels his social media airings have been helpful to his followers and created a sense of community. Which is, of course, exactly the sort of influence the programme makers are concerned about – 'blue ticks' influencing in the wrong way.

Regardless of his beliefs and their veracity, the description of the programme in the email (which he forwarded to me to read) to Ward's sister appeared to be quite one-sided, describing the 'big issues' of people with 'huge numbers of followers' sharing disinformation. They didn't specify what the disinformation consisted of in Ward's case though.

The email nodded to mental health issues, but this would be a very sensitive area for the documentary makers to manage without psychologically harming their contributors and the family members they are talking about. I spoke with Ward about how the approach, made to his family behind his back, had affected him. 'I feel like I am easy-pickings because

I spoke about mental health and suicidal thoughts in 2018,' he told me. 'Messaging my family feels very personal. This is especially painful because the BBC was my employer for years. My sister was quite worried about it the first time they approached her and now she is livid. She doesn't think they really have the content they need and that's why they need her.'

Ward's sister did not want to contribute to the programme and the request had a sobering affect on the two of them. One can imagine that if families weren't 'ripped apart' before the documentary, they might be after.

This chapter belies my own fascination with conspiracy theory and, of course, this is an ideal area of exploration for a documentary, but there is a danger of upholding the tropes so favoured during the epidemic of the 'Covidiot' and 'conspiracy theorist', and using denigration to suppress dissent, as discussed in Chapter 13, 'The climate of fear'. Media appears never to have been so partisan and propagandist, even while purporting to be the opposite

I decided to research people who fall under the umbrella term 'conspiracy theorist'. To be honest it was easy to uncover all kinds of theories among all kinds of people given that the gap between rationality and reality was more of a chasm. I interviewed two men, Steve and Alex, both of whom had pronounced theories and had taken action upon them.

Steve's camouflage clothes and olive green Land Rover would have been well disguised in woodlands, but he was immediately obvious to me in the B&Q car park. Although cafés were open at the time, he'd wanted to meet somewhere anonymous, and suggested our salubrious setting. I got a coffee from the hot dog van and got into his car.

I knew Steve from his job as a security guard in a local shop. I'd been chatting to him throughout lockdown about how business had been, how people reacted when face masks were mandated, if the people in the store had caught Covid – every shopping trip is a research opportunity! In our many conversations we'd talked about what could be behind the UK government's pandemic policies. We'd arranged to meet away from his place of work so he could tell me about his theories.

'All my life I have been prepping. I am always doing risk assessments in my head,' he told me. 'You have car insurance. Why not have a year's supply of rice?' I said I thought that constantly planning for the worst sounded exhausting, but he was cheerful: 'It's not exhausting, because it's not happened yet. Hope for the best, prepare for the worst. I don't think this is it. I think this is a test run. In peacetime you prepare for war.'

I was curious about when he had started prepping. 'Back in the 1970s we had power shortages. I remember going down to the shops and not being able to buy sweets, so I started hoarding sweets. It started there. I was also in the army,' he said. I was a child of the 70s too, and I remember the drawer always full of candles and matches, and that we needed them. I don't have a year's supply of rice, but I have a drawer of headlights, candles and matches, and I know that preparation for power cuts comes straight from my childhood.

We talked about why he felt suspicious. 'I can smell a trap. What are the restrictions and the masks for? They aren't going to affect a virus, so why are they doing it? I think we're being trained for obedience.' I had sympathy with this view. It seemed very likely that the UK had performed a U-turn on masks for psychological not medical reasons. We know that behavioural scientists think masks give a 'signal', which would inspire obedience to the lockdown rules. In a sense, Steve's interpretation is correct. If you perceive manipulation by the government it creates mistrust. So far, so reasonable. And as he said, 'things are a conspiracy theory until they happen.'

Steve continued: 'The Coronavirus Act is an Enabling Act like the Nazis had. And it's scary that governments around the world are acting similarly. Is someone else dishing out the control?' I could see where he was coming from. The Coronavirus Act and Public Health Act were terrifyingly draconian (see Chapter 15, 'Tyranny') and one could potentially draw parallels with the Nazi legislation. And why did governments around the world adopt similar policies at the same time? These policies didn't come from existing pandemic planning literature and expertise – in fact, they were counter to it – so why? Were they copying each other, in a political version of playground psychology? We had to lock down, Sir, the other boys did it! Or were policy changes being driven by another source, a sinister cabal of globalist puppeteers?

I decided to test how 'out there' Steve's beliefs might be. Did he believe aliens might be involved in controlling governments? 'I don't know,' he said. He asked me if I thought there was intelligent life in the universe which might have visited earth. Yes, I thought that was possible. His satisfied face told me he could rest his case. I asked whether he thought a 'Covid conspiracy' was operated by the Masons or Illuminati? 'I'm not a Mason, so I wouldn't know.' Fair enough. So, what was his theory?

'I think the virus could be man-made or released,' he asserted. At one point this definitely would have sounded conspiracy-esque, or at least highly speculative. But by the time he and I met, the WHO still hadn't been granted access to the laboratory in Wuhan, China, and at the time of writing, British scientist Professor John Watson, who was involved in the eventual investigation, said he could not rule out a leak from the lab.[3]

Steve also thought that the pandemic response was 'to destroy the economies of the world', and said 'we can't service all this debt. If you can't pay the debt you are in someone's pocket. Are we going to be living like China with a social credit? Is this about getting us all to have digital ID?'

We had hit another inconvenient truth. Something that was seen as 'conspiracy theory' – that Covid was an excuse to impose a digital ID system upon us – looks more likely in 2021. A logical conclusion to a pandemic in an age of technology? Opportunism by political leaders who want to bring in digital ID anyway? Or a pre-determined plan? The UK government announced it would review a Covid certification scheme, or 'freedom app' or 'vaccine passport'. The European Union put forward a legislative proposal for a 'Digital Green Pass' that provides proof of vaccination or test results. Israel introduced a 'Green Pass'.

I pointed out that although he was open-minded he didn't seem to know what was going on. 'That's right,' he agreed, 'I don't know. All I know is you have 1% who have everything. Then a few more percent under them who control all of us. The middle classes are going now. I think we are sinking down lower and lower and those that control us want a small number of super rich and the rest super poor.' Well, there had been a huge upshift in wealth during the epidemic, so I could see why he thought this. US billionaire wealth grew $1.3 trillion between mid-March 2020 and February 2021.[4] Two thousand of the world's wealthiest billionaires grew their collective wealth by 27.5%.[5] Yet overall labour income dropped 10.7% globally,[6] mainly in lower-income countries, and 150 million were expected to be pushed into extreme poverty by 2021[7] by the pandemic, or rather the lockdowns and restrictions.

I had a lot of sympathy with some of Steve's views. I even shared some to an extent, although I couldn't say whether these end results were the result of sinister secret conspiracies, opportunism, disaster capitalism, or just bad luck. Steve was sure something was going on, but also didn't know what. His genuine curiosity about the world, plus an appetite to read and communicate with others of similar views, seemed to have combined with a childhood predilection for 'being prepared'. While many would call him a conspiracy theorist and 'prepper' I think his beliefs were more nuanced. He would have predicted digital ID, a destabilised world economy and a wealth grab by elites at the beginning of the pandemic, and he would have been right. On the other hand, he thought aliens could be the masterminds of it all.

Steve's Land Rover was a cornucopia of useful items. He had freeze-dried food, water canisters, spare fuel, tools, spare clothes. He told me he could drive into the woods and survive for days. I asked why? What did he think might be coming? 'I've been ready this year to pack my bags and go. My wife believes in all this reluctantly. She doesn't want to believe something else is going on, but she does. I'm always prepared because you never know.' He told me they had bought some woodland and were building a cabin, so that if the time came, they could live off-grid. He described them as being in a 'transitional period' as they prepared for the worst-case scenario. They had a ready supply of fuel, a log burner and a year's supply of rice. He had been buying small pieces of gold for years and had a good supply of carbon arrows. Arrows? That sounded apocalyptic! Would we be shooting each other with bows and arrows? 'I practise archery. I like it, it's a hobby. That doesn't detract from the fact that it's a post-apocalyptic survival skill.'

I asked Steve what was next? 'Tier Three or full lockdown around Christmas. I think worse is coming. 2021 something will happen. There could be riots when people come off furlough. We can't go on like this forever.'

I talked to Alex over Zoom. Although we could have met during the dizzying freedom granted by the government during the summer of 2020, he'd already moved to Sweden. He told me that he'd 'had enough of England, the government and the media'. He had been shocked at how quickly the British public acquiesced to the restrictions on their lives, and said he and his family decided not 'to play the game' but to try life somewhere else.

'The public health and political systems are somewhat uncoupled, so it's less crazy here. You don't read about Covid on signs everywhere, it's not in the media 24/7. Sweden didn't turn Covid into a political game,' he told me. 'Despite what you see in the media in the UK, the Swedes are quite proud of the way they responded. No one here thinks they could or should have done a lockdown.'

I asked how he had felt when the pandemic started, and he told me that Fright Night had a profound effect on him – just as it had on me. 'It was weird, like the Queen's speech on Christmas Day. The whole family was together. I was in the moment. I get chills when I think about it. It was like a show. Boris came out with buffoon hair. They hadn't brushed it, which seemed a bit odd.'

I was impressed by the swift escape to Sweden. I think it was an enviable move. In truth, most people would have enjoyed life in Sweden better during 2020. No-lockdown Sweden is an awkward counter-factual to locked-down UK. The country followed existing pandemic protocol and didn't try the brand new lockdown experiment. The Swedes have largely been entrusted with government guidance rather than law and, as a result, life has carried on more normally and the economy saw a much milder downturn than the UK, with a 2.9% contraction in GDP,[8] rather than the UK's 11.3%.[9]

Lockdown fanatics think Sweden pursued a reckless strategy and fared less well than its Scandinavian neighbours, while lockdown critics praise the gods that a control exists to show how a pandemic can be managed without putting people under virtual house arrest. When Sweden did not lock down, gloomy modellers predicted 100,000 deaths[10] by 1 July. In fact, there were only 5,490 deaths.

I asked how they managed to travel there. 'It was easy,' Alex laughed, 'Travel wasn't as restricted then as it is now. We packed up and drove here! We barely even needed masks on the way. We knew we had a window to travel and then the restrictions would get worse in the UK.'

Curiously, he was right – travelling did become harder. So, what were his theories about why this was happening? 'This isn't about Covid. This is an excuse to crash the economy. I've known it's coming for years. I just didn't know it would be a virus,' he told me. 'Governments are printing the shit out of money. Wealth is shifting upwards more, and the rich are using this "new" money in a wealth grab to buy resources, like land. We're playing a massive game of monopoly. I don't think we ordinary people can win anymore. We can't throw the board over and say we're not playing the game anymore. It's too late for that.'

And so he moved to Sweden because the economy will be stronger? 'No. I think we're about to see the collapse of the Western world. A lot of people will die. You have to be prepared to be one of them. I don't think Sweden will escape from this. All countries will get there in the end. I'm not under any illusion that coming here is a permanent escape. But there are 10 million people here and a lot of land. There are 70 million in the UK. I think it's going to be messy and I'll do what I can to keep me and my family out of it.'

Well, we are quantitative-easing the 'shit out of money'. Hmm, this was a bit frightening (fear is contagious!) because his theory echoed my own early fears. Knowing that the government was pursuing such an economically harmful policy had frightened me. However, I had tried to remain observant about concerns and emotions, and I'd talked to a variety of friends about their interpretations of events in order to sense-check myself. I asked Alex if he thought he was paranoid: 'No. There is nothing new going on right now. Plenty of people have predicted this. The virus provides cover for crashing the economic system and bringing in a new system that will purport to be for the people but is not. There will be digital ID, we'll go cashless, you won't be able to travel anywhere without being vaccinated up to the eyeballs and there will be a grab of the tangible assets. I've been predicting an economic crash since 2012.'

By the time of publication more of Alex's predictions seem to be bearing fruit. I asked how he thought this worked: how and why would our democratically-elected leaders coordinate to crash the world economy? 'There's insane worldwide money printing,' he said, 'so this is obviously a worldwide plan. Johnson and Starmer aren't in charge. They are high-level Masons. They are working for others.' Who? 'Who do you think?' I didn't know, that was why I was asking him. Alex didn't want to go into much more detail.

'At no point in this so-called pandemic did I ever feel fear about it. I always knew I'd be fine. I'm healthy,' said Alex, when I asked if he was scared. 'What frightened me was seeing everything I've read about and believed would happen, come to pass at warp speed. They aren't playing games, they are going for it. Knowing where this could go is scary.'

Theories flourish in the gap between what we know makes rational sense and our lived reality. So much of the response to the Covid epidemic did not make sense. World leaders did act similarly. They used the same language. Was this evidence of coordination behind the scenes, or was it linguistic contagion? Were they acting in sinister lockstep or were they copying each other? They pursued lockdown strategies that might save lives, although there was no evidence that they would, while knowing they would cause economic and societal harm which would cost lives. What is an intelligent and imaginative person to theorise?

Broadly, we might assume government plans were carefully considered, or that a conspiracy was driving events, or that it was all a big cock-up. The initial response looked wise, precautionary and justifiable to many people, and it still does to some. By this point my lockdown critical colours are nailed firmly to the mast. Conspiracy can be as extreme as believing that aliens are pulling strings behind the scenes, or that 5G masts are going to poison us, or it can be more believable. How about the World Economic Forum's 'Great Reset'?[11]

Some people think the government's response to Covid is a smokescreen to disguise their participation in this reset; a radical restructuring of the economy and society. The World Economic Forum also uses the slogan 'Build back better'. My first thought when I heard that was that, if we are 'building back', a degree of destruction has been wrought first. Might I suggest a modest refurbishment instead?

The Great Reset is no 'conspiracy theory', it's a manifesto, a plan, laid out in black and white. And does it tie in to Covid? Yes, if Professor Klaus Schwab, the founder and Executive Chairman of the World Economic Forum, has his way. He said: 'The pandemic represents a rare but narrow window of opportunity to reflect, reimagine, and reset our world'.[12]

The World Economic Forum published an article by Ida Auken, one of their Young Global Leaders and a Danish Member of Parliament, entitled 'Welcome to 2030: I own nothing, have no privacy and life has never been better'.[13] It's supposed to be a provocative enticement to consider the sort of future the WEF imagines, but I would retitle it 'Welcome To 2030: I am a serf and have never been so gullible'. It's an incredibly unpalatable imagining of the future. Every Englishman's home is his castle, and I think that owning nothing and squatting in a communal living space is going to be a very hard sell in this country indeed.

In February 2020 a World Economic Forum tweet stated 'Lockdowns are quietly improving cities around the world' and celebrated the closures of factories and the deserted streets while earthquake scientists can work more effectively. This is by no means evidence of a 'conspiracy' but does suggest an incredibly out-of-touch technocratic approach to life. The tweet did not hit the right note and they deleted it.

Maybe influential international organisations, world leaders and business are conspiring to bring about certain changes in the world. That would be for another book, it strays too far from my remit, and there are thousands of digital rabbit holes for you to explore. Or maybe the answers lie in cock-ups? Of course governments, international organisations and individual scientists make mistakes. Fear clouds rational judgement. Then they might try to hide their mistakes. Maybe between conspiracy and cock-up are conflicts of interest and convergent agendas. Less over-arching than a grand 'conspiracy theory', they could account for lobbying, sympathetic media exposure and high-level handshakes and contracts.

News about conflicts of interest seeped out slowly during the epidemic. SAGE members' financial interests have still not been published at the time of writing. The *BMJ* reported in December 2020[14] that the government was withholding SAGE and other advisory bodies' competing interests, such as whether they had financial interests in pharmaceutical companies receiving government contracts.

The *BMJ* reported that 'Throughout the pandemic, allegations of financial conflicts of interest have circled many public and private actors in many jurisdictions. In the UK the government's Chief Scientific Adviser, Patrick Vallance, made headlines when he was shown to have financial ties to the drug company GlaxoSmithKline.'[15] The journal also reported on the the Wellcome Trust's conflicts of interest; its pharmaceutical investments overlap with its research efforts. Both Wellcome and the Gates Foundation are 'positioned to potentially benefit financially from its leading role in the pandemic response'. And the 'UK government acted unlawfully in failing to publish details of dozens of contracts awarded without competition for goods and services such as personal protective equipment'.[16]

Governments enact controversial policies and businesses

profit from the exploitation of natural disasters, while a population is understandably distracted and looking at danger. This is 'disaster capitalism' as described by Naomi Klein in her book *The Shock Doctrine: The Rise of Disaster Capitalism*. This is cashing in on chaos rather than shadowy conspiracy theory. When people panic, they are pliable. When people are pliable, there is profit to be made.

Is it any wonder that once the initial impact of fear has receded, some minds race? Government leaders emulated cult leaders (albeit unintentionally, one hopes), manipulating our emotions, weaponising our fear against us, wreaking havoc on the economy, culture and mental health of the nation, and behaving in eerie unison with other countries, even parroting the same slogans ('Build back better', for instance). This creates the perfect crucible for 'conspiracy theories'. If the inevitable inquiry is halfway decent, no doubt it will uncover some uncomfortable truths. These may ultimately reveal an alchemy of careful consideration, conspiracy and cock-up.

It is tempting to blame the whole mess on a malevolent cult, a cabal or an evil leader. After all we could then find them, expose them and take them down. They can't hide in the shadows forever. While I don't think we will find anything so simple, convenient and predictably evil lurking in the shadows, I think we should look to our own shadows for the answers.

Carl Jung wrote about the 'shadow' and the danger of psychological projection. Our shadow is the instinctive and irrational side of ourselves. Essentially, it is more comfortable to remain ignorant of our failings, so we project them onto other people, or mythic figures: 'baddies'. The devil is the ultimate projection of our shadow. Jung recognised that there is a tendency within collectivist movements to project elements from the shadow onto others. The vast scale of the global fear response to Covid and the shocking social re-engineering it has instigated leads me to intuit that there are deep, collective unconscious forces at work.

Although Covid is a real disease and SARS-CoV-2 is a real virus, some of the response felt 'unreal' if you were not caught up in the cult-like response. We have not just endured and tolerated but even demanded the curtailment of our freedoms, for a disease which has a median Infection Fatality Rate of 0.05%[17] for under 70-year-olds globally. Our response felt unmoored from the gravity of the threat – why?

I spoke to Jungian psychotherapist, James Caspian, about mass delusions. He pointed out that Jung lived through the striking and destructive collective movements of the world wars and the Cold War. What he said then about mass movements, the shadow and projection can be applied to what is happening in the world now. 'In times of distress people turn to visions of Utopian or Apocalyptic scenarios,' Caspian said. 'Jung said the really dangerous point is when insight and reflection are crushed by the mass movement and the state succumbs to a fit of weakness in that scenario. I think that's happening. The state is afraid of some of the mass movements, such as political correctness. Rational argument is only possible if the emotionality of a situation does not exceed a critical degree. In that case reason will be supplanted by slogans and fantasies. A collective possession develops which turns into a psychic epidemic.'

The looming collective shadow has resulted in mass delusions and mass hysteria before. Humans do this, more often than you would think. Here is a collection of eclectic examples. During the Salem witch trials in 1692–93 there were hundreds of accusations of witchcraft and ultimately 19 executions. A laughter epidemic in a girls boarding school in Tanganyika in 1962 saw up to 159 girls laugh continuously for days in an outbreak of mass hysteria. The 'glass delusion' was a mental illness particularly affecting the noble classes most common in the 16th and 17th centuries, whereby aristocrats believed they were made of glass and could literally shatter to death. The 1528 'dancing plague of Strasbourg' was an inexplicable instance of mass delusion, with hundreds of people compelled to dance, some to the death.

In other examples of mass hysteria, if not psychic epidemics, *The War of the Worlds* radio broadcast caused panic among listeners in the United States who thought the Martians really had invaded. And James Thurber wrote in

My Life and Hard Times about the day when everybody in his town, Columbus, thought the nearby dam had broken and ran miles to escape, shouting 'Go East!'. The dam hadn't burst and, regardless, the water never could have reached the town anyway. It was a fascinating insight into the contagion of fear and its ability to affect the rational mind. No one had questioned where the rumour started, or noticed the reassuring lack of water, and they hadn't even got on their horses or started their cars. They just ran, like lemmings.

I asked Caspian how people can protect themselves, and how can societies protect themselves, from psychic epidemics? 'Jung wrote a book called *The Undiscovered Self*,' Caspian told me, 'and he talked about the plight of the modern individual. To become truly individual that person would need to mis-identify from the collective. Most people are caught up in the collective and in movements and live out their life like that. It's easier and more comfortable to be swept along. To individuate means in practice that we say there is a collective movement but we think critically about it and we are not prepared to be swept along by it.' Jung said that it is not microbes, not cancer, but man himself who is the greatest danger to man.

If the UK, and maybe much of the world, is suffering a psychic epidemic, how do we learn from this experience and recover now, but importantly protect against the next one? A psychic epidemic has the potential to be far more devastating than the worst of natural catastrophes. The supreme danger which threatens individuals as well as whole nations is a psychic epidemic, not a viral epidemic.

After Hitler's defeat, Jung concluded, 'The phenomenon we have witnessed in Germany was nothing less than the first outbreak of epidemic insanity, an eruption of the unconscious into what seemed to be a tolerably well-ordered world.' The role of the government should be to moderate and contain a psychic epidemic and mass delusion, not to exaggerate and multiply it. If fear was an open door in spring 2020, the UK government did not allow us to walk through it, but used a battering ram to knock it down.

JOSEPH, 60, COUNSELLOR

I am working with a lot of clients who are struggling with guilt and fear.

One client feels guilty about not getting into an ambulance with their loved one who later died. They tried to get in the ambulance but were told the police could be involved if they carried on. They feel guilty that they didn't try hard enough. The deep sense of letting people down creates a serious trauma. If you are grieving normally, someone would hug you or hold your hand. There is less of that now. We aren't dealing with grief in the normal ways, and the grief and trauma are greater.

I also have clients who have felt marginalised and ignored, when their relatives died and the diagnosis switched from something to Covid. Some have relatives with dementia in care homes who are frightened and confused about the changes and not seeing their families.

This is a time of judgement. People are frightened to break rules and hug people and do all the things that are normal.

A lady who lives locally to me has a lot of co-morbidities. I went to see if she was alright. She was terrified to come out of the house and spoke to me through the window.

The problems she already had were compounded by terror, because she would religiously watch the Number 10 press briefings. The politicians on podiums told us to be terrified – so it's not any wonder that some people were terrified!

When the rules relaxed and the time came to leave her front door, she couldn't do it. It was like Stockholm syndrome.

I started going round to help her by walking with her, but staying 20 feet away, just to keep her company. These were not therapeutic exchanges, she was a neighbour who needed help. She is much better now.

I think the nation has been bullied and gaslit. This was supposed to be about protecting us, but it hasn't protected us. It's disgraceful that the government tried to frighten us. This is a crime against the people. I can't understand why the official bodies like the British Psychological Society aren't talking about the ethics of what has happened. It's like people are turning a blind eye to what's happening.

15. TYRANNY

'When tyrannies take over it is because people volunteer their liberty voluntarily.'

Lord Sumption

A bold pronouncement, but what we came to expect from Lord Sumption, former Supreme Court judge, in his campaign to defend civil liberties under lockdown.

What could persuade people to volunteer their liberty? Fear, in a word. Emergency situations called for emergency measures. The government responded swiftly and the emergency regulations were nodded through Parliament to applause rather than opposition. But were the UK's emergency laws and regulations proportionate, the least intrusive available, strictly necessary and based on scientific evidence?

Lockdown was enforced under the Public Health Act, originally designed to immobilise and treat people who are infectious, not the entire population. During a House of Lords debate on the imposition of the Regulations, several peers expressed their concern that the Regulations were ultra vires, that is exceeding the legal powers of the UK government.

What made Covid the first disease to ever merit quarantining an entire population of the healthy? It was feared that the NHS would be overwhelmed. Other countries had already locked down under emergency legislation, setting a 'template'. I asked Sumption about this striking authoritarian template, which surprisingly became a norm across the liberal democratic countries of Europe: 'There is a herd instinct in governments and it gave them political cover. Sometimes the best thing is to do nothing.' It's an important point. The media and the public wanted government to act, when sometimes leadership in a crisis involves waiting, or less dramatic and less visible action.

The government reviewed emergency legislation behind closed doors, leaving MPs and the public in the dark about the evidence for the emergency regulations and their proportionality. Repeated requests for a cost-benefit analysis to determine the proportionality were ignored until an attempt to quantify the impacts of lockdown and restrictions was finally published on 30 November, in the report *Analysis of the health, economic and social effects of COVID-19 and the approach to tiering*.[1] 'Vague' might be a good descriptor for this report. It doesn't even mention QALYs – quality-adjusted life years – which are the routine way that the government and NHS quantify the value of a life saved. Presumably this value was not included in the report because it would definitively show that the 'cure' has been worse than the disease.

The lockdown imposed by the government to contain Covid was enforced mainly through the Health Protection (Coronavirus, Restrictions) (England) Regulations 2020, known as the 'Lockdown Regulations', imposed under powers delegated by the Public Health (Control of Disease) Act 1984 ('the 1984 Act'). In addition, the Coronavirus Act 2020 contains the notorious Schedule 21 which allows for you to be forcibly detained, tested, treated and quarantined.

The strict lockdown laws meant that various basic liberties were curtailed, including: the right to protest, worship, maintain relationships, vote (elections were cancelled), the right to education was affected as many pupils had haphazard online provision for months, and you could not leave your house except for a non-exhaustive list of exemptions. These are not trifling privileges, but basic liberties.

On 23 March the Prime Minister ordered people to stay at home. The next day Matt Hancock underscored that these were 'rules', not guidance. But the law didn't change until 26 March. 'A huge proportion of the British population do not understand the difference between guidance and regulation,' said Sumption. 'The government said "you must" and people assumed that was a rule, when it was not. I think that the government knew that people did not understand the difference and exploited their confusion.'

People might have been able to forgive and trade a three-day hiatus from law in exchange for being kept safe from the perils of a virus, but will they mind the government's next foray into despotism? And will they even notice if it happens one statute at a time?

Once these 'rules' were announced on the 23rd, police forces across the country started to enforce them. Derbyshire police tweeted that they would be breaking up groups of people in the streets the next morning, provoking Sumption's outburst, as he described it, on the BBC's *World at One*. He told me, 'they had no business doing anything in a national crisis except enforcing the law. They are not there to give effect to their own views on what a national crisis might require and they are not there to give effect to what a Prime Minister's views might require in a national crisis. They are citizens in uniform who should apply the law and nothing else.'

London's streets were eerily quiet when I visited barrister Kirsty Brimelow's chambers in the summer. Echoing Sumption, she told me that what troubled her most about lockdown law had been the obfuscation between law and guidance by using the term 'rules', and the wrongful convictions that subsequently led to. I asked her if the government deliberately misled the public and the media? Perhaps, but she also blamed a 'chaotic approach and huge incompetence'.

She pointed out that although citizens must follow the law, we are allowed to decide for ourselves whether to follow guidance and she would like the government to stop using the term 'rules'. The confusion between guidance and law led people to be 'wrongfully arrested, wrongfully convicted and that is not only a bad thing for the person concerned, but also for society and the rule of law in general.' To give one example, in England there was a 'rule' we should be two metres apart. There may be stickers on the ground, and it might very well be sensible guidance, but it has never been law. It was and is a request that people may choose to follow, or not.

What compelled Brimelow to speak out were the miscarriages of justice. *Times* journalist Fariha Karim contacted her about the conviction of Marie Dinou, who had been arrested at Newcastle train station right at the start of lockdown. She was held in cells for two nights (under no powers), 'treated appallingly' by the District Magistrate, given a criminal conviction under the wrong legislation and fined £660. Dinou's case was not exceptional, BAME communities were disproportionately targeted, and every single prosecution (a staggering 246)[2] under the Coronavirus Act had been overturned at the time of writing.

'Criminalisation should be removed from these laws', said Brimelow. 'Too many people sitting together having a picnic should never be a criminal offence.'

She hoped that there would be sensible messages from our police chiefs to regulate those police officers who might overreach. Instead 'we had police stepping beyond their powers, fining people for sitting on park benches and police threatening to inspect people's shopping trollies.'

Police officers had a difficult task enforcing complex, fast-changing and sometimes, frankly, illogical laws. However, there were some concerning and heavy-handed tactics, from the use of degrading spit hoods, to police dogs when dispersing a party (leading to tragic life-changing injuries),[3] to carrying firearms when telling a gym to close. Whether through confusion or over-enthusiasm the police mistakenly fined people for not wearing masks despite being exempt, moved people on erroneously from park benches, and threatened people swimming at the beach with fines, among other examples. People driving cars were stopped and turned around or fined, when they had broken no laws, only breached 'guidance'. There are many regrettable examples of mistaken and misused laws, documented throughout 2020 by Big Brother Watch, a small NGO which defends civil liberties.

Perhaps some of the confusion arose from the lack of parliamentary scrutiny – the usual checks and balances were not in place in 2020. The first emergency laws were understandably brought in quickly, but remarkably no primary legislation was brought in all year. We are still under emergency law at the time of publication. Brimelow said the fact that primary legislation has not been debated 'can only mean government control and seeking to bypass the democratic system.' Her grave concern is that the law will be so emasculated it may not be there for us the next time we need it.

Fines were set at life-destroying levels. Individuals who broke the new coronavirus self-isolation regulations faced fines of £1,000. Worse, if an 'authorised person' considered you were 'reckless' in coming into contact with someone, the fine was raised to a crushing £4,000. Fines for organising protests or parties were an inconceivable £10,000.

In any year, these fines are enough to break most UK households financially. But it was a year of rising unemployment, salary cuts and businesses running at half-mast. ONS data shows that average disposable income (after tax and benefits) was £30,800 per year before lockdown. For the poorest fifth, this was just £13,100. Even prior to the current recession – the deepest in modern times – disposable income was falling by more than 4% each year.

The police have never before had the power to issue such large fines to individuals, and there are good reasons for this. Normally, fixed-penalty notices are £100 or £200. For example, driving distracted could land you a £100 on-the-spot fine. The fine can only be higher (increasing to up to £5,000) if it is issued by a court. To keep fines within people's means, some are linked to salary, typically limited to 50 or 75% of a weekly wage. But a £4,000 fine would be a staggering 16 weeks of salary for someone in the bottom fifth of earnings. If these fines were unpaid, resulting in an appearance at a magistrates' court, they would probably be adjusted to be means-tested.

There is simply no equivalent in modern Britain to these disproportionately high fines. As I said in Chapter 7, 'The tools of the trade', they have more in common with the Weregild and 'blood money' of the Dark Ages than any modern-day fixed-penalty notice. 'Recklessly' leaving self-isolation and potentially transmitting the virus would cost you about the same as murdering a 'non-prospering Welshman' would have in the ninth century. Welcome to neo-feudal justice.

'Emergency legislation was alright at the beginning but it's not alright now,' echoed Adam Wagner, a human rights barrister. 'If I was in charge it's what I would do if I could get away with it too.' This was an interesting admission, if a little surprising. I challenged him – would he really? 'If you are in the teeth of a crisis and you think you are saving lives, I can understand the motivations.'

Wagner expanded his reasoning: 'When society is fearful, people search for strong man approaches to politics. These are danger times. Physical danger leads to the legislation (IRA, terrorism, coronavirus) and people will allow a devil's bargain with the state to address it. And I am very sympathetic to it myself. I've spoken about feeling threatened after 9/11. It felt like the world was coming apart. In my feelings, in my mind, I felt the pull of 'go to war', let's blow something. I wouldn't have supported torturing people, but I felt the pull. I realised if I felt it, then anyone else can. What do we do in these times when our values change temporarily?'

This was a refreshingly honest and important insight into how fear of physical danger can shape our reactions to law, society, even war. Wagner agreed that we 'fight the same battles every generation. The same stuff happens in human societies over and over again. If people have too much power they will abuse it.'

I questioned what lessons we had forgotten from previous generations. 'When I first started out at the bar I was involved in an inquiry on the use of torture on Iraqi detainees,' said Wagner. 'They used the five stress techniques of psychological and physical torture that were used in the time of the IRA. The military said in the 1970s that they would never use those tactics again. By the 2000s no one knew about this judgement. Both possibilities are troubling: they either forgot or ignored it.' This seems to encapsulate our problems in one depressing example.

Silkie Carlo, Director of Big Brother Watch, put it to me plainly that we are living through 'the greatest loss of liberty in modern Britain and it has happened by diktat. This is how autocracies and dictatorships emerge, for the "greater good", measure by measure.'

Carlo said we should be vigilant about the Big Tech response and state surveillance. 'I'm struggling to understand how some of the mistakes have been made. It's been a cacophony of disaster. With contact tracing, the government wanted to collect as much data as possible and hold it centrally. They were basically asking people to be on a state-issued digital tag. We warned them that there are serious risks with this. A lot of public money has been wasted. The government doesn't understand that they need public trust, but that doesn't come from rhetoric and finger-wagging. You can't force people, you need a high degree of trust. That trust did not exist with the app.' Also, more covert surveillance powers may be being used, including 'sentiment analysis'. I asked if she meant our private Facebook timelines? 'Facebook and "private" don't belong in the same sentence,' she shot back.

Normally the use of new technology in policing would follow substantive public debate, but Covid has accelerated the take-up of drones and facial recognition software. Carlo cited the example of a police force in Wales using a drone to disperse people who had been standing in line outside a pharmacy for prescriptions, a 'dehumanising and intimidating' form of policing.

She was also cautious about the introduction of thermal scanning. There is no evidence it is an accurate measure of whether someone has a fever. It also ignores that people know better than an infrared scanner when they are ill. After all, we don't send our children to school or visit the Apple Store with a fever. It can also lead to what she called 'surveillance stacking': 'First it's thermal scanning, then they might add facial recognition, then automated age, gender and behavioural data-gathering. We have to be cautious it doesn't lead to a society with diminished freedoms.' Of course, if it doesn't actually work, it's also a pointless pantomime of public health and a waste of money.

I had to agree to one of my sons having his temperature taken before a dental appointment, or he would have been declined care. As though I would not know if he had a fever and was ill? I'll admit I sent one son on a Duke of Edinburgh trip with a slightly broken arm, but I definitely know when they are so ill they have a fever. More to the point, they know when they are ill. Pointing temperature guns at our heads before we cross thresholds does not improve public health.

Like Sumption and Brimelow, solicitor Stephen Jackson explained that he was so concerned about the misrepresentation of guidance as law that he felt compelled to act. He founded the website Law or Fiction to help ordinary citizens as well as employers make sense of the emergency legislation. 'I was astounded to read that the government had only "requested" schools to close in the Simon Dolan[4] case. But I watched the Prime Minister tell us all on television that schools must close. The government has behaved duplicitously towards the public. It shows a worrying level of disdain,' he said.

He said he'd received many messages from confused and worried people, some quite heartbreaking, such as a new mother who needed a doctor to examine her burst and infected episiotomy stitches. Astonishingly, she was not offered an appointment, but was asked to send a photograph of her genitals to an unsecured practice email address. This inconceivably insensitive and intrusive request is no substitute for proper medical care.

'People think physical contact is not allowed,' he said. 'There are sad cases of people thinking that they must only wave through the window at family, grandparents think they can't hug their grandchildren. But they are allowed. And imagine the barbarity of not being able to say goodbye to loved ones on their deathbed. This creates permanent scars.'

Barrister Francis Hoar wrote an article[5] arguing that the emergency regulations were incompatible with human rights. On reading it, a businessman called Simon Dolan, who also believed that the government had acted illegally and disproportionately, contacted Hoar. Together with solicitors Wedlake Bell they mounted a legal challenge against the government. They argued that the lockdown regulations removed the right to liberty by restricting people to stay in their houses, the right to a private and family life, the right to freedom of religion and expression of that, the right to protest and free assembly, plus the damaging effect on business interests and education. Another important part of the challenge was whether the government was right to make the emergency laws under the Public Health Act, and that the government had fettered its discretion by providing the five restrictions which all referred to the virus and did not refer to anything else.

I visited Hoar in his chambers. A portrait of his ancestor Sir Nicolas Tindal hung on the wall, a judge whose judgements protected many from execution by codifying the protection of insane defendants from conviction. This same passion was evident in Hoar: 'I don't mind being an outsider. There are a number of times that the establishment has got it wrong before. I'm in a profession where one is supposed to protect the outliers and the vulnerable. The great heroes of mine have often done that, even when the prevailing opinion was extremely unpopular. That's what a barrister should do.'

I met Hoar before the ultimately unsuccessful Judicial Review and subsequent appeal. When we met he was uncertain but hopeful about protecting the vulnerable, but observed that 'What is terrifying is that this wasn't just imposed by governments, people wanted it. Of course people can choose to stay in their homes, but they wanted it to be law, to impose these restrictions on others.'

Sumption, Brimelow, Carlo, Jackson, Wagner and Hoar were united in their dedicated efforts to speak up for the law and democracy, during a year when most of Britain was more worried about loo roll than the rule of law, and had not understood the seriousness of what was happening to the country.

Sumption was visibly tired during our interview, ready for the holiday he was departing for the next day. Presumably the campaign he had waged had taken its toll. He took a few minutes during the interview to prune his beautiful garden. In the garden I asked him if he felt his public defence of civil liberties was a duty, or a mission. 'No, it wasn't a mission, that smacks of fanaticism. It was not my duty, it was the duty of politicians. The reason I have done it is that I thought this was an outrage which was deeply damaging to civil liberties. No politician was prepared to put their head above the parapet and say that this was disgraceful and profoundly damaging to our traditions and to the people who are least affected by the virus because they are young. Somebody had to say it.' It may not have been his duty, and his interventions as a former Supreme Court judge have come in for criticism, but his campaign does seem to have been driven by a sense of moral duty and public service.

When Carlo and I sat in the lounge of her modest flat in London, she told me she worked 20-hour days in the early weeks, reviewing the legislation and producing Big Brother Watch's monthly reports for parliamentarians. 'I'd never let my team do this, but I had to put in those hours. I feel a sense of duty. I couldn't live with myself if I didn't do everything that I can. There were days I didn't leave this room, I'd sleep for three hours on the sofa, because that's all the time I could take.'

Sumption and Carlo live in the same city but are socially and economically miles apart. One is an ex-judge and OBE of considerable standing, and the other heads up a small NGO. Ordinarily, this should be an insignificant detail, but I found myself comforted by the fact that people across the spectrum of society were prepared to speak up, more concerned with character than reputation, and compelled by a sense of moral duty to do what they know is right, no matter how difficult.

Francis Hoar said the country needed more lawyers to do their part: 'The rule of law does not exist in isolation. It depends upon lawyers and judges prepared to defend it against government power: not just through their cases but through condemning the state for stripping individual liberty. It is our responsibility as lawyers to do so.'

The law is ours. As Roger Scruton said, 'English law is the property of the English people and not the weapon of their rulers.' The British public needs to remember that. Johnson and Hancock, along with all Members of Parliament, are public servants. They have a duty to enact and use law wisely, proportionately and respectfully. Protecting the law and deserving its protection are one and the same. We should all be custodians.

Is it time to release democracy from quarantine and resuscitate the rule of law?

SAM, 30, PARAMEDIC

I've seen a lot of mental health problems, distress, and suicide attempts this year. We're always at the local bridge with people who want to jump.

O ne thing that's different about this year is that a lot more middle-class and upper-class people are suffering and trying to take their lives because they can't get jobs. I've also come across a lot of grief; people haven't had the opportunity to grieve properly for people who have died this year and that causes a huge psychological impact and trauma. Fear and grief can affect us more than the physical.

Young people having anxiety episodes because they are so worried about having Covid. People have called us out because they want a Covid test and they don't want to leave the house.

I talked a 25-year-old woman off the bridge whose mental health had got a lot worse in lockdown. She'd had problems for years, had then got better and was off medication, but in lockdown she went badly downhill. Weirdly, it was the first time as a paramedic I could relate to that. I sympathised and told her I agreed that the lockdown measures were too hard to live with. I said it in front of the police who were there. Jobs like that hit me the most. There's no bloody need – a 25-year-old woman should not be on a bridge in despair and so isolated she wants to die. These measures are not normal, it's not right for human beings to live like this.

16. TERRIFYING IMPACTS

T his is a collection of some of the ways we were impacted by fear and restrictions during the epidemic. Some of these impacts are as a direct result of fear, and some as a result of lockdown, which is related to fear. After all, could we have consented to lockdown and complied with the rules if we weren't scared into submission? I have not included the impacts caused by Covid itself.

DEATH
- 40,000 excess deaths from the economic impacts over the next 50 years, as reduced income, unemployment and anxiety reduce life expectancy.[1]
- 32,000 excess deaths among adults in social care by the end of March 2021 due to reduction in support and people being discharged from hospital early.[1]
- 18,000 deaths due to cancelled operations.[1]
- 10,000 deaths due to disruption to emergency care.[1]
- 4,000 deaths due to not seeking help, even when suffering a heart attack or stroke.[1]
- There was a 52% increase in excess deaths of people dying of dementia during the first wave.[2]
- The equivalent of 560,000 lives will be lost as a result of lockdown. (This was calculated before the third lockdown.)[3]

MENTAL HEALTH
- The number of adults who experienced some form of depression increased from one in 10 to one in five during lockdown, by June 2020.[4]
- 15% of people reported depression, anxiety, or fear as a direct result of government pandemic advertising.[5]

- One in eight adults developed moderate to severe depression during lockdown.[6]
- Nine out of 10 autistic people worried about their mental health during lockdown.[7]
- Autistic people were seven times more likely to be chronically lonely than the general population during lockdown.[8]
- Half of 16 to 25-year-olds said their mental health has worsened since the start of the pandemic.[9]
- 1.5 million children and 8.5 million adults will need support for depression, anxiety, post-traumatic stress disorders and other mental health difficulties in the coming months and years.[10]
- One in three adults increased their consumption of alcohol during the first lockdown to cope with stress.[11]
- There was a 16.4% increase in deaths from alcohol-specific causes between January and September 2020 compared with the previous year.[12] (An inquiry is needed to understand this, but I'm putting this impact in the mental health section for obvious reasons.)
- There was a 20% increase in opiate addictions and a 39% increase in number of relapses among addicts.[13]
- There were 15,541 calls relating to suicide or attempted suicide recorded by London Ambulance Service in the first six months of lockdown, from March to November 2020, compared to 11,703 calls over the same period in 2019.[14]
- 87% of people with an eating disorder have seen their symptoms worsen because of social isolation.[15]
- 161,699 fewer people per month in 2020 were able to contact mental health services than in 2019.[16]

HEALTH

- Six in 10 people reported worse sleep since lockdown was announced.[17]
- Psychological stress is associated in a dose-response manner with an increased risk of acute infectious

respiratory illness, so fear and lockdown measures would probably have increased infection.[18]

- 27 million missed GP appointments by October 2020.[19]
- 350,000 missed specialist referrals for cancer.[20]
- Cancer Research estimated there could be 35,000 avoidable cancer deaths as a result of lockdown.[21]
- 30% of those who had a stroke during the pandemic delayed seeking emergency medical attention due to Covid-19. There were 825 excess deaths for stroke and 1,834 excess deaths for cardiovascular diseases (including cardiac arrest) as a result of delays to seeking help (or potentially the result of undiagnosed Covid-19).[13]
- Deaths from diabetes were 161.6% above average, potentially due to delays in care, from anxiety about seeking care or an overburdened healthcare system.[13]
- Until 8 September 2020, birthing partners were prevented from attending scans and early labour, causing stress and leaving women to endure difficult labours, traumatic news and miscarriages alone.

SOCIETY

- 45,000 extra homeless people since the start of lockdown.[22]
- More than three-quarters of councils across England saw an increase in homelessness in their area since the start of the pandemic. More than four in 10 have seen a significant increase.[23]
- Half of children entitled to free school meals did not have access to the scheme during Covid-19 lockdown in the UK.[24]
- 20% increase in babies suffering non-accidental harm.[17]
- There was a rise of 49% in the number of calls to domestic abuse services.[25]
- Two-thirds of domestic abuse victims were subjected to more violence from their partners during lockdown.[26]
- 5.6 million people are struggling to afford essentials or have borrowed to make ends meet. The amount of arrears and borrowing among this group attributable to the

impact of coronavirus is £10.3 billion.[27]

- A 25% reduction in pre-pandemic learning for primary school children and a 30% reduction for secondary school children.[13]
- The first lockdown saw the cancellation of 15,000 theatrical performances resulting in a loss of £303 million.[13]

ECONOMY

- The UK's GDP fell by 9.9% in 2020, the worst result of any G7 country, and worst contraction the UK economy has experienced since the Great Frost of 1709.[28]
- The increase in public sector net borrowing (March to November 2020 rise in OBR estimates) could be as much as £385.2 billion.[13]
- Unemployment is expected to increase by between 450,000 and 2.45 million above pre-pandemic levels.[13]
- More than a quarter of pubs do not believe they will stay in business after lockdown.[13]
- The creative industries project a loss of £77 billion in 2020.[13]
- The manufacturing sector faced a Gross Value Added (GVA) loss of £71.7 billion from the first two lockdowns.[13]
- The construction sector faced a GVA loss of £40 billion from the first two lockdowns.[13]
- The retail sector faced a GVA loss of £33.8 billion from the first two lockdowns.[13]
- The impact on hospitality was a £37.4 billion loss.[13]

ELLA, 47

My fear is authoritarianism. That other people will think they know what is best for us. I don't believe in our leaders, so I can't trust my environment and the world feels unanchored.

People have lost their minds with fear this year. We aren't used to fear anymore. They are searching for a crescendo in life, an epiphany which they normally get from Netflix. They've imploded with the crisis of Covid. I think if people practised more mindfulness, if they were more present in the moment, they would have managed better.

This year has been a wake up call that people are shit with knowing they are temporary. I am OK with dying; we are here for a finite time. I'd like my children to live longer than me, but I don't think I'm entitled to a longer life than I am going to get.

Lockdown has taught people to ignore feelings and ignore faith. When churches close, when schools close, and isolation becomes the norm, you cannot experience faith in the full. I am not a Christian, but I know what is right and wrong and I trust my faith. The government killed God. It's as simple as that. To put protecting yourself from death above everything is killing God. I wasn't brought up with religion, but I have faith. I believe my consciousness will live forever.

The art of living is not just about having brilliant things happen, it's also about carrying the burden of loss. Life is about feeling.

Courage is fear in disguise.

17. WHY FEAR SHOULD NOT BE WEAPONISED

'Nothing in life is to be feared, it is only to be understood. Now is the time to understand more, so that we may fear less.'
Marie Curie

In the introduction I confessed my discovery that I was more frightened of authoritarianism than death, and more disturbed by manipulation than sickness. Has my fear helped or hindered me? For several weeks into lockdown in the spring of 2020, fear gave me a sick feeling of dread in my stomach a few seconds after I'd woken. Oh God, this is real, it's not just a bad dream. That can't have been a healthy way to start the day. Many studies have shown the link between psychological stress and the immune system.[1] Fear also disconnected me from the usual pleasures of life and my senses were dulled. Even the spring blossom smelt sad. I was not in control of these responses; fear took over. But fear also gave me new intellectual and creative direction. It's made me reconsider what I want from my government. Fear made me write a book.

Fear, like hope, can be very motivating and is not inherently bad. It is an adaptive emotion that mobilises our energy to respond to threat. The challenge is to identify when fear is being used deceptively or to manipulate, or is not well-calibrated to the actual threat and overwhelms us. If we are nudged towards a 'greater good' we play no active role in deciding what 'good' is. We have handed over the big decisions. We are like children being guided by adults who know best. If rule is by 'science' and we, the ignorant population, don't get to review the software code of the models behind our new commandments, it is akin to the peasantry enduring sermons in Latin before the first English translations of the Bible.

The obvious argument in favour of fear is that the use of fear is acceptable if it works, if it kept us safe and if there is a net benefit for society. What did the government policies – lockdown, restrictions, a blitzkrieg of behavioural psychology – keep us safe from? Not unemployment, not other types of ill health, not death and certainly not fear. In fact, they couldn't keep us safe from Covid-19 either. Lockdowns don't work. Now these are strong words. You may splutter – 'but, but, but!' – and think my position is ludicrously counter-intuitive. But many international studies now offer the empirical evidence that lockdowns failed to contain the virus, and at the same time they are a blunt tool which causes great harms. The efficacy of lockdowns is not central to the tenets of this book, but if you want more of my thinking on lockdowns you can read the 'Lockdowns don't work' essay in Appendix 2. Now, back to fear and why it should be not weaponised:

1. FEAR SLOWS RECOVERY

'Fear is a disastrous way to do public health messaging,' said Lucy Easthope, 'and goes against everything we know about how to do health risk communication. Working on CBRN threats (chemical, biological, radiological and nuclear weapons) taught me that weaponising fear to get the response you want causes you insurmountable problems in long-term recovery. Health risk communication is a science but most of that science has been ignored, not followed, during the Covid epidemic.'

Easthope told me 'it's going to take a long time for us to come out of this', because the government deliberately exaggerated the risks of the disease. Fear will slow recovery. And then the next problem is that the 'government don't know what normal looks like. They are genuinely muddling through, but they don't know that recovery is when the birds are singing and children are playing in the playground, not mass testing and death dashboards. The humanistic recovery planner would say stop the dashboards. Stop. We don't do it for *Clostridium difficile*.'

It is obvious and intuitive that fear will inhibit our recovery.

In fact, Easthope said it means recovery will be '1,000 times harder'. But let's flesh out an example. As an MP told me, masks were introduced to give people confidence to go shopping. People were scared and the economy didn't bounce back hard enough after the first lockdown. Thus, masks were mandated.

Introducing a measure without an exit strategy can create more problems. In this case, it is that we are still wearing masks. They have turned the UK population into walking billboards that announce we are in a deadly epidemic. Every time you go into a public space you are reminded by masks of the epidemic. And then the idea that they help (even if they do not) is reinforced. Did you survive your trip to the supermarket? Only because you were wearing a mask! Did you contract Covid on the Tube? No? It must be the mask that saved you! The unintended consequence of the masks is that they keep the fear alive and modify our behaviour, and this has proven useful as far as the behavioural scientists are concerned. As late as January 2021, David Halpern was referring to the useful 'signal'[2] masks give.

Fear also slowed the reopening of schools, as Gavin Morgan, SPI-B advisor, told me, because parents and teachers over-estimated the dangers. Fear means the 'roadmap' to recovery is measured in the tiny tottering steps of battle-weary statesmen who must avoid the landmines of error, lest they detonate public condemnation and media derision. Of course, it makes total sense that our rulers wield fear against us, when we realise that they are also ruled by fears.

If we want to recover, if we want life to go back to normal, we need to dial down the cortisol. One of the simplest measures the government could take would be to remove the mask mandate. They are not backed up by convincing scientific evidence or medical necessity (at least, the government hasn't shown us this evidence) and they are primarily a behavioural psychology tool which is a perfect example of unintended consequences. Masks are a visual metaphor signalling danger, perpetuating the fear and disrupting the human connection and communication which will be vital to society's recovery.

2. THE PUBLIC HAVE NOT BEEN CONSULTED ON THE ETHICS, OR CONSENTED

If psychologists wanted to make people very frightened in a lab experiment, it would be difficult to obtain the ethics approval, especially for an experiment which mimicked this scale and severity. Informed consent for participants would be essential though. Participants would not be allowed to leave the lab unless they were as happy and in as well a state as they arrived. They would certainly not be left in a state of fear.

The British Psychological Society has a *Code of Ethics & Conduct*.[3] Under 'Ethical Principles', it states: 'Psychologists value the dignity and worth of all persons, with sensitivity to the dynamics of perceived authority or influence over persons and peoples and with particular regard to people's rights.' It goes on to say that in applying these values, psychologists should consider consent, issues of power, self-determination and compassionate care.

It seems to me, and to the psychologists who wrote to the BPS, that the behavioural psychologists advising the government have blatantly failed to practise in a way that is consistent with those stated ethical values regarding the fear messaging.

Importantly, we the public have never been consulted about the subliminal methods of manipulation they wield against us. Perhaps we didn't take it seriously enough when they were pushing forward seemingly innocuous changes like making cigarette packaging plain, or encouraging prompt tax returns. But using fear, shaming and scapegoating manipulate our emotions in far more serious and harmful ways.

Ultimately, do campaigns of fear express the best of humanity? Do we imagine a healthy, virtuous and pleasant society populated with scary ads designed to force us into following rules? Is that really what we want?

3. FEAR CREATES COLLATERAL DAMAGE

The use of fear intrudes on our private lives, our minds and our physiological health. The messaging of fear exposes us, against our will, to harmful and offensive messages and creates unnecessary anxiety. That is exactly why the

Advertising Standards Authority has codified against the use of fear.

The fear salesmen – the government, the psychocrats advising them, the media and the scare-mongering scientists – peddled their wares to us throughout 2020 and into 2021. There is no money back guarantee, no refunds or exchanges, the sale is now complete. Was fear a bad purchase?

Chapter 16, 'Terrifying Impacts', provided a brutal list of the impacts of the policy of fear and the social and economic restrictions that were enabled by the compliance that fear generated. The government has been remiss in not quantitatively analysing the costs and benefits of its Covid policies, probably because the numbers will not look good. On 22 March 2021, just one day before the anniversary of lockdown, Chris Whitty acknowledged in a press briefing that the government had known 'right from the beginning the lockdown was going to have really severe effects on many people's health'.[4] He added: 'For many people, physical or mental wellbeing have been very badly affected by this. Ranging from increased levels of domestic abuse, loneliness – particularly in older people who felt very much isolated in their areas – physical health, people maybe exercising less, greater amounts of alcohol consumption.' He also said that coronavirus restrictions would affect livelihoods for years, with government able only to 'reduce and not eliminate' those effects.

At the worst end of the scale there is concern that fear and isolation might have driven suicide attempts, but it is too early for the data. Humans are intensely social and as Patrick Fagan observed in a comprehensive essay on fear, self-isolation and confinement at home can contribute to many 'psychopathological outcomes – such as fatigue, sleep disorders, cognitive impairment, delusions, anxiety, depression, hostility, loss of self-esteem, and lower wellbeing – as well as, ironically, a compromised immune system'.[5]

One of the most distressing collateral damages is the mental health epidemic among children. Children as young as eight 'are self-harming amid an unprecedented mental health crisis fuelled by the stress of lockdown',[6] said accident and emergency consultant, Dr Dave Greenhorn. It is estimated that 1.5 million children and 8.5 million adults will need support for depression, anxiety, post-traumatic stress disorders and other mental health difficulties in the coming months and years, according to the Centre for Mental Health.[7] As their chief economist said, 'the numbers are stark'.

It is the personal stories which illuminate the crisis. Quantitative analysis for the policies is overdue, but the analysis must also be qualitative – we need to hear people's stories. This is why I interviewed a range of people whose lives were affected by the policies of fear.

I followed up with a few of these interviewees, to see how they were feeling. I was pleased to hear that Susan, 15, felt much better and stopped self-harming once she was back at school. Jane had started taking anti-depressants and felt better once she was back at work. Unfortunately her husband had been diagnosed – very late due to healthcare delays – with a rare and difficult type of cancer. Mark was trying to challenge his agoraphobia by going shopping occasionally and this time felt the benefit of the return to the office. Jimmy, who tried to kill himself, is now, thankfully, coping with the support of his family. Sadly, Dave, the doctor, told me that the woman with children who suffered irreversible brain damage following a suicide attempt died soon after we had spoken.

An onslaught of scare-mongering is known to be a health risk. The report *COVID-19 and the 24/7 News Cycle: Does COVID-19 News Exposure Affect Mental Health?* found, unsurprisingly, that 'the 24/7 news cycle covering the virus may amplify perceived threats and have harmful effects on mental health'.[8] And in the US, the CDC (Centers for Disease Control and Prevention) suggests that after a disaster people take care of their emotional health by taking 'breaks from watching, reading, or listening to news stories. It can be upsetting to hear about the crisis and see images repeatedly. Try to do enjoyable activities and return to normal life as much as possible and check for updates between breaks.'[9]

The links between fear and anxiety and health cannot always be proven to be causal, but there is obvious cause for concern and potential for fear messaging to reduce health and happiness. It serves us to remember the basic Hippocratic principle: 'First, do no harm.'

4. LEADERS BUILD FALSE MORAL AUTHORITY AND PROFIT

Sometimes, those who rule do not have our best interests at heart. A little scepticism is healthy, even necessary. Of course, we won't solve this conundrum by saying we don't trust politicians and by retreating from political life. The opposite: we need to ask questions, even when we are being encouraged to fall into line.

Norman Baker, former Liberal Democrat MP, wrote an article[10] for the *Daily Mail* about the day that anthrax was deliberately released in a tunnel on the Northern Line by scientists from the UK government's Porton Down laboratory. As he explained, it was far from the only time they've used Britons as guinea pigs for experiments. These are the kinds of incidents in British history which would startle and horrify most people, who assume unethical experimentation is the preserve of the Nazis.

We had a conversation about the Covid crisis. He emphasised that 'even in a democracy we should never assume the government of the day is right or even well-intentioned. That's not how a democracy works. Even now, at a time of a public health crisis, it is our duty to question. That doesn't mean to assume the government is lying. We know enough to ask whether governments are acting in your best interests or theirs. People have a very low opinion of politicians, and recent reasons have included the Iraq war and the expenses scandal. But, for some reason, they believe the government unwaveringly about an issue of their security, such as an epidemic.'

So, did he think the public ought not to believe the government about the epidemic? 'They've made all sorts of errors,' he said, 'but, worse, we know they have behaved in ways which are inappropriate, such as giving contracts out to their mates and to Tory donors. There's no doubt in my mind we've wasted money on mates to the government.'

As I said in Chapter 14, 'Cults, conspiracy and psychic

epidemics', we must be aware that 'disaster capitalism'– a complex series of networks and influence employed by private companies and governments that allows them to profit from disasters – happens during shock and fear. Governments create fear, then cultivate and exploit it. We won't understand the convergent agendas, the lean to authoritarianism, or how chaos translated to cash until later, and certainly not until we can assess rationally. To think rationally we need to be less frightened. I put this to Baker and he concurred, saying that he believed people had suspended their 'analytic powers because they are worried about dying' and felt 'powerless'. It is at this point more than ever he believes people need to ask the difficult questions.

5. THE USE OF FEAR IS ANTI-DEMOCRATIC

'The use of fear is anti-democratic,' sociologist Dr Ashley Frawley told me. 'There is a lack of belief in the human subject, a subject that is seen as animalistic, incapable of understanding risk, and weak. The behavioural psychologists saw people's proportionate responses to risk as a problem that needed to be overcome. The use of fear assumes you could never deal with this epidemic by using democratic means. And then it becomes a self-fulfilling prophecy, because fear affects our ability to assess risk.'

The weaponisation of fear is a particularly destabilising tactic in the behavioural psychology toolbox because it clouds our judgement, which in turn increases reliance on government, which then creates more fear, which paralyses us further, creating a self-perpetuating doom-loop. William Sargant said that successful brainwashing demands 'the rousing of strong emotions'. Your pliability is exaggerated by your fears.

Governments understand that fear is an unarguable fact of human psychology. History shows us that they will leverage fear, supposedly in our interests, 'for our own good', at the same time as advancing other interests which might not suit us so well. A government that nudges does not trust the people. A government that nudges has given up on debate and transparency and opted for covert manipulation – that is something to be wary of, if not frightened.

During the Covid epidemic, the UK government threatened us with longer lockdowns or tougher restrictions if we misbehaved, and rewards such as the return of the 'rule of six' or garden meetings were dangled in front of us if all went well. The relationship between government and citizen was reminiscent of a strict parent and child relationship, with alternating use of the naughty step and then offering sweets for good behaviour. Citizens were not treated like adults. We were told frightening 'bedtime stories' every day via the news and Downing Street briefings to ensure compliance with a set of ever-changing and sometimes bizarre rules.

There is something intrinsically infantilising about nudge. The behavioural scientists sometimes let the paternalism show through the chinks with their references to locking up the biscuit tin, or comparing us to children who don't need to be asked if we want to learn to read, as though whatever they plan for us is exactly the same as reading.

Claire Fox, Director of the Academy of Ideas, has crossed swords with the behavioural psychologists in the past and is also concerned about the impact on democracy. 'Libertarians have argued in favour of nudge because it avoids state regulation and rules and outright coercion. Instead nudge theories are used to get the outcomes the government wants,' she said. 'It's not a surprise that this government consider themselves to be libertarians and use nudge. And then the political left likes nudge because the left has also lost faith in ordinary people's decisions. Nudge is worse than the nanny state. The nanny state tells you what it is doing, you can push back against it.'

I agreed with her. You know where you are with a clear regulation, you can debate and dispute and change it, but often we can't detect the use of nudges. Did she think of nudge as a sneaky way to manipulate people? 'Yes. You should be free to make decisions about your lifestyle regardless of the outcome. A scientist can tell you not to smoke because it is a killer. That is the right thing to do. They should tell you that and then walk away. You decide whether to smoke or not. But today's public health scientists have decided how the model citizen lives and, for them, the model citizen is not drinking excessively or eating the wrong food or smoking or all kinds of things. But who agrees that that is the best way to live? The 'Good Life' is disputed all the time. It is humanity's struggle to discover the Good Life.'

In *Propaganda*, Edward Bernays said: 'The systematic study of mass psychology revealed the potentialities of invisible government of society by manipulation... the group has mental characteristics distinct from those of the individual, and is motivated by impulses and emotions which cannot be explained on the basis of what we know of individual psychology. So the question naturally arose: If we understand the mechanism and motives of the group mind, is it not possible to control and regiment the masses according to our will without their knowing it?'

His work built on Freud's belief that there is a divorce between a person's conscious thoughts and their suppressed feelings. According to Bernays, it is this which makes human beings manipulable. Governments can therefore design propaganda or psychological operations that go beneath the conscious and rational mind of the individual, targeting suppressed emotions and desires instead, making it possible to manipulate people without them being aware of the underlying motivations.

The suppressed fear of death is supremely powerful combined with the rationally imposed ideas of solidarity and conformity and protecting others. The unconscious mind is manipulable using the most morally virtuous rational reasons, rendering people pliable. And thus, 'three weeks to flatten the curve' morphed into living under a year of emergency laws, to hundreds of statutory instruments passed by ministerial diktat, to the proposal of a potential new medical digital ID. If you believe in democracy you must be suspicious of the use of psychology to manipulate you against your will. Nudge is anti-democratic. The use of fear is a sinister form of control.

18. HAPPY ENDINGS ARE NOT WRITTEN IN THE LANGUAGE OF COERCIVE CONTROL

The vaccine programme appears to be the Happy Ending to the Horrible Story of the Covid-19 pandemic. But I am cautious. Not because I am 'anti-vax', but because I have observed that this stage of the story is also being written in the language of emotional manipulation and coercive control.

Some of the vaccine messaging is optimistic, proud and forward-looking. Some is straight from the behavioural science handbook. The message 'Impfen = Freiheit' which translates as 'Vaccination = Freedom' was projected on a TV tower in Düsseldorf, Germany. Proud optimism or blatant propaganda?

The term 'vaccine hesitancy' is now used to describe the attitude of people who have decided not to get vaccinated. It implies a slight pathologisation, that those reluctant to have a vaccine may have some sort of mental condition, rather than be making an individual choice based on risk analysis and rational preferences. It is designed to denigrate the vaccine sceptic, to make them look a bit silly. It also implies the 'hesitation' is just a step towards the inevitable, part of the process – come on dear, we'll get you over that hump and you'll have your vaccination in the end. Surely an ad hominem attack is less ethical and robustly persuasive than evidence would be?

Some of the language around Covid vaccines ticks the boxes of Biderman's 'Chart of Coercion' (p142–3). In December 2020, the NHS published a document for health professionals called *Optimising Vaccination Roll Out – Dos and Don'ts for all messaging, documents and "communications" in the widest sense.*[1]

Although I talked about the possible propaganda aimed at encouraging vaccine take up in BAME communities in Chapter 8, 'Controlled spontaneity and propaganda', this messaging is a broader departure from the public health language for the wider population. Certain recommended phrases are emotionally manipulative in a way that would affect informed consent. For instance, 'normality can only return for you and others, with your vaccination' and 'if you want to be able to do what you want, then having the vaccine is the fastest and safest way to achieving this'. Why can normality only return after vaccination? If you do not get vaccinated is the message that you prevent everyone else getting back to normality?

I discussed it with psychologist Gary Sidley, who said this 'fits the definition of blackmail' although 'the blatant nature of it is a little surprising'. Public health expert and doctor Jackie Cassell agreed that the document contains 'pretty extreme language' and that 'the whole approach is very much from the SPI-B playbook'.

Cassell was deeply uncomfortable about this extreme language. 'I can't imagine how a doctor could use these arguments,' she said. 'Using peer norms as a direct form of persuasion is not something that comes readily to doctors and we don't speak that language. It goes against our professional training. A vaccine is a medical intervention and people have to consent to it. I wouldn't use the arguments in this document in these ways.' I wondered why the language was so at odds with how doctors are trained to work, and she responded that 'it brings up some interesting disciplinary perspectives, if not fault lines. The behavioural scientists and nudgers occupy a very different space. They are thinking like psychology-trained advertisers, like they are trying to get us to buy fashion or whatever. Asking health professionals to use this kind of language could be profoundly damaging to the trust in government and health services.'

The coercive language in this NHS document shows how integral the behavioural psychology approach now is. This is also apparent in the recruitment of new behavioural science roles in the NHS, Public Health England and various government departments in recent months and years. And not everyone in public health agrees with it. If behavioural psychology is here to stay then it's clear that, at the very least, the different disciplines need greater synergy to ensure that reflective thought about ethics and informed consent is not a thing of the past.

On the world stage, politicians as well as representatives of the WHO, United Nations, Gavi (the Vaccine Alliance) and the World Economic Forum have all parroted the same phrase: 'No one is safe until everyone is safe'. Language is being coordinated – but by whom? The phrase is literally not true: if you have the vaccine, you have the protection it confers.

Boris Johnson announced on 25 March 2021 that 'there is going to be a role for vaccine certification'.[2] He justified the imposition of Covid certificates that might allow businesses to bar unvaccinated customers by saying that the public 'want me as prime minister to take all the action I can to protect them'.[3] *The Sun* duly ran the headline 'No Jab, No Pint'.

There's a feeling after a year of restrictions that people will do anything to 'get back to normal'. But declaring your health status to use businesses and services has never been normal. The introduction of a health status ID to access products and services will cross a rubicon.

Some people are now overly anxious about other people's immune status. In fact, the constant requirement for reassurance, through certificates and checkpoints, could actually 'end up promoting fear and anxiety that are not proportionate to the perils involved', according to Robert Dingwall, sociologist and government advisor.

Once the over-50s and vulnerable categories have been vaccinated, 98% of the risk of death and 80 to 85% of the risk of serious illness will have been eliminated.[4] On that basis, the vaccine programme is a success for at-risk individuals and for society as a whole. So, what would the point of Covid certificates be? After all, the only thing that matters is your own immune status. If you are vaccinated, you are protected. If someone is not vaccinated next to you at the bar, it will not matter because you are vaccinated.

The push for certification is reminiscent of yet another behavioural science strategy. The kinds of people who populate the advisory panels close to government are very risk-averse. They are focused on the importance of vaccination, and 'forcing' their view of good health on to us, and perhaps dismissive of ethical and social considerations. Allowing private businesses to discriminate against the unvaccinated allows the government to avoid mandating vaccinations, but at the same time makes it impossible for people to go about their normal lives without vaccination. It is a form of coercion.

I asked Dingwall if he thought this push for vaccine certificates is a behavioural psychology 'nudge'. 'It's a nudge for low-risk groups, once the high-risk groups have been vaccinated', he said. 'Perhaps the worry is about vaccination uptake among younger people. But why not cross that bridge if we come to it? Public health should not be about bullying people, it should be about advising them.' Jackie Cassell also had reservations about certification: 'Vaccines tap into our relationships with personhood and state. I hate the idea of biosecurity. We don't have a passport for measles because, by and large, we have a fantastic vaccination scheme and uptake. Biosecurity won't make people get vaccinated, feel safe, or have confidence in government and the NHS.'

Is this a case of the government capitalising on disaster? Matt Hancock said in September 2019 that the government was 'looking very seriously'[5] at making vaccinations mandatory for school pupils. Is Covid-19 being used as the excuse to usher in a change that the government already wanted? He said at the time that 'when the state provides services to people then it's a two-way street – you've got to take your responsibilities, too'. But this is autocratic thinking in disguise, where 'responsibility' means doing what you are told. He said he thought that 'the public would back us'. I think that would have been unlikely at the time, as it would have been a huge change for the British socially, ethically and legally. But there's nothing like a pandemic for shifting the dial on mandatory vaccines. Indeed, in March 2021, Hancock announced that the government was looking at making Covid-19 vaccines mandatory for care workers, to the consternation of unions who attacked the plans as 'heavy-handed' and 'authoritarian'.[6]

During the epidemic, public opinion polls functioned like crystal balls, allowing us to gaze at the plans of politicians. While polls are ostensibly supposed to tell the government what we think, they are quite useful for telling us what the government wants us to think and what it wants to do next. And when the results are revealed to us they guide us, through social conformity and the herding instinct, into a preference we never knew we held. As Peter Hitchens said, 'Opinion polls are a device for influencing public opinion, not a device for measuring it. Crack that, and it all makes sense.'[7] In an IPSOS MORI report, David Halpern made a similar comment: 'In a world of behavioural economics, public opinion surveys are themselves a "nudge" – a signal to both policymakers and our fellow citizens about what's acceptable and what's not.'[8]

On 30 September 2020 YouGov asked, 'Once a vaccine has been found, would you support or oppose the government making it compulsory for everyone to receive a vaccination against the coronavirus?' The options allowed you to support, oppose or select 'don't know'. That question was a fairly clear indication of the government's direction of travel at a time when emergency authorisation of a vaccine had not even been granted in the UK. The next question hinted harder at the desired destination: 'And once a vaccine has been found, would you support or oppose the government prosecuting and fining people who do not get a vaccination against the coronavirus?' Before the vaccine had been authorised, long before we would know whether the vaccine interrupted transmission of the virus (that is still not certain at the time of writing) the government was checking to see whether the public would support fines for not having the vaccine.

Just as Hancock's pre-epidemic enthusiasm for mandating vaccines mirrors his post-epidemic interest, might the government's flip-flopping on vaccine passports also align with a previous inclination for such schemes? The European Union published a *Roadmap For The Implementation Of Actions By The European Commission Based On The*

Commission Communication And The Council Recommendation On Strengthening Cooperation Against Vaccine Preventable Diseases[9] which proposed countering vaccine hesitancy, and the development of a common EU vaccination card between 2019 and 2021, to be followed by a 'vaccination card/ passport for EU citizens' that is 'compatible with electronic immunisation information systems and recognised for use across borders' by 2022. Well, that seems to be remarkably on schedule.

Fear has created a morality play where heavy-handed discussions about society-wide vaccine mandates and Covid certificates, or vaccine passports, are privileged over personal responsibility and risk. Does your Happy Ending involve personal responsibility or state mandates? In the desperate desire to end the Horrible Story of the Covid-19 pandemic we are rushing towards a conclusion without being certain enough of our values.

The minister entrusted with reviewing the use of Covid certificates is Michael Gove. As he once said, 'Once powers are yielded to the state at moments of crisis or emergency, it's very rarely the case that the state hands them back.'[10] It will be interesting to see whether the spirit of those words influences the review.

19. MAKING SURE IT NEVER HAPPENS AGAIN

The argument in favour of using fear to command and coerce people during a crisis cannot be justified when we consider the ethics, the collateral damage, and the impact on recovery. How did it work so well? Could fear have taken such a hold if the terrain was not fertile?

In a prescient 2007 article,[1] sociologist, author and fear expert Frank Furedi wrote:

> 'Fear plays a key role in twenty-first century consciousness. Increasingly, we seem to engage with various issues through a narrative of fear. You could see this trend emerging and taking hold in the last century, which was frequently described as an "Age of Anxiety". But in recent decades, it has become more and better defined, as specific fears have been cultivated.
>
> The rise of catchphrases such as the politics of fear, fear of crime and fear of the future is testimony to the cultural significance of fear today. Many of us seem to make sense of our experiences through the narrative of fear. Fear is not simply associated with high-profile catastrophic threats such as terrorist attacks, global warming, AIDS or a potential flu pandemic; rather, as many academics have pointed out, there are also the 'quiet fears' of everyday life.'

Furedi notes that fear is often said to be the defining cultural mood in contemporary society. These fears have led to the ascendancy of public health and safetyism and the heavy leaning on the precautionary principle. The terrain could not have been better ploughed and prepared to grow fear in an epidemic.

History shows us that mass delusions will come and go. Are we particularly susceptible to fear and mass delusions now? When I interviewed psychologist Patrick Fagan, he told me he believes 'we need a discussion about the level of emotional bombardment from all sources: apps, social media, television, government messaging. We're being blown about by our passions. There is a perception that modern technology has made us more rational, when the truth is probably the inverse. Research has shown that smartphones, social media, and the internet more broadly tend to produce a shallower style of thinking – that is, more emotional, more impulsive, and more stereotyped. One paper outlined a case study of a woman driven to psychosis by Twitter, seeing patterns in tweets' characters in a way eerily reminiscent of QAnon. This is all to say nothing of the well-established effect of news content on poor mental wellbeing. Being bombarded with emotional and impulsive content and notifications on a continual basis likely makes us more susceptible to mass hysteria than ever.'

We may look back and wonder if social contagion was more of a threat than epidemic contagion. Social media is awash with bots and trolls, while clever data analytic campaigns behind the scenes manipulate the emotional temperature. And on social media, news travels fast. The study *Bad news has wings: dread risk mediates social amplification in risk communication*[2] examined how bad news stories can turn into mass hysteria when passed from person to person through social media channels. Stories became more negative and tended towards fear and panic as they passed through a message chain.

Think back to those first Chinese videos of 'Stunt Covid' which were viewed many millions of times. Rapid mainstream media coverage ensued, fanning the flames of fear. Social media was the perfect terrain of dry tinder to exaggerate fears. Ideally, mainstream media would dispassionately report and also vigorously fact-check and verify sources, but that didn't always happen. Chapter 2, 'Fear spreads in the media like an airborne virus', looked at the various ways in which the media was complicit in leveraging fear, not least in compensating journalists who generate the most clicks. Finally, at this stage, the fire raging, do you want your government to attend to the flames with bellows or a fire hose?

Recent governments have presided over and benefited from evolving behavioural science, data analytics and propaganda techniques. Dominic Cummings, the political strategist and former chief advisor to Boris Johnson, has been open about the role of data science in the Leave campaign. At the Ogilvy 'Nudgestock Conference' in 2017, he said: 'The future will be about experimental psychology, and data science. The reality is that most communications companies are populated by bullshitting charlatans, and most of them should be fired. Silicon Valley will take over this industry in the same way they've taken over other industries.'[3]

The current government has become expert in 'blowing us about by our passions'. One of the memorable Vote Leave videos was made by agency Topham Guerin, and featured Boris Johnson starring in a pastiche of a *Love Actually* scene. It was amusing but insubstantial puff. If the country votes for leaders based on that level of messaging, it's no surprise we are still being blown about by the same puff. From social media shtick to sophisticated data analytics, we are being manipulated in increasingly effective ways.

There is obviously a need for a robust, honest public inquiry into the management of the Covid-19 epidemic. As a result of my investigations I offer suggestions for some calls to action in the sections below. This book's most important clarion call is for a specific inquiry into the use of behavioural science by government.

How we make sure this never happens again:

1. EVIDENCE-BASED PANDEMIC PLANNING AND PREPAREDNESS
It's worth repeating the following quote from the anonymous scientific advisor deeply embedded in Whitehall. They told me they warned government that there would be severe consequences for excess deaths if the country locked down. 'Lockdown was not the way to go,' they said. 'Bluntly, you should try and power through an epidemic. Lockdown was

obviously going to tank the economy. We have never trained for a lockdown like this. You don't do it for a coronavirus. I've been through all my papers. It's just not something we do.'

But we did do it. Strangely, the narrative in the media and from politicians drifts further towards the idea that we should have locked down earlier and harder. It is still too early to proffer the absolute judgement on excess mortality and the costs and benefits of pharmaceutical and non-pharmaceutical interventions. A robust and honest inquiry must do this.

Lucy Easthope told me that the UK's response has been 'what I would expect to see for a much worse disease. There are no secret plans for a more serious disease like Ebola. People don't know what has been lost for a coronavirus. There wouldn't be a greater loss of liberty for any other disease. This was a massive over-reaction. One of the main problems is we don't have enough critical care beds for an epidemic. We didn't have the PPE. And the government tore up the pandemic plans.'

Why didn't the UK follow the existing evidence-based and rehearsed protocols? Chapter 2, 'Fear spreads in the media like an airborne virus', offered explanations about the pressures which came from social media, and possible bad state actors operating through social media, as well as the traditional press and broadcast media. Chapter 4, 'Fear is a page of the government playbook', looked at how governments use fear to (not necessarily deliberately) ratchet in size and to advance other interests. And I also explored the political bias and motivations of various advisory panels and the 'psychocrats' who have assumed so much power in the decision-making. But there is another more prosaic reason.

Robert Dingwall told me that 'the infrastructures for pandemic planning had been disbanded and the people involved had dispersed. The Department for Health was never supposed to have the role it has taken on. The Cabinet Office for Civil Emergencies Unit should have led across government.' He explained that plans and documentation are simply not always handed over from one generation of civil servants to the next. Think of our pandemic preparedness as languishing in a forgotten filing cabinet.

2. RESPONSIBLE MEDIA

In one of the most unsurprising findings ever, a Dutch study[4] found that exposure to media increased fear. One take-away from the study was that 'stronger messages in the media may induce more fear and therefore more compliance with the social distancing and lockdown policies imposed. However, we caution against using media messages to induce more fear in the general public. There is evidence that suggests that such "fear appeals" do not work very well to promote behaviour change, particularly when people have little coping strategies. Under such circumstances, which may apply to the current COVID-19 crisis, it may not be very helpful to maximise fear, as this may only increase distress. Furthermore, a substantial proportion of respondents in our sample was concerned about the role of (social) media, mass panic, and hysteria. Hence, fear appeals in the media should be used carefully and whether fear appeals work for the current situation requires empirical evaluation.'

Where government and their advisors are using the media to convey policies, to leak news, or for advertising, this is a very important finding to consider. The 'Fourth Estate' has played an enormous role in the behaviour but also the mental health of the population and now in the slow advancement of post-pandemic recovery.

Sometimes the media created insecurities where there were none. We've been here before. Stefanie Grupp wrote in *Political implications of a discourse of fear: the mass mediated discourse of fear in the aftermath of 9/11* that 'fear is decreasingly experienced first-hand and increasingly experienced on a discursive and abstract level'. She also wrote that 'there has been a general shift from a fearsome life towards a life with fearsome media'. It is incumbent on the traditional and social media platforms and outlets to consider their responsibility to their audience in terms of verifying information, and prioritising verified news over clickbait.

A public inquiry should consider: the effect of Ofcom's strict guidance during the epidemic, which stifled essential debate; the incentives and remuneration of journalists to produce clickbait which stokes fear and hysteria; the nature of relationships between editorial and politicians, which is on a scale from uncritical reporting of a ministerial policy to the rumour that there is an MI5 operative in every newsroom; and whether the government's advertising spend compromised editorial integrity.

Big Tech companies wield enormous power in defining the acceptable framework for debate. Their censorship of credible scientists and news articles needs close scrutiny. Also, the social media giants are permitting bad actors to run amok, covertly manipulating public opinion with the use of bot and troll Twitter campaigns and 'fake' grassroots campaigns. Just what are they doing about that? Even more disturbingly, these bad actors may even be UK government departments.

3. EXPERT PANELS

All science is inherently political, and the social sciences are thought to be particularly so. There is a natural tendency for those heading up panels to recruit those who think like them. Checks and balances are needed to make sure that panels include different academic disciplines, industry backgrounds, and political beliefs, and that group participation is structured to permit and encourage challenge and debate. Lucy Easthope recommends that panels 'should also be made to operate adversarially so somebody could argue against their science.'

We can't fix our basic psychological make-up but we can ameliorate it. I heard from different sources while I was investigating this book that 'wild cards' and dissenters were edged out of advisory panels. This is dangerous. MP Steve Baker said in the House of Commons that 'we need to introduce competitive expert advice with red team challenge, because experts are only human and we have been asking the impossible of them in the context of the challenges that they face.'[5]

4. INDIVIDUAL ACTION

Asking you not to be frightened is futile. Fear is hardwired. In fact, to disregard fear would be to put ourselves in mortal danger. We feel fear for a reason. Our evolved psychology and physiology dispose us towards fearing actual and potential threats. To conclude this book by asking you never to feel fear again, to simply switch it off, would be impossible and harmful. But what action can you take to inoculate yourself from disproportionate fear?

My own investigation of fear in the last year has taught me that, regrettably, we must evaluate the claims of those in power, and be sceptical of information from even our most trusted sources. I don't want to suggest you live life in a state of perpetual hyper-vigilance and scepticism; that would be exhausting. However, there are some simple actions you can take to help you achieve balance.

In an article about fear and politics, Leonie Huddy, Professor of Political Science at the State University of New York at Stony Brook, said, 'some media outlets are more likely than others to carry highly emotional content which can exacerbate anxiety. There is evidence that highly emotional content is more likely to be shared on social media, such as Twitter and Facebook, and it may be better to avoid reading news on those platforms and consume less highly-charged coverage that is more common on mainstream news platforms'.[6] Quite obviously, turning off the TV and internet news dams the river of doom. Some of the people I interviewed about fear were able to reach a happier place simply by turning off the news. Lockdown and self-isolation led to greater social atomisation, and people developed tunnel thinking. They were able to put their fears into perspective just by meeting up with others socially.

Taking action can also be helpful. It's been inspiring to witness community support and outreach for the isolated during lockdown, and also the swelling of activism. Despite the restrictions on gatherings, political protest was not truly illegal, and people were able to express their political will and agency through demonstrations and protests.

The other way out of this is to start disregarding the 'rituals of fear' as soon as possible. Masks, dots on the floor and social distancing may be required according to government policy, but they keep us separate from each other. Human connections help us feel good and isolation increases anxiety and depression. Some of this was inevitable. According to psychologist Patrick Fagan, 'The behavioural immune system is our evolutionarily hardwired response to the threat of disease, and it has a raft of predictable outcomes – including becoming less tolerant and more insular. In short, focusing on purity will turn people into puritans.' Various research studies show that contagious diseases encourage intolerance and conformity, a psychological response designed to keep us safe when there are infectious diseases.[7] We shun outsiders and express disgust about things that could be dirty and contagious. But we are through the teeth of the crisis and to rebuild society and mental health we need connection, faces, hugs and conviviality.

If you have read this far, then I hope *A State of Fear* has helped you. Once you know how nudge works, it is much easier to spot it happening. You should be more psychologically resistant to behavioural psychology techniques, including the weaponisation of fear. Think of this book as an anti-nudge handbook. Patrick Fagan has kindly shared an excerpt from an essay which continues this 'Fight back against the nudge' in Appendix 3.

5. AN INQUIRY INTO THE ROLE OF BEHAVIOURAL PSYCHOLOGY AND NUDGING

Cass Sunstein, the godfather of nudge, said that humans are more like Homer Simpson than homo economicus.[8] It's not a great compliment. Well, behavioural psychologists are humans too. What of their limitations, and those of the politicians who wield nudge to influence and manipulate us? Psychology has been used to understand, influence and help individuals. I believe it is now time for us, the individuals, to ask psychologists to turn their expertise back on themselves and on the government. How did their fears influence them? Why did they weaponise our fear against us?

In March 2020, an induction into a 'Cult of Fear' started without us even being aware of it. It began with our leader telling us to stay in our homes, except for necessary and reasonable exemptions, and obviously the Thursday evening ritualistic clapping and pot-banging for the NHS. It continued with the government attempting to manage the minutiae of our lives, including the advice to take our own serving spoons to someone else's house for Christmas dinner.

Fear messaging was used to encourage compliance with the rules. This has changed our lives and our relationships with each other. It has also changed our relationship with the government. This was predicted in the report *MINDSPACE: Influencing behaviour through public policy*,[9] which warned:

> 'People have a strong instinct for reciprocity that informs their relationship with government – they pay taxes and the government provides services in return. This transactional model remains intact if government legislates and provides advice to inform behaviour. But if government is seen as using powerful, pre-conscious effects to subtly change behaviour, people may feel the relationship has changed: now the state is affecting "them" – their very personality.'

Indeed, the use of behavioural psychology and specifically fear has affected our personalities, our mental health, our sense of agency. And this model of governance has been followed without the public consultation that the same document proposed.

David Halpern has said that 'if national or local governments are to use these approaches, they need to ensure that they have public permission to do so – i.e. that the nudge is transparent, and that there has been appropriate debate about it'.[10] Furthermore, the *MINDSPACE: Influencing behaviour through public policy discussion* document he co-authored recommended a public consultation about the use of behavioural insights.

The Science and Technology Select Committee's 2011 report *Behaviour Change*[11] noted that there are 'ethical issues because they involve altering behaviour through mechanisms of which people are not obviously aware' and 'ethical acceptability depends to a large extent on an intervention's proportionality'. Well, using fear to make people obey lockdown rules was a huge intervention.

The report goes on to acknowledge that changing people's behaviour is controversial and that the 'evidence-base of any proposed behaviour change intervention' and 'why it is a necessary and proportionate means of addressing a well-defined problem' should be given. Evidence and a cost-benefit analysis for non-pharmaceutical interventions, such as lockdowns, tier restrictions and face coverings, was not submitted to MPs or the public.

The report also makes an important point that the government argues that non-regulatory approaches are more 'respectful of the freedom of the individual' but that the report authors disagree. Well, quite.

Since 2010 there have been a few gentle suggestions that consultation and debate about the ethics of behavioural psychology are needed. We are still waiting. I emailed the Behavioural Insights Team in December 2020 and March 2021 to ask David Halpern for his views about why the public have not been consulted about the use of the MINDSPACE and EAST behavioural psychology tools. Halpern and BIT did not reply. I also asked Laura de Moliere, Head of Behavioural Science at the Cabinet Office, and again received no reply.

I went back to two of the SPI-B advisors to discuss the ethical considerations and need for public consultation.

SPI Two is the advisor who memorably told me that thoughts of the potential dystopia we might be entering kept them awake at night and that 'psychology has been used for wicked ends'. I asked what we needed to do to develop a good and trusting relationship with government. They flipped it around: 'We need the government to be honest and trust people. That's not been the case. There is also an issue with the advisers. A lot of SPI-B are numbers driven. They look at the "R", and they don't see people. Humanity is missing from the discussion and decisions. We need to consider our relationship with the state. We should consider what we allow government to do to us, including mind control by governments.'

I spoke to Gavin Morgan, the educational psychologist on

SPI-B, several times in the course of researching this book. He was keen to defend his profession: 'Psychology is a much misunderstood and often maligned discipline. It is something that should be positive, and act as a force for good in people's lives and across the whole of society. When I was invited to join SPI-B I thought this was a great opportunity to demonstrate how psychology can do this. The public perception of a psychological role in SPI-B may be to see this as something like manipulation and how to coerce the public to behave in certain ways and in ways that they do not want to. This is not how I saw the opportunity that came my way.'

Fair enough, but SPI-B did suggest tactics that are manipulative and coercive. 'I would hope to think that all psychologists are guided by high moral principles and would use their knowledge, experience and expertise for the cause of good – which is why perhaps recommendations are often at odds with what the government is hoping to hear,' he told me. 'Clearly, using fear as a means of control is not ethical. What you do as a psychologist is co-construction. Using fear smacks of totalitarianism. It's not an ethical stance for any modern government.' So why did SPI-B suggest it? 'The government were frightened people wouldn't obey instructions. To some extent it's why they held off in locking us down. I don't know if using fear was even a conscious decision by the government. But by some sleight of hand the public clamoured for lockdown, so it became inevitable we would lock down,' Morgan said.

Was it ethical to use fear, I asked? 'Well, I didn't suggest we use fear.' But your colleagues did. What do you think of that? He paused. 'Oh God.' Another reluctant pause. 'It's not ethical,' he said.

Finally, I was curious what Morgan had learnt during the epidemic and his role on SPI-B: 'By nature I am an optimistic person, but all this has given me a more pessimistic view of people. People are passive and biddable. A lot of people don't question, their thinking is shaped by other people, especially the media and social media and that is a dangerous thing. As a society we are set up to encourage a passive and biddable population.'

When MPs questioned David Halpern and Stephen Reicher during a Public Administration and Constitutional Affairs Committee on 19 January 2021,[12] not one MP asked about the ethics.

We mustn't let the calls for consultation about the ethics and acceptability of the use of behavioural science, especially about something as profound as fear, drift into a pre-pandemic past. Good ethics must never be behind us if we want to fulfil the potential 'force for good' that psychology can offer government.

First, the public must understand how behavioural psychology is used on them. This book is a start. An independent third party must inquire into the use of behavioural psychology during the Covid-19 pandemic. Of course, behavioural psychology didn't start during the pandemic. It also isn't the preserve of the psychologists anymore: we witnessed many clumsy attempts at nudge from ministers 'having a go'. Rather, the pandemic response has revealed the psychocratic influence deeply embedded in various government departments, the NHS and Public Health England. So, an inquiry should start with a historical literature review of behavioural psychology and the use of it by government to understand its trajectory and to contextualise its use during the pandemic. There should be a full analysis of the tactics used and their impacts, by experts including psychologists, behavioural scientists, mental health specialists, politicians, political scientists, sociologists, civil liberties organisations and lawyers, as well as representatives of the public. The results must be shared and debated and consensus reached on the acceptable and ethical use of nudge in the future.

20. THE END, OR IS IT A PREQUEL?

As I finish *A State of Fear*, it is one year since Fright Night, when our prime minister, Boris Johnson, told us that 'the coronavirus is the biggest threat this country has faced for decades. All over the world we are seeing the devastating impact of this invisible killer... From this evening I must give the British people a very simple instruction – you must stay at home.'

The past year will have meant many different things to many different people. Your experience will have coloured your view of an extraordinary year. It was a year of death and illness, from Covid and also illnesses which lost out in priority, one way or another, to Covid. It was a year of more contentment for some, as they evaded the rat race, life became simpler, they spent more time with family. It was a year of separation, loneliness and hardship for others. It was a year of liberties lost. It was a year of fear.

Some fears we relish and return to: the scariest rollercoaster or the made-you-jump-the-most-times horror film. I think once this debacle is over, people will want to forget the worst and romanticise the best, to storify the saga into a bearable memory. But that would be dangerous. We must use the emotional distance and space to critically assess which rubicons were crossed.

When I started investigating this book, the idea that our fear had been weaponised against us was not popular currency, but is now starting to circulate. At the time of this strange anniversary, a *Guardian* front page headline read 'Covid checks at pubs "could *nudge* young people to get vaccine"'[1] [italics my emphasis], explicitly noting the blatant use of behavioural psychology. In the same week, Professor Tim Spector told *Times Radio* that the prime minister's warnings of a third wave were designed to 'keep the population fearful'.[2] Variants are now often referred to as 'scariants' in an acknowledgement of increasingly obvious attempts to scare the British public into complying with the rules.

Although the vaccine programme has been successful in its aims, and cases, hospitalisations and deaths are falling, the campaign of fear continues. More punitive fines are dangled like threatening bombs, most lately a £5,000 fine should you dare to take an overseas holiday. We have been warned that restrictions will not be eased if we break the rules. A government minister urged the public to 'call out' friends and family for hugging.[3] In the spring of 2021, a poster in a park in Bromley proclaimed 'Covid-19 is in this park and is now easier to catch!' in black, yellow and red fonts and chevrons, which warn of danger. And the doom-mongering headlines continue at home and abroad. Bloomberg proclaimed, 'We must start planning for a permanent pandemic – with coronavirus mutations pitted against vaccinations in a global arms race, we may never go back to normal.'[4]

Yet there are also cracks in the campaign of fear. Young people didn't seem frightened as they crowded into parks around the country on 29 March 2021 when restrictions eased, basking in sunshine and the sociality of groups of six. Spring worked its magic on a seasonal virus and on the soul.

Despite the best efforts of the fear machine, I have some hope. Fear is not sustainable. And, as it wears thin, it is revealed to be in an inverse relationship with the growing awareness of how it was weaponised. As fear finally melts away we will be able to confront our frailties and strengths, as citizens, scientists, journalists and politicians.

US president Franklin D. Roosevelt said in his inaugural address in 1933 that the 'only thing we have to fear is fear itself'. He had a positive vision of a future where fear would be put in its place by a society that believed in itself. These days, politicians are far more likely to advise the public to fear everything, including fear itself. But we can ask for better: from them, the media, the unelected psychocrats and from ourselves. People do not want to live in a state of fear and they do not want to be manipulated. I think the handling of the epidemic should teach us to be wary, if not frightened, of Bernays' 'invisible government' which nudges and forces behaviour change through manipulating our emotions.

It is the duty of us all to think about what type of society we want to live in, which values we treasure, the styles of governance we approve of and reject, and what constitutional protections we may wish to introduce.

It is ironic that in recent years, governments around the world have started to consider frameworks of 'wellbeing', yet they launched campaigns to frighten their populations to implement lockdowns. (Although one sounds friendlier than the other, be aware that both frameworks see our emotions as the province of the state.) When I spoke to Steve Baker MP in the summer of 2020 he offered some thought-provoking comments about how to envisage society: 'I think we need a deep conversation about values and how we want to become. At the moment authoritarian collectivist values are being used. I would dearly love to see politicians of all parties learn from what has gone on during this crisis and say, let us not return to that dystopia, let us choose to be greater and commit to liberal and tolerant values. Normally everyone would say they subscribe to that.'

Gavin Morgan pragmatically told me 'we are always being manipulated whether we are aware of it or not. Politicians try to be good at this manipulation and often have the media on their side to promote a certain narrative – this then becomes how we think and respond. It goes unchallenged – which is why ethical psychology needs to be a positive influence in society. We have a moral imperative and a responsibility to say when we know something is wrong and damage is being done. There is a responsibility for psychology to take a lead role in shaping a better future. We don't know what this will look like, it needs to be shaped by us all. Co-constructed by the nation.' It is hopeful that there are psychologists who want to co-construct. That is a far cry from the psychocrats who see themselves as the architects of our emotions and behaviour.

Some advisors close to government have held our emotional happiness and freedoms a little less dearly than we do ourselves. When he described the inception of the UK's lockdown and the comparison with China, Professor Neil Ferguson said 'It's a communist one-party state, we said. We couldn't get away with it in Europe, we thought. And then Italy did it. And we realised we could'.[5] We could 'get away with it' is a very revealing way to put it. Having got away with it once, is the government likely to inflict an authoritarian measure like lockdown again? And would they rely on our learned obedience, our muscle memory, or would they use fear again? Without the strongest objections from all of us, an inquiry and resistance against these tools, I think their future and repeated use inevitable.

The Covid-19 epidemic may prove to be the biggest campaign of fear the UK, and the world, has ever seen. I'm not sure we even needed it. Fear was an open door – naturally, because we were in an epidemic. The government didn't need to so much as knock on the door. It didn't have to open it for us, and politely say, after you. It certainly didn't need to use a battering ram.

The almost imperceptible stripping away of rights and freedoms, as the people and their government gradually separate, is an old story repeated throughout history, but avoidable if we choose to learn from it. A German professor recounted the process, movingly, in *They Thought They Were Free,* by Milton Mayer:

'To live in this process is absolutely not to be able to notice it – please try to believe me – unless one has a much greater degree of political awareness, acuity, than most of us had ever had occasion to develop. Each step was so small, so inconsequential, so well explained or, on occasion, "regretted", that, unless one were detached from the whole process from the beginning, unless one understood what the whole thing was in principle, what all these 'little measures' that no 'patriotic German' could resent must some day lead to, one no more saw it developing from day to day than a farmer in his field sees the corn growing. One day it is over his head.'

How far has the corn grown? It is known that fear induces a desire for authoritarian control.[6] Here in the UK, one of the cradles of democracy, fear has created the right emotional temperature for the toleration, even enthusiastic welcome, of increased surveillance, reduced rights to protest, and breaches of human rights.

The policies of the last year affected our daily lives, weakened our social bonds, and also disrupted the most intimate human rites of birth, marriage and death. We need to be cautious about policies of fear which invade our humanity. We mustn't let a medical crisis strip us of our freedoms or our ideals.

In the introduction I said I wanted to invite you to write the end of the story. The textbook of tyrants is written in the language of coercion and cajolement. And sadly there is no mythic Happy Ever After. But you know that. The truth is that we live in a permanent prequel, as the story always goes on. The way to change the story is simply to believe in our power to change it.

We seem to have forgotten that no one is safe. You have never been safe and you never will be. Nor will I. In the blind global panic of an epidemic we have forgotten how to analyse risk. If you don't accept that you will die one day, that you can never be safe, then you are a sitting duck for authoritarian policies which purport to be for your safety. If too many individuals immolate their liberty for safety, we risk a bonfire of freedoms.

Nudge undermines free will; it removes our choices without us even knowing. If we continue to allow ourselves to be nudged towards a greater good, we have given up on determining what 'good' looks like. The weaponisation of fear undermines democracy, liberty and humanity. Nudge is not 'fair play'.

The use of behavioural psychology and specifically the weaponisation of fear were symptoms of a government that had given up on trust and transparency. If we truly believe in freedom we must also believe we deserve it. Personal responsibility is not a conduit to danger. Let us reject living in a state of fear. As we recover from an epidemic, we must also recover the trust and transparency that we deserve.

DATA

The UK Government began its attempts to increase and generalise fear at the end of March 2020. Although risk was highly patterned, the public health messaging was designed to expand risks so the entire population felt threatened. The risk of dying from Covid might be smaller and also more age-specific than you imagined.

US CENTRES FOR DISEASE CONTROL

'Current best estimates' of the infection fatality rate (IFR)[1]

0-17 years	0.002%
18-49 years	0.05%
50-64 years	0.6%
65+ years	9%

IMPERIAL COLLEGE LONDON

Report 34 - COVID-19 infection fatality ratio estimates from seroprevalence[2] from Imperial College London concluded that 'We find that age-specific IFRs follow an approximately log-linear pattern, with the risk of death doubling approximately every eight years of age.'

0-4 years	0.00%
5-9 years	0.01%
10-14 years	0.01%
15-19 years	0.02%
20-24 years	0.03%
25-29 years	0.04%
30-34 years	0.06%
35-39 years	0.10%
40-44 years	0.16%
45-49 years	0.24%

50-54 years	0.38%
55-59 years	0.60%
60-64 years	0.94%
65-69 years	1.47%
70-74 years	2.31%
75-79 years	3.61%
80-84 years	5.66%
85-89 years	8.86%
90+ years	17.37%

WORLD HEATH ORGANIZATION

The WHO published *Infection fatality rate of COVID-19 inferred from seroprevalence data*[3] by Professor John P.A. Ioannidis. The report says that:

'Covid-19 has a very steep age gradient for risk of death. Moreover, in European countries that have had large numbers of cases and deaths, and in the USA, many, and in some cases most, deaths occurred in nursing homes.

Locations with many nursing home deaths may have high estimates of the infection fatality rate, but the infection fatality rate would still be low among non-elderly, non-debilitated people... The median infection fatality rate across all 51 locations was 0.27% (corrected 0.23%)... For people younger than 70 years old, the infection fatality rate of COVID-19 across 40 locations with available data ranged from 0.00% to 0.31% (median 0.05%); the corrected values were similar.'

LOCKDOWNS DON'T WORK

This is a book about fear, not about the efficacy of non-pharmaceutical interventions, namely lockdowns. But lockdowns would probably not have been accepted in the first place, nor tolerated for so long, without the weaponisation of fear. You have to be more frightened of a virus and the consequences of ignoring the mandate to stay at home, than you do of losing your livelihood, income, or real-life human connections.

You might think all the UK government's policies were worth it if they worked. Of course, you might not, and I would argue that the consideration of how we became a state of fear can be and should be separate to whether lockdowns work or not. These are extricable issues. The use of fear to encourage adherence to lockdown rules has its own merits and demerits. Your attitude towards a strong state, the use of behavioural psychology and the leveraging of fear will be ideological to some degree. Sadly, I would also argue that belief in the success or failure of lockdown is also ideological to some degree, because belief in the effectiveness of lockdowns does not seem to be based in firm, unequivocal empirical evidence, as I will demonstrate here.

There have been unqualified assumptions in the media that the differences in case and death rates in different countries are explained by lockdowns and interventions such as masks. But this falls into 'Illusion of Control' thinking as well as being, frankly, lazy thinking. And it suits governments to perpetuate the idea that lockdowns work, since they have enacted them.

I may or may not persuade you that lockdowns do not work. The jury may even still be out, if we're being generous. I may be a victim of my own ideological prejudice. But I do hope to at least rock your faith in this new orthodoxy.

The use of universal lockdowns in the event of a new virus

has no precedent. Why haven't they been used before? They are blunt and brutal tools. They breach human rights. (See Chapter 15, 'Tyranny'.) They are destructive to individuals' lives and jobs, to businesses and the economy, which ultimately impacts the health of the nation. There was no good evidence that they do work, and in a world which till now has valued evidence-based interventions, that used to be an extremely important consideration. Since the mass quarantining of healthy individuals from 2020, there is a growing body of evidence that this extraordinary measure does not work in achieving its goals.

After a year of global lockdowns, assumptions behind the modelling – that they successfully control the virus and without them hundreds of thousands more would die – have become accepted truth. This 'truth' is close to religious dogma here in the UK, where we have endured one of the strictest lockdowns in the world, according to an analysis by Oxford University's Blavatnik School of Government.[1] Only two governments, Venezuela and Lebanon, have introduced tougher policies. Questioning the efficacy of lockdowns is akin to heresy and might earn you the accusatory title 'Covid denier' or 'covidiot'. Have the UK's restrictions created a population with Stockholm syndrome?

A 2019 report[2] *Non-pharmaceutical public health measures for mitigating the risk and impact of epidemic and pandemic influenza* by the World Health Organization (WHO) warned of the flimsy empirical basis for epidemiology models such as the one developed by Imperial College London. 'Simulation models provide a weak level of evidence,' the report noted, and lacked randomised controlled trials to test their assumptions.

The report is about preparedness for influenza, but there would be much similarity in strategies and effectiveness for coronavirus (this was touched upon in Chapter 1, 'Fright Night', and is referenced further in the endnotes). It said that non-pharmaceutical interventions (which include hand hygiene, respiratory etiquette, face masks for symptomatic individuals, surface and object cleaning, increased ventilation, isolation of sick individuals and travel advice) can be effective:

'by reducing transmission in the community, the epidemic may be spread out over a longer period, with a reduced epidemic peak. This can be particularly important if the health system has limited resources or capacity (e.g. in terms of hospital beds and ventilators). Also, overall morbidity and mortality can be reduced even if the total number of infections across the epidemic is not reduced.'

Isolation of 'sick individuals' is 'recommended' although the evidence is 'very low'. Note that these are 'sick' individuals. But 'quarantine of exposed individuals' is 'not recommended in any circumstances'. Mass quarantine measures – lockdowns – are 'not recommended' due to lack of evidence for their effectiveness. Similarly, evidence for closing schools, contact tracing, avoiding crowding, internal travel restrictions, border exit and entry screening is 'very low'.

'Case isolation' is defined as 'separation or restriction of movement of *ill* persons with an infectious disease at home or in a health care facility, to prevent transmission to others' [italics my emphasis]. The Covid epidemic is the first time that cases have been accepted to be positive PCR or LFT results without a clinical diagnosis. Normally to qualify as a 'case', you must be unwell and have symptoms associated with the disease. In this report, even case isolation has a 'very low overall quality of evidence', and that's for people who are sick, not just in receipt of a positive test result.

In summarising the section on isolation, this report, which included the same 2006 influenza model that Ferguson adapted to Covid-19, concluded: 'Most currently available studies on the effectiveness of isolation are simulation studies, which have a low strength of evidence.'

(Incidentally, nowhere in the chapter 'Communication for behavioural impact', in the same report, is the use of fear to encourage adherence to NPIs recommended.)

It cannot be stressed enough that the WHO and the UK have never included mass quarantining of healthy people – lockdowns – in epidemic or pandemic preparedness planning. There was no evidence that lockdowns would work, and the harms were acknowledged to outweigh the potential and unproven effects.

Why did we lock down in the UK? SAGE observed the 'innovative intervention' out of China, but they initially presumed it would not be an acceptable option in the UK, a liberal Western democracy. In an astonishing interview for *The Sunday Times*, Professor Neil Ferguson of Imperial College London, a member of SAGE, said, 'It's a communist one party state, we said. We couldn't get away with it in Europe, we thought… and then Italy did it. And we realised we could.'[3]

Neil Ferguson's Imperial simulation model was described in an article in *The Telegraph* as 'the most devastating software mistake of all time'.[4] The modelling used outdated code and contained multiple flaws. (There is more on the modelling in Chapter 10, 'The metrics of fear'.)

The doom-laden modelling grabbed headlines around the world and is credited with some of the responsibility for shifting policies on lockdown. And in circular and fallacious reasoning, the success of lockdown in the UK is measured by deaths 'saved' against those predicted by the unsubstantiated simulated forecasts of the modelling.

Aside from the reportedly dismal coding, was it robust? Models based on assumptions in the absence of data can be over-speculative and open to over-interpretation. Professor John Ioannidis of Stanford University issued a strong warning[5] for disease modellers to recognise the deficiencies in reliable data about Covid-19, which in time proved to be transmission, fatality rates and T-cell reactivity (See Chapter 10, 'The metrics of fear', for more detail.)

The modelling also did not take take into account the spread of the virus in hospitals, care homes and prisons. When 40%[6] of deaths are care home residents and up to two thirds of infections leading to serious illness are contracted in hospital,[7] it cannot be over-stated what a major omission this was.

Journalists, politicians and pundits state that lockdowns work, as though it is undisputed fact. As a result, politicians tighten and loosen the lockdown screws at will. There is no serious opposition. How have lockdowns become the new orthodoxy, when they were never recommended before 2020 and there was no evidence that they worked? Rather than opposition to the evidential and conceptual framework for lockdown, the problem, as defined by the political opposition, and Boris Johnson himself, is that we didn't lock down 'earlier and harder'.[8] We appear to be doubling down on false assumptions.

Regardless, lockdowns cannot be judged solely according to whether they avert death and illness from one virus. If we put aside all consideration of the acceptable reach of government and the imposition on our liberty, there are economic, social and health costs caused by lockdown. The government has shied away from a quantitative assessment of the policy, presumably because the numbers just would not stack up. Civitas[9] produced a report using the standard UK government and NHS's QALY (Quality Adjusted Life Years) calculations and found that the cost per QALY saved ranged from £96,000 to £1.97 million, depending on how successful lockdowns might have been (and the assumptions in the report are quite generous). To contextualise this, the NHS's upper limit is £30,000 per QALY.

But did lockdowns save lives?

Deaths in England and Wales peaked on 8 April 2020, which (given the lag between infection and death), implies that infections peaked and started to decrease before the lockdown on 23 March. This has been acknowledged by Chief Medical Officer Chris Whitty, who said that the R-number was decreasing before the national lockdown.[10] This has been attributed to both voluntary behaviour changes and to the natural bell curve of a virus.

Simon Wood, a professor of statistics at the University of Edinburgh, wrote for *The Spectator* that 'although the estimated fatal infections were in retreat before each lockdown, the daily deaths were surging each time that a lockdown was called. The psychological pressure that this puts on the decision makers is obvious.'[11] This is very plausible – when the pressure is at its worst, politicians are under greater pressure to 'pull a lever', to do something to slow transmission. Less generously, the lockdowns also happen to have been timed to almost be credited with declines which had just begun.

It feels counterintuitive that restrictions do not limit the spread and death toll of coronavirus in the way that the Imperial model expected. However, there are now 34 studies and analyses which show that lockdowns do not work, with countries and states with fewer or no restrictions frequently outperforming countries and states with some of the most strict lockdowns. The American Institute for Economic Research[12] has listed and summarised the 34 reports, which would be an ideal resource for those interested in learning more.

In the interest of balance, I should say that the WHO published an article[13] on 31 December 2020 which said 'large scale physical distancing measures and movement restrictions, often referred to as "lockdowns", can slow COVID-19 transmission by limiting contact between people'. It did not link to any evidence supporting this, but I have collated a few papers which find evidence in favour of lockdowns in the endnotes.[14]

Assessing mandatory stay-at-home and business closure effects on the spread of COVID-19,[15] from academics at Stanford University, concluded: 'in summary, we fail to find strong evidence supporting a role for more restrictive NPIs in the control of COVID in early 2020. We do not question the role of all public health interventions, or of coordinated communications about the epidemic, but we fail to find an additional benefit of stay-at-home orders and business closures. The data cannot fully exclude the possibility of some benefits. However, even if they exist, these benefits may not match the numerous harms of these aggressive measures. More targeted public health interventions that more effectively reduce transmissions may be important for future epidemic control without the harms of highly restrictive measures.'[16]

Oxford University's Centre for Evidence-Based Medicine (CEBM) analysed excess mortality for 2020 across 32 countries. They used excess mortality instead of 'Covid deaths', to avoid problems with recording and classification of deaths and they used age-adjusted mortality to take into account differences in the average age of populations. It's a simple matter to look at the table and see that excess mortality does not obviously correlate with the severity of lockdowns.

To highlight one example, Sweden is often cited as a counter-factual to the UK's policies because it did not impose strict lockdown measures throughout the year. It kept all retail and hospitality and most schools open and imposed no restrictions on private gatherings. According to CEBM, Sweden only had a 1.5% increase in age-adjusted mortality. England and Wales, with the strictest lockdown in the developed world, saw a 10.5% increase in age-adjusted mortality.

Johan Carlson, Director of the Public Health Agency of Sweden, said: 'Some believed that it was possible to eliminate disease transmission by shutting down society. We did not believe that and we have been proven right.'[17]

How does the Imperial modelling handle this counter-factual? Interestingly, as Simon Woods noted in *The Spectator*, 'to accommodate this anomaly their model treats the final March intervention in Sweden (shutting colleges and upper years secondary schools) as if it was lockdown. As many others have pointed out, that's a strange way to model the set of data that most directly suggests that lockdown might not have been essential.'[18]

As economist David Paton pointed out in his article 'The myth of our "late" lockdown',[19] the November national lockdown in England 'had no observable impact on hospitalisations or deaths at all. And although both have fallen very significantly over the past couple of months, all the indicators tell us that infections were decreasing well before the third national lockdown in January, even in regions not already placed in the highest Tier 4 restriction level.' Often, proponents of lockdowns do not take the time lag between infections and hospitalisations and deaths into account, but hope to discern effect where there is none.

Paton highlights the example of the Czech Republic, a country which, on 16 March 2020, locked down early and hard with border controls and the first national mask mandate in Europe. The early, strict lockdown in Czechia 'did nothing to stop an autumn surge and second lockdown, then an even bigger December surge and yet another lockdown. Most recently, despite introducing even tougher restrictions at the end of January, Czechia experienced yet another big surge in cases throughout February and early March. As it stands, the Covid-related death rate in Czechia is the highest in the world (excluding the microstates of Gibraltar and San Marino) at 2,245 per million – 20% higher even than the UK.'

Voluntary behaviour change might impact transmission more than mandatory lockdowns. *A first literature review: lockdowns only had a small effect on COVID-19*[20] from the Centre for Political Studies in Denmark found that 'Studies which differentiate between the two types of behavioural change find that, on average, mandated behavioural changes accounts for only 9% (median: 0%) of the total effect on the growth of the pandemic stemming from behavioural changes. The remaining 91% (median: 100%) of the effect was due to voluntary behavioural changes. This is excluding the effect of curfew and face masks, which were not employed in all countries.'

Aside from a possible small effect attributable to mandated lockdowns and the further impact of voluntary behaviour change, what else affects the course of Covid? I would stray too far from the remit of my book and my armchair expertise to offer definitive conclusions, but having immersed myself in articles for the last year, hypotheses include: age of population, number of people in care homes, prevalence of obesity and other co-morbidities, number of nurses per capita, Vitamin D, previous exposure in the population to other coronaviruses, herd immunity, the volume of testing determining how many deaths are attributable to Covid, contact tracing, use of face masks and other NPIs. All of the uncertainties should remove the certainty that people place in one brute intervention.

Viruses cannot be turned on and off like a tap by governments. This is difficult for the politicians – the enactors of lockdowns – to admit. This is partly due to the sunk cost fallacy, whereby a decision with destructive consequences traps the decision-maker in a cognitive cul-de-sac – they can't admit the mistake and they keep going. The same is true for governments around the world. Lockdowns don't work, so they impose more. It is difficult for the opposition to admit as they called for harder, earlier and longer lockdowns. It is hard for the lockdown-cheerleading media to admit. If lockdowns hurt more than they helped, this is a painful truth for us all to admit. Yet it is a truth that must be acknowledged if we want to save ourselves another wave of unnecessary lockdown pain.

FIGHT BACK AGAINST THE NUDGE

This is an excerpt from an essay by behavioural scientist Patrick Fagan.

There are three solid tactics that you can use to fight back against nudges.

1. UNCOVER

Firstly – forewarned is forearmed. There is evidence that education and training can mitigate the effects of cognitive biases. Research by Professor Carey Morewedge, in particular, has found that people can be 'debiased' by teaching them about a given nudge through interactions, games, or videos, making them less susceptible to it; Morewedge has demonstrated that this debiasing effect can apply to real-world decisions and can last at least two months.

In other words, understanding that your decisions are liable to be nudged, and being able to recognise these nudges in the wild, is key to psychological independence. Being aware, for example, that the government is using fear to manipulate you is the first step towards spotting and resisting that manipulation.

Additionally, behavioural science insights can be used to manage one's own environment to reduce persuasibility. For example, one of the biggest psychological manipulators is conformity – that is, feeling pressured to follow and even believe the crowd in defiance of all reason – and research has discovered a number of mediators of this effect. Conformity is reduced, for example, when decisions are made in private; and so we can make an effort to make important decisions away from prying eyes to ensure a degree of rationality.

2. UNPLUG

However, although debiasing may be possible, there is also

plenty of evidence that biases persist even if you are aware of them. It is a bit like an optical illusion: even though you may rationally know it is an illusion, your brain still cannot unsee it; likewise, even though you may know that Apple use tricks like scarcity and social proof to make their iPhones seem attractive, you still want one. As an experimental example, participants in one study were taught about a nudge called anchoring and adjustment, and they were told that it was about to be used on them – and yet their decisions were still biased by it.

This happens because much of our thinking and behaviour is influenced by external stimuli of which we have little-to-no awareness; messages take hold subconsciously. For example, product placements make people more likely to buy the brand even if they don't consciously remember having seen it; similarly, priming research has consistently shown that subconscious or incidental exposure to symbols influences thinking (with, as just one example, people voting more conservatively when polling is held inside a church). Since these effects bypass conscious systems, it is difficult to think one's way out of them.

As a result, messages still shape your mind and influence your behaviour, even if you view them critically. As Gustav Le Bon noted in his classic, *The Crowd*, persuasion occurs not through rational thought but through affirmation, repetition, and contagion. Do you think, for example, that anyone would watch an advert for Lynx body spray and rationally believe wearing it would cause buxom women to chase after them? And yet the subconscious associations are made, and behaviour is influenced. To make an analogy, an expert nutritionist will get fat and poorly from eating McDonald's every day, even though they are consciously aware of the food's nutritional make-up. We ought to take as much care with what we put into our minds as we do with our bodies.

All this is to say that the second tactic for fighting nudges is simply to avoid them – or else they will get you eventually. As the saying goes, if you hang around in a barbershop long enough, sooner or later you're going to get a haircut.

Of course, it is important to keep well-informed, but this is achievable without being manipulated. Avoid highly-emotional or sensationalist sources of information; in particular, avoid video content as much as possible. The moving image is more attention-grabbing, emotionally engaging, and persuasive than text; it engages pre-conscious brain systems. In short, unlike reading, video doesn't give you the breathing room required to think critically. What's more, reading improves cognitive function – that is, books make you smarter.

3. UPLIFT

This brings us to the third and final tactic: raising your level of consciousness. There are steps you can take in life to give yourself more conscious brainpower, enabling you to make more reasoned decisions and better resist external manipulations.

Namely, reducing cognitive load will free up your rational mind to make better decisions. To avoid being manipulated by the news, for example, be sure to avoid consuming the information when you are tired, hungry, stressed, or distracted: approach it with a clear mind. Similarly, reduce decision fatigue by minimising the amount of inconsequential choices you have to make throughout the day, and avoiding being overwhelmed with information; limiting emotional overstimulation will likewise make you less prone to emotional thinking. This means cutting down your consumption of 'dopamine hits' throughout the day – use social media less, eat less indulgent food, watch less television, and stop watching porn. The word decadence is derived from the word decay: the more decadent you are, the less structure you have in place, and the more liable you are to be blown this way and that by external forces. As for internal distractions, obsessive thoughts and negative emotions can be cleared away by mindfulness meditation.

Ultimately, the goal is to give your brain room to think by reducing chaos in your life. To paraphrase William H. McRaven and Jordan B. Peterson – make your bed and clean your room.

ACKNOWLEDGEMENTS

I am grateful to everyone who allowed me to interview them while researching this book. I can't publicly thank the anonymous contributors, but you know who you are. I hope that everyone I interviewed feels that I have done justice to their expert contributions or personal stories.

In addition, I'd like to thank Patrick Fagan for providing an excerpt from an essay on how to combat nudge. Piers Robinson kindly helped me understand how the UK's laws changed as a result of the war on terror. Gary Sidley was particularly helpful when I researched Chapter 7, 'The tools of the trade', and within that chapter I have referenced an excellent article by him. The 'scientific advisor deeply embedded in Whitehall' generously gave me lots of time, insight and information while treading the careful line of never revealing any official secrets. Thank you R. Whitehead for providing expert insight into public health and propaganda.

My thanks to all readers of this book in its various drafts for their time and suggestions, especially Lucy Easthope, Zoe Harcombe, Harrie Bunker-Smith, Piers Robinson, Fergus Drennan, Joanna Williams, and Francis Hoar.

REFERENCES

INTRODUCTION

1. assets.publishing.service.gov.uk/government/uploads/system/uploads/attachment_data/file/887467/25-options-for-increasing-adherence-to-social-distancing-measures-22032020.pdf
2. www.worldometers.info/coronavirus/
3. www.ons.gov.uk/peoplepopulationandcommunity/birthsdeathsandmarriages/deaths/bulletins/monthlymortalityanalysisenglandandwales/january2021
4. www.civilserviceworld.com/professions/article/government-chief-scientist-explains-lack-of-eyecatching-measures-in-coronavirus-fight
5. www.kekstcnc.com/media/2793/kekstcnc_research_covid-19_opinion_tracker_wave-4.pdf
6. www.bbc.co.uk/news/uk-55631693
7. www.kekstcnc.com/media/2895/kekst-cnc-covid19-opinion-tracker-wave-5.pdf
8. www.cam.ac.uk/research/news/uk-public-most-concerned-about-coronavirus-more-than-spain-or-italy-study-suggests
9. www.ipsos.com/ipsos-mori/en-uk/britons-least-likely-believe-economy-and-businesses-should-open-if-coronavirus-not-fully-contained
10. www.bsg.ox.ac.uk/research/research-projects/coronavirus-government-response-tracker#data
11. NHS England stats to 20th January
12. Computed from Office of National Statistics data by experts at Oxford's Centre for Evidence Based Medicine at Oxford University. Reported: www.dailymail.co.uk/news/article-9157627/One-six-hospital-patients-caught-Covid-19-treated-illnesses-figures-show.html
13. www.dailymail.co.uk/news/article-8539541/200-000-people-die-delays-healthcare-report-warns.html
14. www.spectator.co.uk/article/is-the-cost-of-another-lockdown-too-high-

CHAPTER 1: FRIGHT NIGHT

1. Operation Cygnus referred to influenza, but the planning would also translate to and be effective for coronavirus. As veteran disaster planner Lucy Easthope told me, 'There are review documents for SARS and MERS. It is a common

misapprehension that we weren't prepared for coronavirus. The effectiveness of Operation Cygnus would be effective for either. For instance, the *National Risk Register of Civil Emergencies* lists coronavirus and SARS in the 'New and emerging infectious diseases' section. Interestingly, it notes the need for contact tracing and isolation of affected individuals but not 'lockdown': assets. publishing.service.gov.uk/government/uploads/system/uploads/attachment_data/file/211867/NationalRiskRegister2013_amended. pdf Additionally, after the SARS outbreak in Toronto, the SARS commission was published in 2007 and was known to disaster planners: www.archives.gov.on.ca/en/e_records/sars/index.html

2. www.telegraph.co.uk/news/2020/06/04/coronavirus-infections-england-wales-hit-peak-days-lockdown/

CHAPTER 2: FEAR SPREADS IN THE MEDIA LIKE AN AIRBORNE VIRUS

1. Video of people collapsing in China, Daily Mail: www.dailymail.co.uk/news/article-7923981/Coronavirus-Disturbing-videos-claim-people-collapsing-Wuhan.html
2. www.cambridge.org/core/journals/american-political-science-review/article/how-the-chinese-government-fabricates-social-media-posts-for-strategic-distraction-not-engaged-argument/4662DB26E2685BAF1485F14369BD137C/core-reader
3. www.propublica.org/article/how-china-built-a-twitter-propaganda-machine-then-let-it-loose-on-coronavirus
4. www.tabletmag.com/sections/news/articles/china-covid-lockdown-propaganda
5. www.bbc.co.uk/news/uk-51828000
6. twitter.com/HuXijin_GT/status/1238864397713305600
7. www.the-sun.com/news/378365/coronavirus-patients-welded-into-homes-in-china-as-death-toll-spirals-to-813/
8. 'Section 11: War, Terror and Emergencies - Guidelines' from the BBC's Editorial Guidelines
9. www.telegraph.co.uk/women/life/grimmilestone-need-glimmer-hope/
10. lockdownsceptics.org/the-future-shape-of-things/
11. www.lbc.co.uk/news/matt-hancock-tells-lbc-how-film-contagion-alerted-him-to-global-vaccine-scramble/
12. www.bbc.co.uk/news/health-54598728
13. www.pressgazette.co.uk/poll-journalists-have-not-donea-good-job-at-covid-19-briefings-majority-of-respondents-say/
14. www.pressgazette.co.uk/press-gazette-poll-shows-half-believe-trust-in-journalism-has-fallen-since-covid-19-outbreak/
15. www.pressgazette.co.uk/coronavirus-public-distrust-journalists-despite-relying-on-news-media-for-daily-updates-survey-shows/
16. order-order.com/people/piers-morgan/

17. www.bbc.co.uk/news/health-54696873
18. www.telegraph.co.uk/news/2020/11/19/many-could-immune-covid-despite-never-having-infected-study/
19. www.acpjournals.org/doi/10.7326/M20-6817
20. www.telegraph.co.uk/news/2020/05/05/britons-scared-coronavirus-infection-rest-world/
21. www.campaignlive.co.uk/article/govt-spent-184m-covid-comms-2020/1708695
22. www.ofcom.org.uk/__data/assets/pdf_file/0025/193075/Note-to-broadcasters-Coronavirus.pdf
23. freespeechunion.org/letter-to-ofcom-following-its-decision-to-sanction-itv-and-london-live/

CHAPTER 4: FEAR IS A PAGE OF THE GOVERNMENT PLAYBOOK

1. www.bi.team/wp-content/uploads/2018/08/BIT-Behavioural-Government-Report-2018.pdf
2. www.gov.uk/government/speeches/pm-global-vaccine-summit-closing-remarks-4-june-2020
3. www.city-journal.org/the-politics-of-fear
4. ibid
5. academic.oup.com/ia/article/96/3/691/5813532
6. www.cato.org/blog/chance-being-murdered-or-injured-terrorist-attack-united-kingdom
7. onlinelibrary.wiley.com/doi/epdf/10.1111/eci.13554
8. www.who.int/bulletin/online_first/BLT.20.265892.pdf (The professor behind this study published by the World Health Organisation, Dr John Ioannidis of Stanford University, assessed IFRs with age specificity which proved very accurate by the end of the year.)
9. www.youtube.com/watch?v=LzmcHAbcoqg
10. Two discussions of the evidence: 1. 'A city-wide prevalence study of almost 10 million people in Wuhan found no evidence of asymptomatic transmission.' - www.bmj.com/content/bmj/371/bmj.m4851.full.pdf 2. lockdownsceptics.org/has-the-evidence-of-asymptomatic-spread-of-covid-19-been-significantly-overstated-2/
11. www.haaretz.com/israel-news/.premium-deradicalize-israel-s-covid-insurgents-before-they-incite-a-civil-war-1.9529626
12. www.thetimes.co.uk/article/uk-officials-hunt-mystery-person-who-tested-positive-for-brazilian-variant-then-vanished-xj3m6ksbp
13. assets.publishing.service.gov.uk/government/uploads/system/uploads/attachment_data/file/926410/Understanding_Cycle_Threshold__Ct__in_SARS-CoV-2_RT-PCR_.pdf
14. www.cebm.net/covid-19/infectious-positive-pcr-test-result-covid-19/

15. www.gov.uk/government/publications/covid-19-management-of-exposed-healthcare-workers-and-patients-in-hospital-settings/covid-19-management-of-exposed-healthcare-workers-and-patients-in-hospital-settings
16. www.theportugalnews.com/news/2020-11-27/covid-pcr-test-reliability-doubtful-portugal-judges/56962
17. www.telegraph.co.uk/politics/2020/12/05/freedom-loving-conservative-cant-wait-get-us-back-living-personal/
18. www.theguardian.com/commentisfree/2021/feb/27/it-is-only-a-matter-of-time-before-we-turn-on-the-unvaccinated
19. www.express.co.uk/news/world/1385597/Germany-Covid-angela-merkel-eu-news-coronavirus-lockdown-detention-centre-refugee-camp
20. www.dailymail.co.uk/news/article-8681001/People-wont-wear-face-masks-likely-sociopaths-study-claims.html
21. www.ncbi.nlm.nih.gov/pmc/articles/PMC5789790/

CHAPTER 5: THE BUSINESS OF FEAR AND THE UNELECTED PSYCHOCRATS

1. assets.publishing.service.gov.uk/government/uploads/system/uploads/attachment_data/file/744672/Improving_Peoples_Health_Behavioural_Strategy.pdf
2. www.thisismoney.co.uk/money/news/article-3202652/The-hidden-hand-pulling-financial-strings-secretive-government-nudge-unit-tries-manipulate-behaviour-help-sinister.html
3. www.instituteforgovernment.org.uk/sites/default/files/publications/MINDSPACE.pdf
4. eprints.lancs.ac.uk/id/eprint/79061/2/Nudge_final_.pdf
5. publications.parliament.uk/pa/ld201012/ldselect/ldsctech/179/179.pdf
6. www.itv.com/news/2020-04-27/coronavirus-related-syndrome-among-children-may-be-emerging-alert-suggests
7. www.bbc.co.uk/news/education-52373829
8. www.societi.org.uk/kawasaki-disease-covid-19/answering-your-questions-24-may-2020/
9. www.independent.co.uk/news/health/coronavirus-children-hospitals-intensive-care-pims-b1796419.html
10. www.telegraph.co.uk/news/2021/01/19/children-admitted-hospital-mental-health-medical-reasons-leading/
11. www.thestar.com/politics/political-opinion/2021/02/21/the-nudge-unit-ottawas-behavioural-science-team-investigates-how-canadians-feel-about-vaccines-public-health-and-who-to-trust.html
12. www.stuff.co.nz/national/politics/opinion/124400849/jacinda-ardern-is-a-great-communicator-but-clearly-not-everyones-listening

13. gript.ie/look-for-ways-to-increase-insecurity-anxiety-and-uncertainty-zero-covid-document/
14. www.welt.de/politik/deutschland/plus225868061/Corona-Politik-Wie-das-Innenministerium-Wissenschaftler-einspannte.html
15. uncommongroundmedia.com/clap-for-carers-a-show-of-solidarity-or-sinister-submission/
16. www.bighospitality.co.uk/Article/2020/09/21/No-evidence-hospitality-responsible-for-Coronavirus-transmission-spike
17. www.theguardian.com/world/2020/nov/21/england-to-enter-stronger-three-tier-system-after-lockdown
18. assets.publishing.service.gov.uk/government/uploads/system/uploads/attachment_data/file/944823/Analysis_of_the_health_economic_and_social_effects_of_COVID-19_and_the_approach_to_tiering_FINAL_-_accessible_v2.pdf
19. www.independent.co.uk/news/uk/politics/nudge-unit-david-halpern-brexit-a8293061.html
20. www.tni.org/en/article/going-global-the-uk-governments-cve-agenda-counter-radicalisation-and-covert-propaganda
21. webarchive.nationalarchives.gov.uk/20200203104056/gcs.civilservice.gov.uk/news/alex-aiken-introduces-the-rapid-response-unit/
22. www.gov.uk/government/news/government-cracks-down-on-spread-of-false-coronavirus-information-online
23. www.thetimes.co.uk/article/gchq-in-cyberwar-on-anti-vaccine-propaganda-mcjgjhmb2
24. www.middleeasteye.net/news/twitter-executive-also-part-time-officer-uk-army-psychological-warfare-unit
25. www.gov.uk/government/groups/independent-scientific-pandemic-influenza-group-on-behaviours-spi-b

CHAPTER 6: THE SPI-B ADVISORS

1. www.bbc.co.uk/news/uk-politics-54421489
2. www.nas.org/reports/the-irreproducibility-crisis-of-modern-science/full-report#ImplicationsforPolicymaking
3. www.telegraph.co.uk/news/2020/03/25/two-thirds-patients-die-coronavirus-would-have-died-year-anyway/
4. www.gov.uk/government/publications/role-of-community-champions-networks-to-increase-engagement-in-context-of-covid-19-evidence-and-best-practice-22-october-2020
5. en.wikipedia.org/wiki/Susan_Michie
6. assets.publishing.service.gov.uk/government/uploads/system/uploads/attachment_data/file/948607/s0995-mitigations-to-reduce-transmission-of-the-new-variant.pdf

CHAPTER 7: THE TOOLS OF THE TRADE

1. www.theguardian.com/culture/2017/sep/04/how-we-made-dont-

die-of-ignorance-aids-campaign

2. www.dailymail.co.uk/femail/article-9183957/NHS-workers-watching-Sin-recall-horrifying-ignorance-faced-AIDS-patients-80s.html

3. www.ft.com/content/38a81588-6508-11ea-b3f3-fe4680ea68b5

4. www.gov.uk/government/speeches/pm-address-to-the-nation-on-coronavirus-23-march-2020

5. www.bi.team/wp-content/uploads/2015/07/MINDSPACE.pdf

6. www.theguardian.com/culture/2017/sep/04/how-we-made-dont-die-of-ignorance-aids-campaign

7. Drawn from MINDSPACE Influencing behaviour through public policy

8. www.instituteforgovernment.org.uk/sites/default/files/publications/MINDSPACE.pdf

9. www.coronababble.com/post/how-the-mean-psychologists-induced-us-to-comply-with-coronavirus-restrictions

10. www.ditext.com/packard/19.html

11. www.bbc.co.uk/news/av/uk-england-london-55396770

12. pubmed.ncbi.nlm.nih.gov/11228916/

13. parliamentlive.tv/Event/Index/2d0e5df7-cb15-434c-89a5-579c051aa8ec

14. www.spiked-online.com/2020/10/06/the-new-covid-fines-could-destroy-your-life/

15. assets.publishing.service.gov.uk/government/uploads/system/uploads/attachment_data/file/882722/25-options-for-increasing-adherence-to-social-distancing-measures-22032020.pdf

16. news.npcc.police.uk/releases/update-on-national-crime-trends-and-fixed-penalty-notices-issued-under-covid-regulations

17. www.independent.co.uk/news/health/coronavirus-news-face-masks-increase-risk-infection-doctor-jenny-harries-a9396811.html

18. royalsociety.org/-/media/policy/projects/set-c/set-c-facemasks.pdf

19. www.chroniclelive.co.uk/news/north-east-news/face-masks-could-compulsory-shops-18598438

20. www.dailymail.co.uk/news/article-9181135/amp/Government-funding-EIGHT-vaccine-passport-schemes-450-000.html

21. www.independent.co.uk/news/uk/home-news/coronavirus-uk-news-professor-chris-whitty-no-masks-advice-a9374086.html

22. www.youtube.com/watch?v=PRa6t_e7dgI

23. apps.who.int/iris/bitstream/handle/10665/337199/WHO-2019-nCov-IPC_Masks-2020.5-eng.pdf

24. www.ecdc.europa.eu/sites/default/files/documents/covid-19-face-masks-community-first-update.pdf

25. www.independent.co.uk/news/health/face-masks-coronavirus-death-rate-covid-matt-hancock-today-a9618306.html

26. www.gov.uk/government/publications/face-coverings-when-to-wear-one-and-how-to-make-your-own/face-coverings-when-to-wear-one-and-how-to-make-your-own
27. www.acpjournals.org/doi/10.7326/M20-6817
28. unherd.com/2021/01/inside-the-covid-ward/
29. https://www.bbc.co.uk/news/uk-england-london-53498100
30. www.express.co.uk/news/uk/1261340/coronavirus-uk-hospital-beds-covid19-uk-number-latest-nhs-response
31. www.dailymail.co.uk/news/article-9157627/One-six-hospital-patients-caught-Covid-19-treated-illnesses-figures-show.html
32. www.express.co.uk/news/uk/1388277/coronavirus-latest-scientists-government-deadly-strain
33. www.parliament.uk/business/news/2020/february/statement-on-wuhan-coronavirus/
34. www.asa.org.uk/type/non_broadcast/code_section/04.html
35. twitter.com/CllrEjiofor/status/1338903582855278593
36. www.telegraph.co.uk/news/2021/01/21/government-discontinue-covid-ad-accusing-joggers-exercising
37. Government Communication Survey 19th-21st March 2021 conducted by Yonder for the Recovery Campaign

CHAPTER 8: CONTROLLED SPONTANEITY AND PROPAGANDA

1. www.middleeasteye.net/news/mind-control-secret-british-government-blueprints-shaping-post-terror-planning
2. www.theguardian.com/commentisfree/2017/may/24/emergency-planner-manchester-heal-terror-hurts
3. twitter.com/adilray/status/1353677950550495243
4. assets.publishing.service.gov.uk/government/uploads/system/uploads/attachment_data/file/952716/s0979-factors-influencing-vaccine-uptake-minority-ethnic-groups.pdf
5. ibid
6. inews.co.uk/news/faith-leaders-vaccine-mistrust-black-minority-ethnic-hesitancy-safe-842317
7. assets.publishing.service.gov.uk/government/uploads/system/uploads/attachment_data/file/933231/S0830_SPI-B_-_Community_Champions_evidence_and_best_practice.pdf
8. www.gov.uk/government/news/community-champions-to-give-covid-19-vaccine-advice-and-boost-take-up
9. *Optimizing vaccination roll out: dos and don'ts for all messaging, documents and 'communications' in the widest sense,* published by the NHS in December 2020. Since removed from the internet.
10. www.timesofisrael.com/israel-sees-60-drop-in-hospitalizations-for-over-60s-in-weeks-after-vaccination/
11. www.gov.uk/government/publications/coronavirus-covid-19-vaccine-adverse-reactions/coronavirus-vaccine-summary-of-yellow-card-reporting

12. fullfact.org/online/foetal-cells-covid-vaccine/
13. blogs.bmj.com/medical-ethics/2020/11/23/the-covid-19-vaccine-informed-consent-and-the-recruitment-of-volunteers/

CHAPTER 10: THE METRICS OF FEAR

1. www.telegraph.co.uk/news/2020/05/05/britons-scared-coronavirus-infection-rest-world/
2. www.kekstcnc.com/media/2793/kekstcnc_research_covid-19_opinion_tracker_wave-4.pdf
3. www.medrxiv.org/content/10.1101/2020.09.15.20191957v1.full.pdf
4. www.spectator.co.uk/article/treasury-reveals-it-didn-t-forecast-economic-impact-of-second-lockdown
5. coronavirus.data.gov.uk/details/healthcare
6. www.dailymail.co.uk/news/article-9157627/One-six-hospital-patients-caught-Covid-19-treated-illnesses-figures-show.html
7. civitas.org.uk/publications/what-price-lockdown/
8. www.telegraph.co.uk/technology/2020/05/16/neil-fergusons-imperial-model-could-devastating-software-mistake/
9. www.statnews.com/2020/03/17/a-fiasco-in-the-making-as-the-coronavirus-pandemic-takes-hold-we-are-making-decisions-without-reliable-data/
10. www.bmj.com/content/370/bmj.m3563
11. www.thelancet.com/journals/lancet/article/PIIS0140-6736(05)73948-9/fulltext
12. lockdownsceptics.org/the-real-fault-with-epidemiological-models/
13. www.pure.ed.ac.uk/ws/portalfiles/portal/14288330/Use_and_abuse_of_mathematical_models_an_illustration_from_the_2001_foot_and_mouth_disease_epidemic_in_the_United_Kingdom.pdf
14. www.express.co.uk/news/uk/1388099/lockdown-end-date-uk-lockdown-rules-covid-news-2021-rules-when-will-lockdown-end
15. www.telegraph.co.uk/news/2021/04/06/government-models-warning-third-wave-based-flawed-figures-telegraph/
16. twitter.com/SadiqKhan/status/1284035605203226625
17. cdn.doctorsonly.co.il/2020/03/COVID-19-Webcast-agenda-March28IL.pdf
18. apnews.com/article/8795470456
19. www.gov.uk/government/publications/covid-19-management-of-exposed-healthcare-workers-and-patients-in-hospital-settings/covid-19-management-of-exposed-healthcare-workers-and-patients-in-hospital-settings
20. www.bbc.co.uk/news/health-55470496
21. www.theguardian.com/commentisfree/2020/sep/21/coronavirus-britain-vallance-whitty-fear-data-alarm
22. www.telegraph.co.uk/news/2021/01/13/uk-records-highest-

reported-coronavirus-deaths-figure-of1564/

23. www.telegraph.co.uk/news/2021/01/18/analysis-second-wave-nothing-like-first/

24. www.dailymail.co.uk/news/article-9363137/Official-charts-lay-bare-impact-Covid-crisis.html

25. www.mirror.co.uk/news/uk-news/covid-caused-more-deaths-year-23722724

26. ibid

27. lockdownsceptics.org/2021/03/16/is-covid-the-worst-infectious-disease-in-a-century/

28. www.who.int/director-general/speeches/detail/who-director-general-s-opening-remarks-at-the-media-briefing-on-covid-19---16-march-2020

29. www.who.int/news/item/19-01-2021-who-information-notice-for-ivd-users-2021-01

30. www.theportugalnews.com/news/2020-11-27/covid-pcr-test-reliability-doubtful-portugal-judges/56962

31. www.independent.co.uk/news/health/coronavirus-vaccine-latest-cases-covid-19-patrick-vallance-b1159462.html

CHAPTER 11: COUNTING THE DEAD

1. www.themdu.com/guidance-and-advice/latest-updates-and-advice/certifying-deaths-during-covid-19-outbreak

2. www.ons.gov.uk/peoplepopulationandcommunity/birthsdeathsandmarriages/deaths/datasets/weeklyprovisionalfiguresondeathsregisteredinenglandandwales

3. tinyurl.com/463ueh37

4. Summary of report in *The Daily Mail*: www.dailymail.co.uk/news/article-9203279/Government-estimates-220-000-true-death-toll-pandemic.html

5. https://fingertips.phe.org.uk/static-reports/mortality-surveillance/excess-mortality-in-england-week-ending-01-Jan-2021.html

6. www.ons.gov.uk/peoplepopulationandcommunity/healthandsocialcare/causesofdeath/articles/leadingcausesofdeathuk/2001to2018

7. documents.manchester.ac.uk/display.aspx?DocID=51861

8. www.samhsa.gov/sites/default/files/dtac/srb_sept2015.pdf

CHAPTER 12: THE ILLUSION OF CONTROL

1. www.itv.com/news/2021-02-17/no-covid-19-outbreaks-have-been-linked-to-crowded-beaches-mps-told

2. coronavirus.data.gov.uk/details/deaths

3. www.bbc.co.uk/news/uk-55382861

4. www.ons.gov.uk/peoplepopulationandcommunity/healthandsocialcare/healthandwellbeing/bulletins/

coronavirusandthesocialimpactsongreatbritain/8january2021
5. www.bbc.co.uk/news/55669736
6. news.sky.com/story/covid-19-in-tier-4-everybody-needs-to-behave-as-if-they-already-have-coronavirus-matt-hancock-says-12168124

CHAPTER 13: THE CLIMATE OF FEAR

1. *Scapegoat Rituals in Ancient Greece*, by Jan Bremmer
2. www.conservativehome.com/podcast/the-moggcast-episode-fifty-three-tuesday-26th-january-2021
3. documents.manchester.ac.uk/display.aspx?DocID=51861
4. twitter.com/ClareCraigPath/status/1352516332995162112
5. www.covidfaq.co
6. www.sciencedirect.com/science/article/pii/S0022103120304248
7. www.bi.team/blogs/policy-tribes-how-allegiances-can-harm-policy-making/
8. www.cnbc.com/2020/09/02/study-refusal-to-wear-face-mask-associated-with-psychopathy-traits.html
9. www.spectator.co.uk/article/why-is-youtube-so-afraid-of-free-speech-
10. www.acpjournals.org/doi/10.7326/m20-6817
11. gbdeclaration.org
12. www.theguardian.com/commentisfree/2021/jan/01/false-hope-pandemic-dangerous-disinformation
13. www.theguardian.com/commentisfree/2020/sep/29/rival-scientists-lockdowns-scientific-covid-19
14. assets.publishing.service.gov.uk/government/uploads/system/uploads/attachment_data/file/961210/S1056_Contribution_of_nosocomial_infections_to_the_first_wave.pdf
15. www.dailymail.co.uk/news/article-9157627/One-six-hospital-patients-caught-Covid-19-treated-illnesses-figures-show.html
16. www.thesun.co.uk/news/uknews/13636531/labour-leader-sir-keir-starmer-demands-full-national-lockdown/
17. 'Exclusive: Reviews of hospital-acquired covid deaths as 'basic' breaches found', HSJ, 24th February 2021

CHAPTER 14: CULTS, CONSPIRACY AND PSYCHIC EPIDEMICS

1. hitchensblog.mailonsunday.co.uk/2020/07/peter-hitchens-weve-all-turned-from-normal-humans-into-muzzled-masochists.html
2. www.telegraph.co.uk/news/2021/03/14/one-year-coronavirus-lockdown-did-boris-johnson-take-long-tell/
3. www.independent.co.uk/news/health/covid-origin-wuhan-who-investigation-china-b1802081.html
4. inequality.org/great-divide/updates-billionaire-pandemic/
5. www.weforum.org/agenda/2020/10/the-rich-got-richer-during-the-pandemic-and-that-s-a-daunting-sign-for-our-recovery/

6. www.ilo.org/global/about-the-ilo/newsroom/news/
    WCMS_755875/lang--en/index.htm
7. www.worldbank.org/en/news/press-release/2020/10/07/covid-
    19-to-add-as-many-as-150-million-extreme-poor-by-2021
8. www.reuters.com/article/sweden-economy/swedish-govt-
    sees-milder-downturn-in-2020-slower-growth-next-year-
    idINKBN28Q1VZ
9. www.civitas.org.uk/publications/what-price-lockdown/
10. www.medrxiv.org/content/10.1101/2020.04.11.20062133v1
11. www.weforum.org/great-reset/
12. www.weforum.org/agenda/2020/06/now-is-the-time-for-a-great-
    reset/
13. www.forbes.com/sites/worldeconomicforum/2016/11/10/
    shopping-i-cant-really-remember-what-that-is-or-how-
    differently-well-live-in-2030/
14. www.bmj.com/content/371/bmj.m4716
15. www.bmj.com/content/372/bmj.n556
16. www.bmj.com/content/372/bmj.n511
17. www.medrxiv.org/content/10.1101/2020.05.13.20101253v3

CHAPTER 15: TYRANNY

1. assets.publishing.service.gov.uk/government/uploads/system/
    uploads/attachment_data/file/944823/Analysis_of_the_health_
    economic_and_social_effects_of_COVID-19_and_the_approach_
    to_tiering_FINAL_-_accessible_v2.pdf
2. metro.co.uk/2021/02/25/every-single-prosecution-under-the-
    coronavirus-act-has-been-unlawful-14143868/
3. www.bbc.co.uk/news/uk-england-bristol-55034697
4. www.crowdjustice.com/case/lockdownlegalchallenge/
5. ukhumanrightsblog.com/2020/04/21/a-disproportionate-
    interference-the-coronavirus-regulations-and-the-echr-francis-
    hoar/

CHAPTER 16: TERRIFYING IMPACTS

1. assets.publishing.service.gov.uk/government/uploads/system/
    uploads/attachment_data/file/957265/s0980-direct-indirect-
    impacts-covid-19-excess-deaths-morbidity-sage-december-
    update-final.pdf
2. www.alzheimers.org.uk/news/2020-06-05/ons-report-shows-52-
    increase-excess-deaths-people-dying-dementia-alzheimers-
    society
3. www.spectator.co.uk/article/is-the-cost-of-another-lockdown-
    too-high-
4. www.ons.gov.uk/peoplepopulationandcommunity/wellbeing/
    articles/coronavirusanddepressioninadultsgreatbritain/june2020
5. Government Communication Survey 19th–21st March 2021

conducted by Yonder for the Recovery Campaign

6. www.ons.gov.uk/peoplepopulationandcommunity/wellbeing/
   articles/coronavirusanddepressioninadultsgreatbritain/june2020
7. www.autism.org.uk/what-we-do/news/coronavirus-report
8. ibid
9. www.standard.co.uk/news/health/covid-pandemic-devastating-
   toll-young-people-mental-wellbeing-b900229.html
10. www.centreformentalhealth.org.uk/news/10-million-people-
    england-may-need-support-their-mental-health-result-
    pandemic-says-centre-mental-health
11. bmjopen.bmj.com/content/10/11/e044276
12. www.bmj.com/content/372/bmj.n317
13. civitas.org.uk/content/files/The-cost-of-the-cure-30-November.
    pdf
14. www.itv.com/news/2021-01-28/increase-in-suicide-related-calls-
    at-half-of-englands-ambulance-services-over-lockdown
15. jeatdisord.biomedcentral.com/articles/10.1186/s40337-020-
    00319-y
16. www.thelancet.com/journals/lanpsy/article/PIIS2215-
    0366(20)30530-7/fulltext
17. www.kcl.ac.uk/policy-institute/assets/How-the-UK-is-sleeping-
    under-lockdown.pdf
18. www.nejm.org/doi/full/10.1056/NEJM199108293250903
19. www.dailymail.co.uk/news/article-8846695/Nearly-27MILLION-
    GP-appointments-England-lost-Covid-19-pandemic.html
20. ibid
21. www.bbc.co.uk/news/health-53300784
22. www.theguardian.com/society/2020/nov/08/tens-thousands-
    homeless-despite-uk-ban-evictions-covid-pandemic
23. centrepoint.org.uk/about-us/blog/locked-out-youth-
    homelessness-during-and-beyond-the-covid-19-pandemic/
24. pesquisa.bvsalud.org/global-literature-on-novel-coronavirus-
    2019-ncov/resource/en/covidwho-728827
25. publications.parliament.uk/pa/cm5801/cmselect/
    cmhaff/321/32102.htm
26. www.nelsonslaw.co.uk/panorama-domestic-abuse-lockdown/
27. www.stepchange.org/policy-and-research/debt-research/covid-
    debt-2020.aspx
28. www.telegraph.co.uk/business/2021/02/12/economy-shrinks-
    99pc-record-annual-contraction/

CHAPTER 17: WHY FEAR SHOULD NOT BE WEAPONISED

1. www.ncbi.nlm.nih.gov/pmc/articles/PMC1361287/
2. parliamentlive.tv/Event/Index/2d0e5df7-cb15-434c-89a5-
   579c051aa8ec
3. www.bps.org.uk/sites/bps.org.uk/files/Policy%20-%20Files/

BPS%20Code%20of%20Ethics%20and%20Conduct%20
%28Updated%20July%202018%29.pdf
4. www.dailymail.co.uk/news/article-9395215/Chris-Whitty-
admits-Government-knew-lockdown-severe-effects-health.html
5. www.thedatapsychologist.com/post/crude-and-unethical-
why-boris-johnson-was-wrong-to-try-and-terrify-us-into-
submission
6. www.bbc.co.uk/news/uk-england-leeds-56417014
7. www.centreformentalhealth.org.uk/news/10-million-people-
england-may-need-support-their-mental-health-result-
pandemic-says-centre-mental-health
8. journals.sagepub.com/doi/full/10.1177/2378023120969339
9. emergency.cdc.gov/coping/selfcare.asp
10. www.dailymail.co.uk/news/article-9231773/Ex-MP-NORMAN-
BAKER-reveals-day-anthrax-released-tunnel-Northern-Line.
html

CHAPTER 18: HAPPY ENDINGS ARE NOT WRITTEN IN THE LANGUAGE OF COERCIVE CONTROL

1. *Optimizing vaccination roll out: dos and don'ts for all messaging,
documents and 'communications' in the widest sense,* published by
the NHS in December 2020. Since removed from the internet.
2. news.sky.com/story/there-will-be-a-role-for-vaccine-
certificates-says-pm-but-it-might-not-be-until-august-12256251
3. www.bbc.co.uk/news/uk-politics-56517486
4. www.spiked-online.com/2021/03/25/what-is-the-point-of-
vaccine-passports/
5. www.theguardian.com/society/2019/sep/29/government-
seriously-considering-compulsory-vaccinations-matt-hancock
6. www.independent.co.uk/news/business/covid-vaccine-care-
home-workers-unions-b1821303.html
7. hitchensblog.mailonsunday.co.uk/2017/05/my-first-epistle-to-
the-corbynites-dont-get-me-wrong-about-the-polls.html
8. www.ipsos.com/sites/default/files/publication/1970-01/sri-ipsos-
mori-acceptable-behaviour-january-2012.pdf
9. ec.europa.eu/health/sites/health/files/vaccination/docs/2019-
2022_roadmap_en.pdf
10. https://twitter.com/BigBrotherWatch/
status/1369272255897812992

CHAPTER 19: MAKING SURE IT NEVER HAPPENS AGAIN

1. www.spiked-online.com/2007/04/04/the-only-thing-we-have-to-
fear-is-the-culture-of-fear-itself/
2. onlinelibrary.wiley.com/doi/abs/10.1111/risa.13117
3. youtu.be/_Tc4bl1yZLw
4. www.researchgate.net/publication/340378068_Fear_of_the_

coronavirus_COVID-19_Predictors_in_an_online_study_
conducted_in_March_2020
5. www.parallelparliament.co.uk/mp/steve-baker/dept/DHSC
6. www.apa.org/news/apa/2020/10/fear-motivator-elections
7. www.ncbi.nlm.nih.gov/pmc/articles/PMC3189350
8. link.springer.com/article/10.1007/s11077-018-9325-5
9. www.instituteforgovernment.org.uk/sites/default/files/
publications/MINDSPACE.pdf
10. thepsychologist.bps.org.uk/volume-24/edition-6/interview-
david-halpern-insight-nudge
11. publications.parliament.uk/pa/ld201012/ldselect/
ldsctech/179/179.pdf
12. parliamentlive.tv/Event/Index/2d0e5df7-cb15-434c-89a5-
579c051aa8ec

CHAPTER 20: THE END, OR IS IT A PREQUEL?

1. www.theguardian.com/world/2021/mar/25/covid-checks-at-
pubs-could-nudge-young-people-to-get-vaccine
2. news.sky.com/story/covid-19-vaccinated-people-should-be-
able-to-meet-up-and-go-on-holidays-says-scientist-12257033
3. www.thesun.co.uk/news/14484775/roadmap-brits-lockdown-
rules-friends-family-hugging/
4. www.bloomberg.com/opinion/articles/2021-03-24/when-will-
covid-end-we-must-start-planning-for-a-permanent-pandemic
5. www.thetimes.co.uk/article/people-don-t-agree-with-lockdown-
and-try-to-undermine-the-scientists-gnms7mp98
6. pubmed.ncbi.nlm.nih.gov/23390971/

APPENDIX 1: DATA

1. www.cdc.gov/coronavirus/2019-ncov/hcp/planning-scenarios.
html
2. www.imperial.ac.uk/mrc-global-infectious-disease-analysis/
covid-19/report-34-ifr/
3. www.who.int/bulletin/volumes/99/1/20-265892/en/

APPENDIX 2: LOCKDOWNS DON'T WORK

1. www.thetimes.co.uk/article/ec-lockdowntracker-24-hsc-
p5q3zzxht
2. apps.who.int/iris/bitstream/handle/10665/329438/9789241516839-
eng.pdf
3. www.thetimes.co.uk/article/people-don-t-agree-with-
lockdownand-try-toundermine-the-scientists-gnms7mp98
4. www.telegraph.co.uk/technology/2020/05/16/neil-fergusons-
imperial-model-could-devastating-software-mistake/
5. www.statnews.com/2020/03/17/a-fiasco-in-the-making-as-the-
coronavirus-pandemic-takes-hold-we-are-making-decisions-

without-reliable-data/

6. news.sky.com/story/coronavirus-40-of-recent-covid-19-deathsin-englandand-wales-occurred-in-care-homes-ons-11986899

7. lockdownsceptics.org/2021/03/10/up-to-two-thirds-of-serious-covid-infections-are-caught-in-hospital-study/

8. www.telegraph.co.uk/politics/2021/03/14/exclusive-boris-johnson-accepts-made-mistake-delaying-first/

9. www.civitas.org.uk/content/files/The-cost-of-the-cure-30-November.pdf

10. www.thetimes.co.uk/article/chris-whitty-blames-poor-planningfor-lockdown-in-bad-tempered-health-committee-d5kb3fmw2

11. www.spectator.co.uk/article/covid-and-the-lockdown-effect-a-look-at-the-evidence

12. www.aier.org/article/lockdowns-do-not-control-the-coronavirusthe-evidence/

13. www.who.int/news-room/q-a-detail/herd-immunity-lockdowns-and-covid-19

14. www.nature.com/articles/s41586-020-2405-7; science.sciencemag.org/content/369/6500/eabb9789; www.bmj.com/content/370/bmj.m2743

15. onlinelibrary.wiley.com/doi/10.1111/eci.13484

16. www.cebm.net/covid-19/excess-mortality-across-countriesin-2020/

17. https://omni.se/folkhalsomyndighetens-chef-i-ku-vi-har-fatt-ratt/a/WOK81g

18. www.spectator.co.uk/article/covid-and-the-lockdown-effect-a-look-at-the-evidence

19. www.spiked-online.com/2021/03/18/the-myth-of-our-late-lockdown/

20. https://papers.ssrn.com/sol3/papers.cfm?abstract_id=3764553

INDEX